7c

BETWEEN
PARENT
AND
SCHOOL

BETWEEN PARENT AND SCHOOL

Murray M. Kappelman, M.D.
Paul R. Ackerman, Ph.D.

The Dial Press/James Wade
New York

3157

To
Lee, Karen, Ross,
Lynn, Terri, Stephen
and a cabin
in the mountains

Published by
The Dial Press/James Wade
1 Dag Hammarskjold Plaza
New York, New York 10017

Manufactured in the United States of America

Second printing

Library of Congress Cataloging in Publication Data

Kappelman, Murray Martin, 1931–
    Between parent and school.

    1. Home and school. I. Ackerman, Paul R., 1934–
joint author. II. Title.
LC225.K32   370.19'31   77–23219
ISBN 0–8037–0544–1

CONTENTS

PARENT POWER

APPENDIX

1 Why You Need This Book – For Parent Power

You certainly remember the pleasure and anguish of that bittersweet moment when your child took his or her first hesitating step toward that strange, unknown building called school.

Many parents experience a profound sense of loss at that moment, a sense that they have relinquished something very important and very valuable to people who may not care or be as accepting as they. This is particularly true in the case of the first child, whose initial day of school causes the first real feeling of separation that the parent has had. Even with each succeeding child, there still lingers a deep concern that the child is entering uncharted waters, where many dangers can come from the unknown. The unknowns are the teachers, the principal, the other important school personnel, the other children, and above all the searing question whether the child will be able to cope, to succeed, to "make it."

After that first day, most parents gradually relinquish their prerogatives during those daylight hours to the "other people," accepting, hoping, and waiting for the appropriate educational and emotional responses to be forthcoming for their particular child. Despite experiences with older children, even the parents of several children stand by without intervention as each child enters the educational "system" with new and unique problems. Usually, parents are fortunate in having a "normal" child without specific health or educational problems. This child is literally thrown into the waters of the new school to sink or swim. Most parents feel they should not interfere with their child's school experience. This feeling often goes back to their own childhood, when they were taught that the teacher was sacrosanct and "always right." The teacher was probably the ultimate authority figure when they were children. She or he was not to be challenged or questioned.

1

Between Parent and School

One kept one's doubts, one's serious concerns about a teacher's judgment, fairness, or partiality, deep within one's own thoughts, sharing them only with a trusted friend.

Somehow, when you were growing up, it was not generally taught that the "school people" were fallible human beings capable of error and bad judgment. This deeply ingrained sense of the "special" nature of the school and its personnel has been etched in the subconscious of many of today's parents so that they hesitate to question, to doubt, or to challenge the teacher, the principal, or other important school figures in their child's life.

Yet a school is run by and for human beings. And human beings make mistakes. We know that our children are susceptible to the occasional misdemeanor, mistake, or inappropriate response. But we are less prepared for such human failings in people responsible for our children within the school environment. They, too, have the same human potential for mistake and misinterpretation in dealing with our children. If we are not prepared to act when we discover these errors, these inappropriate responses, these actions which interfere with our child's emotional and educational adjustment to school, then we are seriously evading our responsibility as parents.

Children see us as their front-line protectors, the persons in their lives who are most deeply concerned with their interests and problems. How must they feel when we turn away from the obvious mistake or unfair action which occurs to them in school? Do *they* believe that the teacher . . . the principal . . . the school nurse is always right? Very unlikely. What they do realize is that their parents are afraid, for some unfathomable reason, to come to their defense at school.

We must be prepared to take up the crusade for our child if we feel that an injustice has been done. We must be ready to start a movement for change if there are deficient educational resources for our child, whether he or she is a normal youngster in the main program or a special youngster with unique educational problems. We must attempt to understand the tasks, the responsibilities, the obligations of the people surrounding our child in school. What are the goals of each? What can and should we expect of this school professional? Whether our child is average or special, are there missing elements in the total school environment which detract from rather than add to his educational experience? And how can we, as parents, either singly or as a group, develop the power to facilitate change and awareness so that our children receive the very best possible educational experience, one which fits each child's specific needs?

This is the theme of this book: to provide the information, the incentive, and the guidelines that will allow parents to feel a sense of authority in being responsible for their child's education.

One of the main reasons that parents feel shut out by the educational system is because they did not fully understand their own school when they were students. They still do not appreciate the intricate details and interactions that constitute a working school system. School remains impregnable—a mysterious edifice into which the parent is allowed entry only during conferences, occasional Parents Teachers Association meetings, and special visiting times.

As a result, parents develop fantasies about the school system—fantasies which are harbored by many whose own memories of school are hazy and clouded by impressions instead of facts. Often these fantasies are negative and cause angry overreaction on the part of parents to letters sent home, evaluations by teachers, homework assignments, class placements, and so on. For the child's sake, it becomes very important to dispel such fantasies and bring out an accurate picture of the way most school systems operate and the roles the various professionals within this system play. A parent can learn the roles and maximum capabilities of each school professional. Then he or she will have the ammunition to request that the full professional potential of everyone in the system be made available to his or her child—and to every other child.

How many parents know what the principal of a public school actually does? How can he or she help you and your child at a time of crisis? Why is a social worker needed in a school? What does a speech clinician offer? In what ways are the school nurse and the school doctor important to your child? Why would the school ask a psychologist to see your child? What else do teachers do besides teach? What can you expect of the teacher in a conference with you? What are you being told about your child? Who is a "special education teacher"? What qualifications does he or she have, and how do they differ from those of the regular classroom teacher?

To deal with these educational professionals when you are called to school to discuss your child or when he or she casually mentions at the dinner table that he or she has had contact with a "new person" in school, you must be fully equipped with the proper information as to who this person is, and what you and your child can expect from him. You must be aware of how you can work with each of these professionals to improve, modify, or innovate the education of your child. One of the major aims of this book is to introduce each of these special people in your child's school life, and to answer all the possible questions you might have about how you relate to them—whether your child is "problem-free," a normal child with special problems, or a special problem child.

The child who needs the most out of the school experience is the child with special problems—the child with unique needs that make his or her educational process more intricate and more individual. But it must be stressed that every child has the potential, some day, of being a "special" child.

If your child has a physical handicap, he or she is special. If he has a chronic physical illness or has ever suffered from a prolonged physical illness that takes him out of the school environment for over two weeks, he fits into this category and needs special school attention. The mentally "slow" child is in need of specific educational programs. The hyperactive youngster usually cannot fit into the "mainstream" and must be handled with a sensitive awareness of his placement. The child suffering from an emotional illness—whether stemming from a severe, immediate personal crisis or more prolonged and severe trauma—will need an individualized approach from the entire school staff and system. The blind child, the deaf child, the child with specific learning disabilities that are preventing normal learning processes . . . none of these are going to be assimilated into the regular classroom without special programming and preparation.

The child who has failed a grade in school, been expelled from school or excluded from activities or specific learning exercises, been physically or emotionally abused by teacher or peer within the school setting— the child with any one of these common school problems fits into the category of special child.

Is your child particularly bright? Are you honestly able to call your youngster "gifted" or talented? If so, he or she needs individual attention from the school system if those gifts and talents are to be developed fully. Any child, no matter how or in what way special, is entitled to an appropriate education which meets his or her potential and needs. It is the legal mandate and *mission* of your school system to provide such an education for your special child. This book attempts to deal with each of these very special children and to point out the ideal educational approaches for them. In addition, it attempts to assist all parents in organizing their thoughts about how to obtain better help if they do not believe that their child is receiving the best educational experience.

Knowing what the problems are for your special child and armed with the ideal possibilities, the parent can approach the individual school, and the entire school administrative system, with a plan of action that demands attention and response. Remember that the child usually cannot fight for himself. You are the ultimate advocate for your child. Without your knowledge, your interest, and your involvement, followed up by appropriate and properly directed action, there is a very strong likelihood that the unusual situation hampering your child's educational progress will *not* be discovered or given the maximum attention.

In many cases, the school system is careful and assiduous in screening, identifying, and helping the children with problems. These systems are to be applauded and given your full support. You will only realize how well your individual school is functioning if you compare the suggestions offered here with the range of services offered by your local school system for each specific educational problem. If your school system is offering or attempting to offer the full spectrum of special programs suggested here, then you must lend your vocal and political support as an individual and as a group organizer to make certain that these efforts are not in vain—that the legislators and responsible officials are aware of the administrative and fiscal support these programs require to succeed.

But if it becomes fairly obvious to you as you read these pages, that your local school system is lagging behind in the innovative yet necessary programs for the average and the special child, then you must speak out alone or create a band of collective voices to cry out in defense of your children's right to the best possible education. This is the basis of "parent power" . . . the ability to know what is needed, to recognize what is lacking, and collectively to demand and facilitate the acquisition of those services needed to give every child the education he or she deserves.

Sometimes parents are fearful of entering the educational world because the language seems so foreign. Terms like "mainstreaming" and "normalization" are thrown at parents. Special psychological tests are referred to without any explanation of their method, interpretation, or significance. Parents feel ignorant and inferior, leaving a school interview with the foreboding sense that their child has moved into a foreign country where he or she cannot be reached. A sense of being desperately uninformed usually pursues the parent for weeks after these encounters. This book tries to cut through the educational jargon and provide a brief but cogent analysis of the types of tests that your child might be facing. So informed, you can understand the language and be able to place the test results in the proper perspective for your child's future.

Parents often underestimate their impact upon the school system. The fact is that as voters they ultimately control it. The individual parent has power—but only when that parent is fully prepared to fight for his/her child's cause with the correct information about a child's special problem and the knowledge of the school's responsibilities to cope with that particular problem. The power of parents expands tremendously when an organized body of parents gathers to influence the school system and the legislators about the changes which must come about if the children they represent are going to get a "fair shake" in the current educational system. These parents can become an important motivating force for change for their children.*

Ultimately, change for the specific child has to occur at the local school level. Each child will be helped only when there is sufficient rapport and understanding between parent, teacher, and school. There must be a willingness to share in the effort to change the system so that it fits the child rather than always attempting to reconstruct the child to fit the system. This teamwork, geared toward creating a flexible school environment that can adjust to every child, should be the ultimate goal of parent, school, and system. To enter this team, the parent must know what the other members do in their jobs, what their expectations and objectives are, and how the team as a whole can best be

*A fine example of this can be seen in the Association for Children with Learning Disabilities, an organization composed primarily of parents of young people with significant specific learning disabilities. To demonstrate the dramatic impact of this group, in November 1975, a series of conferences were requested by the ACLD and granted at the White House to review the current state of learning disabilities and the future legislative and educational strides that were needed from all influential groups. This is what organized, effective parent power can achieve. Both authors attended the first of these White House sessions and were impressed by the respect and consideration the conference received, both from the government officials and from the leadership in the field. Here is how the cumulative impact of parent power can affect every "special" child in the land.

utilized in the school setting. In addition, the parent must understand his/her own child, the special problems and possible solutions, the alternate routes to maximum education, and the options for the future. That is what this book is all about.

THE INSIDERS

2 The School Administrator

Probably the most forbidding figure throughout our entire public or private school career was the principal or headmaster. Whether it was a man or a woman, we always sensed a pervading air of ultimate authority. Everyone in the school was responsible to this person. When our problems could not be handled within the classroom, it was to the principal we were sent. This was the final stopping place before expulsion. Instinctively we knew that no matter who ran the school system or the school board, the autonomy and control of our school was under the rule of the principal, administrator, or headmaster. Most of us simultaneously feared and respected him, but we never really understood his functions. What were his responsibilities? He simply seemed always to be there, always omnipotent, and always the final arbiter in the decisions and problems affecting our lives at school.

Children grow into parents. However, this growth and maturity usually does not carry with it any more knowledge and respect for the school principal, nor does it lessen the sense of deep concern most parents retain when having to approach a principal on issues involving their child.

Therefore it becomes essential for the effective parent to understand the responsibilities and daily activities of the school administrator. It is necessary to know the whole person, the pressures that affect him, and the possibilities of help he can offer you. Only by understanding his entire function will you be able to approach him in the most intelligent and effective way. This is the basis of our attempt to sketch the portrait of the school administrator.

"Excuse me, please, but where can I find the . . . uh . . . the administrator's office?" (Darn! Why can't Linda ever get those telephone messages straight?)

"The what?"

"Mr. . . . I'm not sure how you pronounce it . . . Mr. Carey? I think he's the superintendent." An embarrassed grin, "I've come because of a telephone message my seven-year-old took, so I'm not sure."

"Oh, you mean Mr. Carriker, the principal. He's in charge of this school. The superintendent is in charge of the whole district. There is a Mr. Kelly here but he's an attendance officer, truant officers we used to call them. Your kid been playing hookey?"

"No, we just moved here. I think he'd be afraid he would get lost if he played hookey." (I wonder if all school maintenance men go around asking personal questions to visitors?) "Where is the principal's office then?"

"Way down the hall, on the right." He points, tilting his head so he can try to see past the crowds of children in the hall.

You thank him quickly and hurry. It's a bad start to my day, you think. First that cryptic message from Linda last night that Mr. Carriker wanted to see me about Jimmy, and then the undecipherable time and place, and, to top it off, the impossibility of finding a parking place. Five minutes late and I have to explain to a janitor that my son is not playing hookey. What kind of a man runs a school where people are not more sensitive . . . or professional? What kind of a man thinks I should drop everything and come to see him at such-and-such a time? Well, I certainly hope it's important. Suddenly you shudder because the impact of the words "important" and "Jimmy" become connected. Has Jimmy done something wrong? Are drastic changes going to be made at his school? Is he in trouble? Has the principal discovered something I don't know about? Is he well? And why am I supposed to see the principal rather than Jimmy's teacher? As your hand reaches for the doorknob to enter the principal's reception area, you ask yourself, who is this man and what can I expect?

Generally you can expect the principal or superintendent (and his private school counterparts) to be male (except in elementary public school), Republican, and slightly conservative. He will probably be over the age of thirty-five and will have taught at least five years before moving into his administrative position. His office will usually be private, and you will notice copies of *The School Administrator* and other technical journals resting on his coffee table. His bookshelves will often have his favorite textbooks from graduate school days and will undoubtedly hold several volumes of state education laws and their supplements. Ashtrays are not normally found in these offices, particularly during the last five years. He will usually not invite you to lunch unless the appointment goes into the noon hour. If you are invited, lunch will be in the school cafeteria. He will probably never offer you a drink. He will, on the whole, be friendly, businesslike and prompt. In the best of interviews between parent and administrator, he will guide the conversation from a discussion of the individual child to the actions that should occur and then back to the child. In a less than optimal interview, you may leave with a vague feeling of disappointment. You may have several unanswered questions: "What did I just learn?" "How far can he help me, anyway?" "What is he going to do now?" The most distressing feeling when leaving the principal's office is usually, "Isn't there something that I can do?"

There *is* something you can do; indeed, many more things than you probably have realized. There are rights you have as a parent that you may not be aware of. There are actions that the principal or superintendent can take that are legally sanctioned, and some that are pure bluff. There is information you can and should obtain about your child. There are actions which the superintendent or principal may want to take that you can block if you feel they would be harmful to your child. But the most important thing to remember during this interview is that the law requires that you, as your child's parent, *be given an equal right to help the school provide the best education for that child.* This is legally and morally the reason you both meet. Problems in talking to principals and superintendents generally revolve around a misunderstanding of the partnership involved in educating the child. So if you enter the interview with some advance knowledge about how principals and superintendents work, their legal responsibilities, and their ethical mandate, you will be better able to effect this parent/administrator partnership.

The principal's or superintendent's job is comparable to that of a corporation president; that is, he is responsible for the running of the business—the school—but is given overall direction by his board of directors, the school board. Generally, he is able to make decisions about what happens in the day-to-day events affecting the child. He changes the teachers, modifies the schedules, the discipline, and lunchroom activities; but any major decision, or any decision that affects the spending of the school's money or resources, must have the consent of the school board. Any hiring and firing of personnel must be done by the school board. Therefore, if you think that the solutions to your problems are likely to be such major undertakings as starting a new program in special education or buying new buses, you must be prepared to do some homework with school board members in addition to the principal. That kind of change must be initiated by the principal and receive the approval of the school board.

Usually a school board sets annual goals for the principal or superintendent by which they ultimately judge his worth. They expect him to produce reasonable budgets. He is to keep everyone, especially the parents of his children, satisfied and happy with the school and the board. The school system wants as few dropouts as possible. When the students take standardized achievement tests, they should, as a group, score equally with (or better than) their counterparts throughout the rest of the state and the country. He and his faculty should be sterling examples of well-adjusted citizens and should live exemplary lives without any taint of misconduct or scandal. It would not hurt the school board's feelings if the principal or superintendent hired a coach who produced a winning district basketball team, but they could get easily disgruntled if the team failed to retain its leadership the following year. And with all that federal money available, the administrator should be getting a few grants now and then just to show that the school system is innovative and can use federal monies effectively. Squeezed somewhere in between all these lofty aims, the administrator should be completing the reports, records, and clearances required by the state and federal governments which make money flow from these sources. He must also keep his allocated funds in neat, tight budgets and accounts.

These goals make for an extremely busy day behind the scenes. Follow a principal or superintendent around for a day, and you will observe a person with a high tolerance for diverse, detailed activity, who has to make major and minor decisions with speed and dispatch, and who is constantly besieged by his students, faculty, and staff for solutions, praise, or conciliation.

Most principals or superintendents at some time or other during the day will have to review attendance statistics, make decisions about the daily assignment of personnel for such extracurricular duties as lunch monitor or trip chaperone, hold a conference or two with troubled parents, and maybe discipline a couple of children with firm warnings or even initiate suspension actions. The principal may also review applications for new teaching positions, make decisions on school purchases, write four letters to parents and six pages of a new grant proposal, and receive a telephone call from a concerned school board member. Later he might draft a set of informal remarks for a local education meeting, outline a series of goals for a new five-year plan being requested by the school system supervisor, and skim two new educational journals that have just come in the mail to see if any of his colleagues have gotten published or if there are any interesting articles. As the day draws to a close, he might read and make comments on a new plan for innovation in one of his instructional departments. Finally he will forget, after work, to shop for the three pounds of hamburger which was scribbled on the note in his inside pocket.

With those kinds of back-breaking schedules and almost insurmountable objectives, why would the principal or superintendent want an interview with you, Jimmy's father or mother?

Sometimes the reasons behind the requested interview are as harmless and flattering as an invitation for you to help in the library, be a class mother, or lecture the seventh grade on what it's like to be an airplane pilot. But, unfortunately, the reasons are not usually this rewarding to either parent or principal. As the executive head of the school, the principal or superintendent is generally the person who has to make the final decisions that may dramatically affect a child's educational future and must involve that child's parents.

Your child's school attendance may be one reason for your summons. Most states have laws which make it compulsory for all children to attend school until reaching a stipulated birthday. The administrator is responsible for enforcing these laws, either directly or through his attendance or truant officer. If a child cannot attend school, the principal must be made aware of the problem. In most states, he can excuse the child or, conversely, prevent him or her from attending school by the use of expulsion or suspension. Often prohibiting attendance becomes a matter for discussion under the heading of "discipline." If you are called in to school, and you are aware that your child is having trouble getting to school or staying in school, you should be prepared to talk to the principal about it. When you consult him, attempt to find out the possible reasons for the problem. Is the child over-attached to you or his brothers or sisters at home so that he is balking at separating and going to school? Do problems exist between the teachers and your child? Is he frightened to walk to school because there are bullies on the next block? Is he bored with school and wanders out of the classroom in mild protest? Is he chronically late because of the temptations of the candy counter at the drugstore? Does he oversleep every morning because he watches television too late the night before? Did he get lost during the last two field trips when he tried to find the bathroom and is fearful of this happening again?

Do not let an administrator tell you in simple terms that the problem lies in your child's nonattendance or tardiness—it lies in the motivation for that nonattendance or tardiness. Do not accept a disciplinary action without some understanding of the causes or, at least, some system suggested to find out the causes, such as counselling, testing, or observation. Insist on talking to his or her teacher to find out what school is really like for your child when he gets there. Ask your child to describe a day in his school. Observe him in his classroom and note how much he is rewarded or how often he is subtly punished. Check on your own habits of attendance. Are you and your family prompt, always on time, and interested in staying through events until they are finished, or is there a decided family tendency to tardiness, leaving events that are boring, or avoiding unpleasant activities? You can help your administrator with attendance problems by insisting on receiving answers about your child's motivations and worries in school. Schooling is far too important an experience for both you and your child to allow the child to be excluded or expelled, whether by his own actions or the administrator's will.

Another reason you may be called into the principal's or superintendent's office is to discuss the discipline of your child. If this occurs, you can be reasonably certain that your child's teacher has admitted to the principal that she has tried various forms of discipline, has been frustrated, and failed in her attempts to control the disliked behavior of your child. Chances are good that she has already talked with you about what she is trying to do, but this may not always be the case, particularly if the behavior she is trying to control is hard for her to describe and explain, such as: "He has a bad attitude toward adults," or sexually threatening to her: "He keeps pinching the bottoms of the little girls in the class." If the administrator requests a conference with you, you must expect that he has assumed a major share of the responsibility in prescribing a new form of discipline and will want to discuss his plans with you. Often this course of action will involve you, and require your participation at home; he will ask for your cooperation. If he does not request such cooperation, *you* should suggest it. Define what you can do to change your child's behavior (if it is offensive) and participate in the disciplinary process (if it sounds appropriate). After all, you have been on the job for a long time and have insight and experience as to what will and will not work with your particular child.

He may suggest that the school personnel use physical punishment —a spanking or knuckle wrapping. Accept this only if you practice it at home and the child knows its significance. The issue of physical punishment for children in school has been fought in many courts in this country. Most administrators will be extremely reluctant to use it if you strongly disapprove. (This is dealt with more extensively later in the book.)

The principal could discuss the withholding of privileges. This method is used in many homes, but with the knowledge that the withholding is fair and *temporary*, being the result of a specific misbehavior. As a parent, you should feel obligated to tell your child why you are withholding the privilege. The child should understand what change in behavior he or she must exhibit to have the privilege returned and how long the privilege will be withheld because of the misbehavior. Insist on the same conditions in school. You should make certain during your discussions with the principal that your child knows what he did to warrant the punishment, what he needs to do to avoid it in the future, and how long the school will withhold the privilege. It is better for the person who initiates the punishment to explain this entire picture to the child since that will help the child to connect the act with the consequences; but you as a parent should know both the act and the punishment, treat it factually and reasonably at home, and help to reward the correct behavior when it occurs in school.

The administrator may also have decided that the child should be transferred to another class or to another teacher as a solution to a chronic behavior problem. This is not usually done because the child is "incorrigible," but because it appears that there are irrational and irreconcilable differences between the teacher and a child which require this action. In the past, one of us had to request a transfer of his kindergarten child because the teacher had not spoken to the child for six weeks. Investigation revealed that the author's child, a bright, quiet, slightly immature five-year-old, was the exact image of the teacher's own child at that age. The teacher's daughter, at that time, was entering high school and was having very serious problems in "breaking away" from her mother. She was rebelling in the most flagrant ways. The teacher as a mother could not handle this rebellion, was seeking professional help to deal with the communication problems, and throughout this period of intense personal distress was trying to teach.

Having to face a child, so evocative of her own, every morning was too reminiscent of her own failures; the teacher could not bring herself to speak to the child. When the circumstances were known, the transfer was effected quietly, the teacher was free to be more objective about her own problems, and the five-year-old flourished in a new atmosphere of acceptance and affection. It was important to handle this move without announcement, admonition, or recrimination: the action had to be negotiated tactfully and confidentially with the principal. In this case the positive impact of parent-principal interaction was felt by all.

This is probably the way any move of a child within a school should be handled. Unlike the home, where punishment can be meted out privately, punishment of the same child at school runs the risk of peer reinforcement. A child's playmates should never participate in the child's punishment. They should not be allowed to ridicule or torment the punished child. Sharing the confidentiality of the punishment permits them to label or brand the child "bad," "stubborn," "rebellious," or in any other negative terms that injure the child's image of himself. Punishment is *for the act* and not for the person; it is important that the school administrator as well as the parent emphasize this fact, not only to the child but to his/her friends if and when they are involved. It is up to you, as a parent, to make sure that any punishment or discipline suggested by the administrator is directly related to the child's misdeed. The relationship between punishment and action must be explained to the child by the person who has the most facts about the situation. The punishment should be spelled out in detail, handled as privately as possible, and terminated at a reasonable time. If dramatic moves of the child within the school have to be made to alleviate intolerable situations, parents should have a full understanding of all the ramifications, the need for the move, the expected gains from it, and the possible effects upon the child and his friends. Schools can be valuable allies in the process of helping children grow up by showing them the consequences of bad actions and by rewarding them for good actions; but a child needs the mutual consistency of reward and punishment that fits the offensive action both at home and at school. Only you as a parent can guarantee this after contact with the principal.

The process of transferring a child from one classroom to another is a third reason you may be asked to an administrator's office. Such a request may be routine ("Johnnie's class is overcrowded and I wanted to transfer him to a split-level class") or represent a new direction for your child ("We think Joanne has more ability in math than we first suspected and want to place her in a more accelerated track"). For whatever reasons, a transfer from one class to another after school has started is often a painful adjustment for a child. He or she has to leave one group of friends and make another for reasons he or she may not quite understand. He or she stands the chance of being teased by friends who do not understand the reason for the change. So your job, if you approve of the transfer, is to make the change as painless and profitable as possible. Familiarize yourself with all the details of the move. Become informed about the standards and quality of work demanded by the new class. Talk about the personality of the new teacher and the composition of the new class, and compare the value of the obvious differences with the potential progress possible in the new class. Find out if there will be any overlap in activities that would involve the child's friends from the old class. Talk with the teachers of both classes and agree upon the explanation which your child should receive from each person involved. Discuss with them how the children of the old class should be told of the transfer and see how the children of the new class are being prepared for the "new" child. Ask if there are ways of introducing your child gradually into the new class so that a sudden shift does not have to be made which might create anxiety. Find out if the potential repercussions resulting from the move could be minimized by waiting until the semester or holiday break rather than acting in the middle of a school term. But, primarily, make certain that you agree with the purposes and expectations of the transfer. Once you *do* agree, support the move fully. Help your child feel secure in the change and check up continually to make certain he is being supported by his new teacher and friends.

Discipline, transfer, and attendance are frequent reasons why administrators want to see parents. But why might parents want to see administrators?

One reason you might want to see a principal is to appeal a decision made by your child's teacher. This is going one step higher than the teacher in the "chain of command" of the school, so it should be done only when effective communication with the teacher, after many trials, seems impossible. Always have facts, not merely opinions, prepared when you take this action. Know exactly what you want to accomplish and what you want done on behalf of your child before you go to the administrator. Do not approach him with general complaints about the teacher's attitude or lack of effectiveness in class. Ask yourself what you would do differently if you were the teacher in this situation and prepare your own nonpunitive solution to the problem to present to the principal.

You should be aware that the principal's first reaction will be to defend the teacher. After all, as the leading administrator, he is ultimately responsible for all his teachers' actions and evaluations. The law of survival requires unity between him and his staff. Only if you are armed with facts will you be able to make your case effectively. Then, if you can state the options, you should be able to negotiate effectively with the administrator.

Another reason you might want to see your child's administrator is if you feel that something terribly wrong is happening to your child in school, but you cannot put your finger on it and cannot get information to quiet this concern. Suppose your child suddenly is bringing home weak marks in the fifth grade and has been a straight B student before. The teacher has no explanation other than he or she just "appears not to be trying." You may want to request that your child be tested. You may want the administrator to have the child counselled. You may want to know more about the teacher from a superior. Or you may just want some helpful advice about what to do, where to go, and who to see. A principal has seen a lot of people, students and parents alike, and watched a lot of successful solutions to problems that were thought to be unworkable at the time. Chances are good that he can offer a few remedies you never considered.

Again, you may have been looking through your child's textbooks and found examples of blatant sexism or racism. Or you learn that the school is about to set up a course in human sexual behavior and you want more information on the content and values to be taught. In other words, you are concerned about problems that you feel might affect many of the children, and you want to do something about them. In all these cases a visit to the administrator is in order.

Again, go armed with the facts. You should know if other parents are equally concerned. Are the school-related organizations, such as the P.T.A. (Parents Teachers Association) or the National Education Association, informed and active? What will be the consequences to the children if the projected course of action is continued? What will be the consequences if it is discontinued? Are there other paths open to the administrator? In this case you may be questioning a direct decision made by the administrator. This is your right as a parent and taxpayer, but you must expect some resistance unless the administrator was forced to that decision by law or mandate which he could not control. If your complaint affects many children, enlist the help of their parents. But go to the administrator *first* and explain what you are doing. Don't force him into an uncompromising position—that's a situation which would put anyone on the defensive.

What should you know when you first meet with the administrator? Try to remember the following points:

1. He is a busy, harassed executive who is being pulled in many different directions by many people. Your position will be appreciated when you have thought it through in terms of the facts involved, the options open to everyone, and the actions you are prepared to take in behalf of your child.
2. General complaints about faculty or staff and their "attitudes" will be met with defensiveness. The administrator has to live with his staff and coax the very best out of them so that they will serve the largest number of children with the fewest problems and the highest degree of effectiveness.
3. If any of your problems involve other people, other children, or large issues, before you see the administrator be sure you know what are the feelings of these other people and what is your degree of outside support.One way the administrator can *turn you off* is to show you how alone you are in your position.
4. Try to keep the problems that you will be talking about centered on the child. A comment like, "Mrs. Smith shouldn't be teaching because she's rigid," is too critical and generalized. A comment like, "I'd like Jimmy to have a teacher who is flexible in her approach to solving problems, because Jimmy has shown by his early reading and beginning math concepts that he can tolerate approaching problems in many ways," is child-centered.
5. Realize that if the administrator is arbitrating a problem such as discipline, or transferring a child to another class for behavioral reasons usually this reflects only the teacher's viewpoint. Ask for an honest personal evaluation, and try to listen with as few defensive reflexes as possible. Chances are you will learn something about your child that you did not previously know. Wait until you have obtained some clue as to the motivation behind your child's inappropriate behavior, and then try to work out a reasonable solution. Request that the principal clearly delineate his plans for the punish-

ment of this unacceptable behavior, that there are set limits on the punishment, and that you may join him in a conference with the teacher to discuss a consistent method of explaining the action to your child.

6. Try to talk constructively; in other words, discuss with the principal how these problems can be prevented from happening again. If your child has an attendance problem, you should discuss ways of getting him or her back to school, but at the same time indicate how school can be made a rewarding and exciting place again.

7. Administrators, as in all other professions, use a professional jargon that is sometimes hard to understand. Or when it is used you may think you know what the mumbo-jumbo means, but not in fact understand all the ramifications. Sometimes an administrator will talk jargon to you because he forgets that you are not a professional; or he might be putting you off, keeping you at arm's length from the problem (see Chapter 24). It may be easier and less painful to tell you that Joan has "a cognitive deficit" than that she is suspected of being "mentally retarded." Before you leave his office, make sure you understand the meaning of all the words that he uses. Ask him to explain until you are certain of every suggestion and implication. *This is particularly essential when he reads professional reports on your child, for the words in these documents are liable to go into the child's records and follow him or her for the rest of his or her school career.* Make sure you have grasped what is being said.

8. You do *not* have to accept any major decision made by the administrator. Note that the word "major" was used. Minor punishments, small changes in schedule, altered bus routes—all of these decisions are minor. But if a decision is made to expel or suspend your child, or place your child in a special education class, or transfer your child to a totally different teacher, or send your child to another school, often there are methods of appeal, ways of overriding the decision, appropriate approaches to questioning the action. You can firmly refuse to allow such a decision, pending a better investigation, if you feel that the child will be hurt educationally or emotionally by it. Most reasonable administrators will usually agree to suspend action if all parties are not in agreement. So know your rights, as parents of the children in the school and as taxpayers, and demand them quietly but firmly. Be aware, also, that you are not going to be as objective as you would like to be. After all, it is your child

who is in jeopardy. So seek the advice of a third party who has talent and background knowledge before you block any major decisions.

9. If an administrator has any "papers" describing your child's problem or his proposed actions on that problem, ask to see these papers. Sometimes they will give you a framework which you will not get from your conversation. Most administrators know that under new laws they can no longer withhold records from the parents, so you may insist on seeing any or all of these documents. If reports and documents about your child are not mentioned, ask about them. Explain that you would like to see any professional statements or observations which might describe your child's problems. If, according to your facts the history or observations on these papers are incorrect, make certain that the correct data is placed in the files. These records simply offer you more information about your child; if you are told that they do not go into your child's files, don't battle for correction.

10. Remember that the administrator has a "business" to run—educating children. He cannot spend much additional time helping you solve many of your child's home, disciplinary, emotional, and learning problems. Nor can an administrator solve all of the community's problems. Be reasonable in your requests; fair in your demands; and just in your judgments. If you want a decision implemented, you must be prepared to do much of the legwork. In other words, be ready to share the educational process with the principal as one of his co-workers.

In your attempts to get the best educational opportunity for your child, the principal or administrator will be your second line of action immediately after discussion with your child's teacher. As we stated before, there will be times when you will need to go to the administrator first, but usually you will initially need to speak to your child's teacher for information, background, and facts.

The principal and his teachers comprise a closely knit educational "family." They consider themselves team workers in the task of educating large numbers of children residing in their school district. Occasionally these educators distrust parents because they have had many emotional and irrational meetings with them which resulted in deadlocks. Often the parent sees a child through one set of eyes, while the school sees him or her from a totally different perspective. All too often, with this barrier, the two cannot communicate sufficiently with each other to effect the most advantageous solution for the child's problem.

Although it is sometimes difficult for principals to accept the reality, they do realize that the most profitable addition to their school team is the intelligent, rational, and well-informed parent. But to find a parent who is capable of accepting the team approach, of seeing beyond their subjective feelings about the child and concentrating upon the solutions, who can share the responsibilities and rewards of the educational process with other members of the team, and will stay focused on what is best for the child is, in their experience, a very difficult task.

They look for "parent power" like that described in Chapter 22—rational, logical, helpful power—not hysteria and undirected aggression.

What you, as a parent, have to offer the administrator is an application, a readiness, a knowledge of the conditions necessary to join their team. Your attitude should be: When do I go to work?

5 The Teacher

"Hello, Mrs. Haynes, I'm Jonathon's mother."

She practiced saying it to herself as she walked down the crowded hall. It would be important to be relaxed and friendly, to build up a trust, to share a common interest. She hoped she would be able to talk freely with Mrs. Haynes. She wanted so badly to talk about Jonathon's shyness, so much like hers when she had been younger and so painful to observe in her only child. She considered talking about Jonathon's reading habits, telling Mrs. Haynes that he read for an hour and a half every evening before bedtime, and asking her if she considered that "normal." She wanted to ask her help in locating a sensitive music teacher for the boy. She needed to know if he had any friends, if he was adjusting well to school during his first year, if the move last year from Michigan had upset him. What would be expected of Jonathon this year? What should she and Mike do to help him in school? "Mrs. Haynes, I'm Jonathon's mother reporting for duty," she'd like to say, if she were greeted with enough warmth to permit it.

Jonathon's mother found the door and knocked softly. Inside, the teacher gave a movement of surprise, glanced at the clock, then walked quickly over and opened the door to reveal the tense woman on the other side.

"I'm Mrs. . . . I'm Jonathon's mother," she managed to say after Mrs. Haynes had opened the door.

"Oh, Jonnie's mother." Was it a question or a confirmation? "I must have gotten mixed up. I didn't expect you until tomorrow. But as long as you're here, I'd be glad to talk to you. Won't you come in?" The teacher led Jonathon's mother to a small table with even smaller chairs and gestured her down.

Mrs. Haynes seemed young; she guessed the teacher was about twenty-four years old. Probably she had been teaching only about two years. What would she know about problems of shyness, of sensitivity in music teachers, in "normal" adjustments? What could she ask this very young woman? How could she establish an easy relationship with another person who hadn't expected her and who had let her know, by her movements and expressions, that this would be a short, hurried meeting?

Mrs. Haynes began talking. The teacher's voice was rapid and distant, as if it had been rehearsed and the words spoken so often that they were automatically triggered. Her smile remained constant, and her eyes were fixed abstractly upon the brooch Jonathon's mother wore on the scarf around her neck. The teacher thumbed through an appointment book on the table, finally put it down, and said to Jonathon's mother:

"How careless of me to have you down for the wrong day. I must have been very busy when you called. But thank you for coming anyway. We shouldn't take too long, because Jonnie is one of my favorite pupils. He's so well adjusted in class that I'm constantly amazed. You know, I'm really taken with his artwork. It's the best in the class. I guess you already know that he's only in the middle level reading group; but I want you to know that he's doing O.K. I expect him to improve a little this year; but I'm not too worried about it, because, with his personality and outgoing traits, he should receive a lot of help from the other children. They should certainly serve to reinforce his strengths."

"He's only an average reader?" Jonathon's mother inquired. "I'm really surprised. At home he reads for an hour and a half every night, and he never asks for help with words or anything. Is that only average work here?" She thought of the many times he had read to her, of the smooth flowing sequences of words, of the few small mistakes in pronunciation, of the occasional funny little omissions. She recalled her pride in his achievement, and the praise she had given Jonathon to help him maintain his reading habits. But was that only average for children in this school? She was about to ask Mrs. Haynes these questions when she heard a voice with a slight edge of annoyance.

"Apparently it is. But we'll know more about it in another four months, after we get the results of his standardized achievement tests. I'd be surprised, though, if he scored above the sixtieth percentile in reading."

"Percentile?"

"Oh, I'm sorry. I shouldn't use—uh—*technical* terms. What I meant to say was that I expect Jonnie would be considered average compared to the whole country. In fact, I'm so sure he won't score

The Teacher

higher that I've placed him in the middle—or average—reading group. But, of course, if he does score higher in these next tests then I'll be glad to consider changing him. What worries me is if he's reading all that time at home and is just in the middle reading group, maybe he has a problem that we don't know about. I'll certainly look more closely at him starting tomorrow." She glanced at her wristwatch.

Jonathon's mother felt her throat tighten, which made it difficult to keep her voice calm. Jonathon with a reading problem? It might be important to make light of that remark. "Oh, I think, like you said, that it's probably not much to worry about. Why don't we just wait and see what happens with his reading throughout this year? But could you tell me something about his music? He seems to love music, and I wanted to ask you . . ."

"Yes, that's the problem that I wanted to talk about with you— Jonnie's behavior in the music class. Now as I said before, Jonnie has marvelous peer relationships. He's one of the most gregarious boys in the whole class, probably a natural leader. But music class is where this trait gets him into trouble."

"Gregarious? You mean Jonathon is outgoing and friendly?" a note of incredulity in her voice.

"Of course. Don't you see that at home? Why there's not a child in the class that doesn't interact with Jonnie socially during the course of the day. But in music class, where the environment is unstructured, this characteristic gets him into trouble." She smiled. "That's the class where all the note-passing occurs, and Jonnie's right in the middle of this misbehavior."

"Note-passing?"

"Yes, note-passing!" The teacher paused to allow Jonathon's mother time to register her puzzlement. "But Jonnie's so popular that *his* notes get widely circulated and cause children to talk because they're so . . . so . . . provocative. It's hard to explain. But here, let me show you one of Jonnie's notes." Mrs. Haynes quickly stood up, walked to her desk, picked up her blotter, and retrieved a badly wrinkled piece of paper. She handed the paper to Jonathon's mother and with a conspiratorial wink said: "Wouldn't you react to this note if you were a little girl?"

The note was written in large careless block letters. The message, "BETY TELL JULY HE HAS A HOL IN HS UNDERPATS, JOHN,", contained a backwards N, plus several erasures around "underpats" and a large heart around "Bety." Jonathon's mother gasped. Then she burst out:

"But this isn't my Jonathon's note. He's Jonathon—or Jon—not *J-O-H-N*. Who are we talking about? Is it my Jonathon, Jonathon Pratt? Does my son have the reading problem, or is it this John? Maybe this confusion explains some things I haven't been able to understand in our conversation."

She had barely finished the last sentence when she knew she had said the wrong thing. She saw the muscles around Mrs. Haynes's mouth tightening, and felt trapped. She watched the teacher's face change from amused condescension to professional coolness. She heard in the tone of the teacher's voice the sudden barrier of defensiveness. Communication was blocked totally.

"No, it doesn't explain anything, and I'm sorry if there's a misunderstanding. I guess I merely grabbed the wrong note to show you." The words were measured and low. "Of course, I know Jonathon, and, as I said, although he's not a bad reader, he certainly could improve. I hope you'll try to help him at home. I'm talking about a boy who is gregarious—sometimes. Sometimes he does write notes that get him in trouble, but I guess I don't have one with me now. But frankly, Mrs. Pratt, there is a problem I do want to talk with you about. The times that Jonathon is not gregarious, he actually appears withdrawn to me. He won't take the initiative in sports and classroom activities and has to be prodded. I worry about these things. I think you should worry about them, too. Do you notice this extreme reticence—this shyness —at home?" Now her face had resumed a patronizing attitude; the pace of her voice was quickening as she glanced again furtively at her watch.

Mrs. Pratt hurried her reply. "I sometimes see that, yes. I was hoping to talk about it, but I know you're in a rush now. Maybe another time?" She was stalling, her thoughts confused.

"Certainly." The professional ending to an interview. "Why don't you think about this conversation and make some mental notes for our next meeting. I am concerned about Jonathon, and wonder if he might need some professional help for his . . . uh . . . reticence in the future. But we can talk about this later. In the meantime, you can also help him at home by letting him read to you and correcting his errors as they occur."

She stood up, a signal to Jonathon's mother. But Jonathon's mother did not move for a minute. She was thinking: "My son is Jonathon, not John. My son reads well. My son has a problem with shyness, not 'withdrawal.'" Mrs. Haynes, you don't know about Jonathon. You

28

shouldn't be so defensive. You haven't helped me in any way to understand my child. I can't talk to you about him because I don't think you know him. I feel left out of this school—the whole educational process. And you have my child for six hours a day, five days a week. Suddenly I'm really afraid—and very helpless."

If you had been Jonathon's mother, what would you have done? Gone to the principal and complained? Made an immediate reappointment for a confrontation? Asked for testing for Jonathon? Requested the chance to observe Jonathon in the classroom for yourself? Checked the reputation of Mrs. Haynes as a teacher with the neighborhood mothers? Filed an ethics charge with the National Education Association or the American Federation of Teachers?

None of these actions really would have been sufficient for the confusion, the hurt, the anger you would have felt immediately after that disastrous interview, nor would any of the actions substantively have changed the outlook or effectiveness of Jon's teacher, Mrs. Haynes.

What happened between Jonathon's mother (or you) and Jonathon's teacher (or your child's teacher) represents a classic case of a serious communication problem between teacher and parent. This blocked exchange of ideas occurs time after time, even during transactions between two adults. The causes are many; but, generally, that kind of misunderstanding occurs because both parties involved in the conversation have brought different backgrounds, assumptions, and expectations to the meeting. To illustrate this clearly, we should reexamine the interview between Jonathon's mother and Mrs. Haynes.

What hopes, expectations, and assumptions did Jonathon's mother bring to the meeting? She had come to visit the first grade teacher for one reason—Jonathon's school success. After all, she was Jonathon's mother, expected by her husband and friends to be totally dedicated to his growth in every possible way. Jonathon was the center of his mother's concern, the repository of all her hopes and ambitions, the inheritor of all her values, the proof of her adequacy as a mother. Her expectations of the meeting with his teacher were based on the belief that Mrs. Haynes would and could talk about Jonathon as a individual, that she would be able to discuss his strengths and weaknesses in an almost professionally clinical way, that she would become an ally to Jonathon's mother in Jon's upbringing, *and that the teacher would infer, from her observations of Jonathon, that his mother had been doing a very adequate job in raising him.* Jonathon's mother wanted him to be important to Mrs. Haynes, the very same way that Jonathon was important to her. She wanted Mrs. Haynes to acknowledge her responsibility for the daily care of Jonathon when he was away from his mother; but she also needed Mrs. Haynes to define her role as Jon's teacher, not as a separate person who was competing with Mrs. Pratt for Jonathon's time and attention. She probably hoped that Mrs. Haynes would ask her questions about Jonathon rather than having to be interrogated herself.

Mrs. Haynes, on the other hand, was a person caught in two obvious mistakes and trying to save face. She acknowledged her responsibility to her children and considered herself a professional on the issue of the education of children; but all of a sudden, in this situation she observed herself behaving in a less than professional way. She had miscalculated the time of the interview, had not prepared ahead of time, and was forced to talk about a child in her class in a manner suggesting incompetence. Finally, to her horror, she realized that she had been talking about the wrong child! She thought that if she did not bring the conversation immediately to a halt, she would not only lose the respect of that mother but would have difficulty in facing herself with the knowledge that she had appeared unfit and unprepared to teach a classroom of children. If she believed this of herself, how could she do all that she had to do with her children objectively and dispassionately? So she had to back out. She had to give herself time to think more about Jonathon so she would be ready for the next meeting. She had to bring up some negative traits, so Jonathon's mother would be concerned enough about those things that she would forget the immediate embarrassment of the situation. She had thrown some technical words at the mother to show her that this teacher had been specially trained for her job. She wanted the verbal smokescreen to stop the mother's questions. She was forced to retreat behind a superficial professional facade.

Have any of these interactions and reactions occurred in your meetings with your child's teacher? It is very likely, for these misunderstandings do crop up in far too many interviews between parent and teacher.

You have a right to be uptight. The facts of the matter are that you, as a parent in our American society, have been given an inestimable position of responsibility when you are challenged in the rearing of a child. You are legally responsible for his or her acts until he or she reaches the age of maturity. You are told by all religions that you are morally responsible for the development of your child's values and goals. You are also able to see, as he grows, the adoption of your mannerisms, your feelings, and, often, your lifestyle. Your children are so important to you that an interview with a teacher about any one of them will bring into immediate focus many of your worries and concerns about that specific child. That this happens to you is natural and normal. You should expect and recognize the reaction, so you can work around it.

While you acknowledge that you will always be somewhat emotional about your child, you should recognize too that these feelings will often color your perceptions of the other people who deal with him or her. Your child is leaving home when he or she first goes to school, be it nursery school, kindergarten, or first grade. This will be the first time he or she will be away from you for prolonged periods. You will worry about who is taking care of him or her in approximately the same way that you worry about the quality of the babysitter with whom you previously left your child. If someone is going to have to play parent or parent surrogate to your child, you want that person to be the best possible one. You fantasize that the person ought, in fact, to be a great deal like you. When Jonathon or Joanne goes to school, the child is trusting; you are entrusting. It has to be hard for you both.

But you do send your child to school, not only because the law states that you must but also because you believe in schooling. You believe it is right for your child. You know that without education, your child will not be able to get the job or career you hope for. You know that education can elevate him or her in the social world, and yield the kinds of friends and family you desire. Education can offer new experiences of discovery, reward, and satisfaction. You don't want to deny him or her these experiences. So you send your child to school and to that stranger, the "other parent," the teacher.

You worry about it, however. You wonder if that teacher can understand your child the way you do. Does she (or he) have your patience in hearing your child through the detours in his rambling conversations? You question whether she is teaching him or her the right values. So you often enter the parent-teacher interview with two feelings—one which accepts education as necessary and desirable for your child, and another which doubts whether the teacher is actually good enough or competent enough to teach your child. Unless controlled, these conflicting feelings, these two opposing forces within you will invariably initiate the burst of anxiety in a parent-teacher interview that finally stops communication.

You are not the only one of the pair who can block communication. The teacher is also capable of interfering with the mutual exchange of ideas.

The barriers to communication between you and the teacher are generally only half of your making. Often the teacher also comes to the interview with some intrinsic and firm biases.

One bias is that a teacher is a "professional" and you are not. What that means is that she (or he) believes, because of college orientation and pressure from fellow teachers, that she knows more about teaching and educating your child than you do. She does have an advantage, if you add up her ability to use technical terms, quote the latest educational research, sum up her past experience, and deal with thirty children at one time in her classroom. However, what she does *not* know as well as you do is *your* child. You know best how your child behaves at home, what excites him, what rewards work best for him, what your goals are for him, and what helps him learn. Unfortunately, the "professionalism" of teachers is sometimes translated by them as meaning: "Don't ask the parents, because they think I'm supposed to know." For communication finally to occur, the teacher's attitude must be totally reversed to: "As a professional, I can use the knowledge and skills of Joanne's mother to help me educate her." Sometimes both the parent and the teacher have to recognize the barrier of "professionalism" that exists between them and work through this artificial "job differential" before the two can cooperate as a team in the education of the child.

Another area in which the teacher does not know everything is how to educate each child to the best of his or her ability. If *you* think that she has this total answer and if *she* thinks she has this total answer, then you are both in trouble once again. Modern education has demonstrated clearly that each child learns differently and in his own particular way. It is the teacher's job to find out how a child learns best and to make his educational program as individual as possible, given the large classes and groups in which he will have to function. In order to find the best program for each individual child, however, the teacher often must do a great deal of searching. Sometimes she will need psychological and educational tests; sometimes watching and observing the child will tell her what works best. Often a teacher will have to try different techniques on a child for that child's learning pattern before she recognizes what is best (in a sort of trial-and-error method). During her training period, she is given a library of these techniques; but only experience helps her to use these skills most effectively in finding the teaching method that works best for each child. Therefore, although she needs your basic information about your child, she cannot always tell you immediately what your child is all about. A good teacher recognizes her certain insecurity in starting to teach a class and will ask you for the necessary information. A poor teacher will only tell, not ask. When this occurs, often it will be your task to switch roles as a parent and become the competent "teacher." Obtain the pertinent information from the teacher as to what she has tried that stimulates and catches the attention of your child in school. Then you can add the information about your own home observations. Together you can paint the complete portrait of your schoolchild.

A final hurdle to communication that a teacher often brings to the parent interview is the sheer exhaustion of the daily job. A look around the classroom shows too many children, too little space, not enough equipment, the additional demands of administrative record keeping, untrained aides, outside college coursework which needs preparation, class lessons to be written, and referrals of "problem" children to be made. Add to this the knowledge that most teachers are being underpaid in comparison to their college classmates who graduated at the same time but went into other fields. You have, then, a person who is often tempted to say, "Why put up with overindulgent parents all day when I could be living it up as a junior business executive or a personnel officer?" Somewhat immature? Certainly. But who, after a hectic day with 30 livewires who have been kept indoors by the rain, is not ready to regress into adolescent anger? Sometimes, as with any of your close friends, you might just have to listen to your child's teacher until the frustrations of the classroom have been discussed and are relieved. Then you can move on to the important matters.

And there are many important matters that you may need to discuss with the teacher about your child. Some will be dealt with in more detail in later chapters of the book; however, there are items of information that you can and should receive every time you have an interview with your child's teacher.

For instance, find out from the teacher what the class is doing that is particularly unusual and interesting. This will give you something to discuss with your children around the supper table and reinforce the teacher's daily work in these special areas.

Ask what your child is working at right now and how you can help him/her with it.

Ask her if she has detected any problems developing between your child and the other children in the class that you might investigate before they become more serious.

Ask her what your child is doing best, so that you might compliment him/her at home and reinforce the progress in this area.

These might seem like simple questions, but they are often not given precise consideration by the teacher simply because she works almost constantly in a group environment. Both you and she will be surprised at the insight the answers to these questions can give. The questions must be asked tactfully, gently, with interest, and the responses heard without argument. On the parent-teacher team, your job is to make certain that you follow up, reporting back your responses to the tasks and lessons the teacher asks you to do with your child at home.

There will be times when you will come to your child's teacher with very significant problems. Then you really need the information that can help you make the genuinely important educational and therapeutic decisions required. Occasionally you must respond to decisions that are being made about your child by the school, the courts, or by other agencies outside your control. These are all crucial times when you must communicate with the teacher absolutely freely. You will have to work at this conversation; it may take more than one sitting. You will have to try to keep unemotional and rational. You will have to try to focus on the task, which is making the best decision for your child. Here are some points that might help you in these vital conversations with your child's teacher:

1. You can reward a teacher for good teaching. The ratings of effectiveness that a teacher receives at the end of the year will be determined, in large part, by how satisfied the parents are with the growth of their children and how much each child actually gains in education as measured by tests. Therefore, keep in mind that the teacher will be interested in your reaction to her plans for your child. Listen to her, and ask how she expects these goals to help your child with his/her education. If her plans seem reasonable, give them a try. Let her report to you how the efforts are working. Remember that you can give her a boost at the end of the year as well as a black mark. Reward her if you can; and punish infrequently. Your child will thank you for that positive philosophy.

2. Because of her training, she knows about many educational systems and different techniques. If you feel that what is happening to your child is not adequate, ask her for different options. Ask her what she would do if . . . If your child were a boy instead of a girl with the same problem . . . if she were fifteen instead of thirteen . . . if she went to a structured school rather than an open school. Begin to discuss the new and varied techniques with which you and she might experiment. Ask her where you can learn more about some of these new teaching methods. The school will probably have a library with a section on education; if not, you might try the local teacher's college library. Investigate and find how many exciting, new, and varied options modern education has to offer your child.

3. Every time you go to the toy store or library you will be subjected to "educational" gimmicks and systems geared to making you the "teacher." Some of these so-called teaching systems are worthless. In fact, many can run counter to good modern teaching methods. Ask the teacher about such toys and systems and let her help you find the ones that are helpful and that correlate with the material being used in the classroom. This will give you an insight into the teacher's plans and place you in the appropriate position of "adjunct-home teacher."

4. Every teacher grades differently. Different educators have different opinions about the value of grading. Each teacher looks for better and more valid ways of reporting to a parent than letter or number grades. Discuss grading with the teacher in an attempt to learn what she (or he) is trying to say by the "grades" given your child. Ask her if she grades a child in relationship to his own growth or to that of the class. Ask her if she feels that children generally receive higher grades in her class at the end of the year than at the beginning, and if so, why? Ask her how she would like to report to you if she had her preference—both of you can then determine if that method might be used in the future in addition to the present one. In other words, tune into the formal lines of communication between teacher and parent regarding the child's "grades." Then you can follow up the report card with more understanding. This will serve as a basis for a more profitable, informal discussion as to what the report card is really saying about your child.

5. As a teacher with a full class, she is in the unique position of watching your child every day within a large group—something you can probably never do. You need to know how your child reacts in

this environment, because his or her group actions will determine how well he or she is progressing in the social skills so necessary to productive maturity. Sometimes you can get a sample of how well your child is doing by observing him for a day or two with his friends. But it will still be only a sample. For more information about his social progress you will have to turn to his teacher; and you should respect and pay attention to her answers. But try to clarify them as much as possible. Check up on this social behavior frequently. If you hear what begins to sound like a psychological interpretation or jargon (such as: "Jack seems withdrawn in large groups but outgoing in small groups"), request that the teacher give you specific examples. A teacher is not, and should not function as, an amateur psychologist. Check out the examples; then draw *your own* conclusions. The teacher's specialty is education—not psychology.

6. Finally, your child's teacher often has a wealth of experience with which to place any problems in proper perspective. If you can tap into that experience, and share that perspective, you will be in a better position to be more objective about your child and any problem that arises. Together, you and the teacher can plan additional options. Ask the teacher if she has dealt with children with similar problems. What did she find most effective in those cases? What in her experience has happened if option (A) was selected? Option (B) or (C)? Ask her what kind of home guidance has proved most effective with children of similar problems in her experience. What have other teachers accomplished with children under similar circumstances? How? When? This kind of questioning can have the advantage of broadening the perspective and interpretation of the child's problem for both parent and teacher. The teacher is rarely asked such questions by troubled parents; this is unfortunate since the answers need to be shared by *all* who handle children.

Teachers are the "first line" of education. They are the people in the educational system who mean the most to your child, and, therefore, will mean the most to you as the parents. They are the people who should be consulted first when any major educational decisions are pending, and again when any such major decisions are made and implemented. Because of the nature of a teacher's training, attitude, and job, she (or he) will not always be able to solve all of your or your child's problems as quickly or compassionately as you might wish. But because of your feelings about your child and his education, you too will not always appear as reasonable and rational as you think you should. It is up to you as the parent to bridge any barriers to communication that exist between you and the teacher. You can accomplish this by keeping your talk focused on the educational needs of the child and by consciously agreeing to share the responsibility for your child's education with the teacher. You will have to learn to accept and respect the teacher's ability to guide the educational destiny of your child, even though you cannot afford to do so without questions and continued observation. You will have to give the teacher the information that can help her in making educational decisions about your child, but you cannot expect to tell her what to do in the classroom. Your best relationship with the teacher is one of partnership in the educational process—with the teacher as the senior partner. This is a difficult position for a parent to assume.

But you must try; for the sake of your child.

4 The Special Education Teacher

How many times have you, as a thinking parent, questioned the role of the special education teacher in today's schools? If you were to bring the subject up in casual conversation over a cup of coffee with friends, the dialogue might commonly sound something like this:

"Sure, I know that handicapped kids need some special help. But do they need teachers all to themselves? After all, a lot of very famous handicapped people succeeded without special education teachers. Why, I remember when I was in elementary school about twenty years ago and I knew several handicapped kids. But we had good teachers then; and they handled those kids just right. We included them in our games and tried to forgive their mistakes and really liked some of them. They got along well then. Why not now?"

The answer to this question is not as obvious or simple as it may appear; it has historical, legalistic, humanitarian, and educational roots. But if you put the whole history of progress on special education in perspective, consider the forces which caused the changes, and then simplify the outcomes, you will arrive at the fact that those handicapped children of twenty years ago (with a very few talented exceptions) just got by. *That is all.* They managed. They barely made it. They got by in elementary school, where they were promoted because the teacher felt sorry for them and did not know what to do with them for another year. They got by at home because their parents felt an obligation to shelter them and to keep them fixed in an environment which offered them as little challenge or pain as possible. They skimmed through the first eight grades of school, then just seemed to drop from sight, either taking a job somewhere in a relative's back room, or being committed to a state or private agency, or finally landing in a prison, or just remaining silently and unobtrusively at home with a nonworking mother or guardian. They were promoted by making a marginal adjustment to a structured school situation in the early grades, but dropped out when life became unstructured and more complex and demanding. In essence they were being "maintained"—not taught—in our schools. Their talents and potentials went untested, unchallenged, and were not exercised. Their ability to be useful, happy citizens was never explored. Their human right to be given every possible opportunity was ignored.

Special education teachers have been challenged to reverse this attitude and this situation. They are to look for every possible potential in every child. The special education teacher attempts to help that child grow in every emotional, educational, and physical way as much as is humanly possible. The aim is to prepare and condition that child for as many of life's pleasures and disappointments as he or she can absorb and tolerate. The key to the success of the special education teacher is her (it is usually a woman) ability to ignore the child's disability in favor of his ability.

Does this sound idealistic? It is. And so are many special education teachers, if we may be allowed to make a generalization. In the past, handicapped children would be viewed as having limited expectations by all, and they would be helped to live only up to the level of these narrow expectations. But the special education teacher cannot believe in these preset limitations any longer. She has seen too many handicapped children who have broken the rules about their expected horizons. Today's special education teacher has seen the severely and multiply handicapped child holding down a forty-hour-a-week job and living in an independent apartment with a roommate. The special education teacher has seen children formerly thought to be severely retarded by Down's Syndrome (sometimes called Mongolism) reading a book by age seven, and blind children walking across town with no dog, no cane, no companion. Deaf children can carry on conversations with others by reading their lips and speaking clearly enough to be understood. Crippled children can participate in special modified athletic events which hold the same thrills of competing and winning as non-handicapped athletics. And handicapped children can become handicapped adults who marry, work, pay taxes, commute, play, fight, worry, love, enjoy, and worship just like any non-handicapped person.

A special education teacher maintains and lives to continue that vision.

How will you know a special education teacher when you see one?

After the above description, you might start searching for someone with an eternal smile on her face or sporting an immaculate halo. Not so. Generally the special education teacher is a bit unkempt, harassed, and tired. Teaching handicapped children is extremely hard work. It requires many hours, great patience and flexibility to tolerate the daily unpredictable changes displayed by these children.

So how does the special education teacher differ from the teacher of a non-handicapped child? In other words, what is "special" about the special education teacher?

Nothing basically. The special education teacher is, first and foremost, a teacher. To understand the insights and information she has about your handicapped child, and the appropriate questions you should ask her, re-read the previous chapter on the teacher. Each of the attributes of that regular classroom teacher—each of the expectations —are the same attributes and expectations as those of the teacher of your handicapped child. Indeed, if your handicapped child is being "mainstreamed" (placed in a class with predominantly non-handicapped children), the teacher who is responsible for him or her has had training primarily in teaching the non-handicapped child. She will be often a regular teacher in a regular classroom. (More about this later.)

But assuming that your child has a special education teacher, and that you want to know what is unique about this teacher, some facts which you should know about special education teachers follow.

1. Special education teachers do not always work in self-contained, isolated classrooms. In the elementary school, it is true, many classes are designated as being primarily for mentally retarded children, or for emotionally disturbed children, or for deaf children. One teacher, one team of teachers, or one teacher and aide are with the class of children for most of the day. This is called a self-contained classroom. But very many special education teachers now function as "resource teachers." For example, most blind children do not need to have special self-contained classes. They need to acquire special skills early in their school career such as learning Braille, tape-recording, typing, and how to use the libraries for the blind. When these skills have been mastered, the blind child can join regular non-handicapped classes. Then the resource teacher of the blind child teaches and reinforces these skills in special classes held during the day. She also helps their teachers with special materials when the children are working in the regular classroom—and that

is usually all that is needed by the normal blind child. In high school, often there is a specialized teacher of vocational skills who works with handicapped children on occupational counselling and job training. He or she may be a special part-time teacher of a particular kind of occupation. Another specialized teacher who might be provided for your handicapped child is an expert teacher of "mobility" (how to move around if you are blind or severely physically disabled) or someone specifically trained in "adaptive physical education" (how to exercise when you have limited physical strengths and skills). All of the special education teachers who deal with the handicapped child must blend their talents into an effective, cooperative team.

2. Special education teachers are trained on average for a longer time and with more specialty work than regular teachers. In every state a special education teacher has to be "certified" by the state education department. That means that the teacher has to show a great number of courses and credits in a specialty area of the handicapped, *in addition to* her training as a regular teacher. In most states, the minimum level of educational achievement for a special education teacher is fast becoming a master's degree.

This suggests that the special education teacher is supposed to be informed about a number of educational areas in depth. Since the special education teacher is trained first as a regular teacher, she understands a great deal about the subject matter relevant to the non-handicapped child. She knows what kind of material should be taught in what sequence to each child. Her training also includes both college and practical work in observing and learning different teaching methods to motivate all children and to handle a wide diversity of students, each of whom learns at a different rate.

But the training of the special education teacher goes a step further. And this is the essential step. She learns how to *individualize* or *prescribe* teaching. This means that the special education teacher should be equipped with the knowledge and skill necessary to look at one handicapped child, interpret his or her tests and behaviors, and make up a whole teaching sequence and method that will effectively teach that particular child. Furthermore, the teacher ought to be able to work with each handicapped child for whom she is responsible in an "individualized" way. And in addition to knowing about the usual courses which the non-handicapped child is expected to complete successfully in the course of normal educa-

41

tional experience, the special education teacher is acutely aware of the need to set different educational goals for the handicapped child. These children may not need to spend time on "the history of China," for instance, if such learning will prevent or interfere with their ability to grasp an occupational skill necessary for their future independence and self-sufficiency. So the special education teacher "individualizes" the goals for the special child (with help from other supportive figures such as informed and cooperative parents) and "prescribes" the education being mapped out for this particular child.

Generally this plan will include a heavy emphasis on language— that vital tool which helps everyone to find an easier and smoother path in society. Furthermore, it might redefine math, or communication skills, or motor achievements, in more practical and definitive terms. Math, for instance, might not be set up by this teacher as "knowing beginning algebra"; rather, she might have created the more realistic goal of "knowing how to maintain and balance a personal checking and savings account." Communications might be related to "interpersonal skills in transmitting ideas" (or how to make your feelings clearly known) rather than "writing usable essays." Motor skills standards might be defined as those useful in certain job situations rather than those needed for passing a physical fitness standard. It is true that most special education teachers, because of their primary training as regular teachers, strive to help the handicapped child learn all the content required of a non-handicapped child during the equivalent school years. However, they will sacrifice some of the more abstract areas if this means that they can offer the child more abilities and proficiencies in daily living patterns and in self-sufficiency for the future. And you, as a parent, can team up with this teacher to set these realistic goals, agree to the appropriate objectives, and help your handicapped child prepare for his/her successful later life as a socially contributing citizen.

3. Special education teachers are often more committed and more trained to working with parents than regular teachers. Throughout their college and postgraduate training, the role of the parent in the education and "treatment" of handicapped children is stressed. Many state and almost all federal programs for the handicapped child mandate the existence of provisions for parent counselling or parent education. Colleges and universities are including more experience for the teachers-in-training in both class and individual con-

ferences with parents. Most special educators know, in fact, that if it had not been for parent pressures and lobbies in the early days of special education, they might not have their assignment. These teachers are quick to realize your importance as a parent and as a fellow colleague in planning the education of your child. You may rest assured that if you wish to talk to your child's special education teacher, your note requesting an appointment will be answered (or if not, another note to the supervisor will get a prompt response). You will be considered a valuable team member in your child's education.

4. Special education teachers often have more special resources available to them. They also have been trained to locate and uncover the particular materials and resources your child needs. What does that mean for a handicapped child? It comprises special libraries; unique and individualized curriculum materials; magazines and books of advice or description of programs for parents; names and services of other professionals who are on the team helping your handicapped child, such as pediatricians, nurses, psychologists, physical therapists, and so on; and the latest techniques of education and treatment for the special child. Suppose your child is not blind but has very low vision. He or she will be receiving some remedial help in school, but the special education teacher can help you find a clinic where you can get many low-vision aids individually prescribed and supplied. You will want to know how other parents whose children have problems similar to yours handle the everyday routine of discipline, feeding, play, monitoring, and the like. The special education teacher should be able to help you find the nearest parents' organization to provide you with such information. Or perhaps she will show you a copy of one of the very useful parent's magazines devoted to advising the concerned parents of handicapped children. Are you anxious to help your handicapped child learn at home? The special education teacher can give you practical aid in teaching methods and provide you with special materials for parents which will make teaching your child much easier. Do you want to read more about your child's problem? Try one of her suggestions of a special education library, or a national computer service (Educational Resources Information Center—ERIC) that will automatically search out, for a small fee, all the literature in your specific area and give you an annotated bibliography. Do you want a pediatrician in tune with your child's special needs? Ask the special education teacher for a

list. What of the latest theory of treatment you just read about in the Sunday supplement? Have the special education teacher check it out for you. When you establish yourself as a qualified member of the team that is "treating" your child, you will find that the special educator will share much with you—as a colleague.

Armed with these facts about special education teachers, you are now ready to enlist their aid in helping you provide the best education you can program for your handicapped child—"best" meaning the most productive in terms of your child's personal satisfaction and preparation for later life. Different types of handicaps are covered specifically in later chapters in this book. For now, it is important to realize that you do have an ally—one on the front lines of the battle for your child's successful march toward maturity. You need to be concerned that both you and this ally, the special education teacher, share the same goals.

As you seek this allegiance, there are some things to remember—things that are vital to a full partnership in the team which will be working with your child.

The first thing to resolve is that, as the parents of a special child, you neither have to feel guilty that your child is handicapped nor to assume the full responsibility for his/her education. This may seem obvious, an annoying truism. But consider for a moment. When you first found out that your child was handicapped, didn't you ask if there was something you could have done to prevent it? Didn't you wonder whether some divine will was testing—perhaps punishing—you? Did you in fact dedicate yourself completely to righting your child's wrong? Many parents of the handicapped do feel this way. Even though they indicate that they are enlightened, they still experience a deep, extended sense of binding responsibility. Your ally does not feel that you are totally responsible. That fact may help you establish an easier dialogue with her—she assumes some of this load.

The special education teacher believes that it is her job, as well as that of the parent, to set the educational goals for your child, to help the child realize these goals, and to redefine them as the tasks appear to be accomplished (or thwarted). The school systems, the state constitutions, and the courts also know that the public and private schools are responsible for helping you to educate your handicapped child. Therefore you need not feel that you have to be eternally grateful and acquiescent. Don't just accept the aid of the special educators—become a full partner.

A second fact you must remember is that, as a parent, you cannot always know what is best for your child. So you must learn to share the work with the special education teacher. You must make joint decisions. Try to research and acknowledge your child's needs as carefully and well as your ally is doing. Listen as objectively as possible to the special teacher, contribute your opinion to the decisions, then carry through together.

And, finally, remember that your child is first a child and, secondly, a child with a handicap. Utilize the knowledge of the special teacher as the trained expert in your child's specific problem, but also remember that this teacher has training and skills in the education of all children—with or without handicaps. The more you are able to treat your child as "normal," the more he or she will be able with the special educator's help to adapt to the future. And if you are not sure whether a problem that has arisen with your child is due directly to the handicapping condition or is merely a reflection of the natural growth and development process, do not hesitate to ask the special education teacher for her advice. She watches your child and can contribute her observations and informed opinion.

The special education teacher is more interested in the child than in the handicap. He or she is "special" because of the special challenge. Her job and yours is to work together to meet this challenge, and graduate an adjusted "special" child into adulthood.

5 The Communication Specialist

Speech therapist, speech clinician, hearing therapist, speech pathologist—all these names have been used at one time or another to describe the communication specialist in the schools. One of them may still be used in your school; but no matter what the title, this description essentially designates the person described in this chapter. We have chosen the term "communication specialist," not because the profession has designated that specific title, but because the people most recently trained in this field really can diagnose, prescribe, and treat all kinds of communications problems—from the understanding of a child's hearing to the full spectrum of his ability to make a verbal response.

Few parents are aware of the broad talents of this special professional —talents that are used in daily contact with their child. To find out what a communication specialist does, let us accompany her through a hypothetical work day.

8:00 A.M.: Ms. Allen arrives for work at the Elmhurst Elementary School (her assignment on Monday and Wednesday mornings). She checks in at the front office for any messages or referrals left in her box. There are two from the third grade teacher, Ms. Michaels, about children with possible speech problems. She checks her appointment book and scribbles a reply. Then she heads for the special education office, where she picks up the machine that tests hearing levels, the audiometer, which was returned the day before after an annual check for accuracy. Lifting up the machine in her arms, she turns down the corridor and swings open the door to her office.

She had not expected to see the six-year-old girl, with big frightened eyes, looking startled and struggling to sit upright on the couch in the corner. "Hello, what's this? So early in the morning?" The little girl tries to speak, but the sound is tiny and inaudible, hampered by the thermometer she is holding between her teeth. Her eyes are moist, and she sniffles several times.

Ms. Allen recognizes a mistake—a frequent one—caused by sharing her office with the nurse. "No problem, young lady. Mrs. Simmons [the school nurse] must have forgotten that today's Monday. On Mondays and Wednesdays, this is the speech room—not the health room. Now you go back to Mrs. Simmons's office and wait there for her. Tell her Ms. Allen is in today. O.K.? And don't bite that thing." She shakes her head as she reflects ruefully on her constantly changing working areas. Space is tight in the school and she is the first one to have to share offices.

She opens the stylish cloth bag she has been carrying and takes out the scrapbook of pictures she has made for the first period's articulation therapy.

8:30 A.M.: The first group of children arrives. Six children from grades one through three troop into the small room. All of them have problems in speaking clearly; it is difficult for other children or adults to understand them. The communication specialist seats them around her in a half circle and begins talking to them. She asks them specific questions, and each child responds to her in the sentences she requires in these sessions. (Communication specialist: "What a pretty dress, Carolyn. From what material is it made?" Carolyn: "It is made from cotton.") When a child makes a speech error, she corrects it immediately, asking the child to repeat the correct sound, showing him or her in the mirror what the sound looks like on his or her face, and asking the rest of the children in the group to repeat it.

Then she askes two children to work together on the "r" sound. She gives the pair pictures of rabbits, radios, trains, and cars. The children must correct each other when they hear the incorrect "r" sound. Another group of three children have more errors in their speech pattern than the "r" sound. The communication specialist asks them to look through the magazines and catalogs on the table to find pictures of images with the "st" sound, cut out these pictures, and put them in their speech scrapbooks. That exercise leaves time for Ms. Allen to work with Ronnie, who has so many speech errors that he has difficulty being understood by anyone, including his parents. She suspects that there may be some mild neurological problems that contribute to his problems with speech, but she has not worked with him long enough to discover the entire extent of his difficulties. He has been included in this group session because the communication specialist wants to find out if he can profit from the instructions she gives to the rest of the children. However, Ronnie is still in a diagnostic period as far as she is concerned. Today she opens a picture book that has no words and asks him to tell her a story. As he "talks" she writes down his speech as it sounds, letter by letter, for later analysis. She realizes that there will be many more such exercises before she can specifically pinpoint his distorted speech patterns.

Fifteen minutes before the end of the period, Ms. Allen talks to all the children again. She asks them to tell her what they have just done and share their experiences with the others. She helps to translate for Ronnie, never quite certain that she is using the words he is trying to formulate, hoping his facial expressions will give her a clue. Just as the bell rings, she compliments the children on their progress and sends the group back to their regular classes.

9:15 A.M.: Second articulation session. Now Ms. Allen confronts a group of older children, fourth grade to sixth grade. This group is not as relaxed about their speech problems as the younger group because at this age, the other children are beginning to make fun of them. In fact last year, one of the fourth graders had cried the whole hour during the first two weeks of her sessions because she felt so "different."

Essentially, Ms. Allen uses the same basic techniques with this group as she did with the first. She encourages the use of problem sounds in words, corrects the words, and shows the children how to produce them. She patiently asks each youngster to reproduce these problem words correctly so that everyone can hear them and she can reward them for their success. The games she uses to encourage spontaneous speech are more sophisticated than those she tried with the earlier class. The older children take their lesson much more seriously. But she is pleased to note that the children seem to have a certain warm compassion for each other; they are gentler and more tolerant with one another than they are with their own mistakes. They are patient with repeated errors, and volunteer to demonstrate whatever correct sounds they can make. They comfort those who are trying and are grateful for their individual progress.

10:00 A.M.: Testing and preparation time. Today Ms. Allen must administer two audiological evaluations and one speech test. The two audiological tests are for children, Jack and Mary, in the second and fourth grades. Neither child has been tested for over a year, and their teachers report classroom behavior which could indicate a new hearing loss. Each one seems to have trouble concentrating for long periods of time on the lessons, does not seem to understand directions as well as the other children, and has to be called two or three times before responding.

Ms. Allen works with each child individually. When Jack is seated, she slips the earphone over his head and instructs him to raise his hand when

The Communication Specialist

he hears a sound. The communication specialist tests the child's response to a loud sound and watches closely to make sure that he does not see her press the lever on the audiometer. She must protect against the youngster "faking" the test. Then she tries different tones at different volume levels, and notes on her charts when the child responds. In this way, she fills out an accurate audiogram—a pictorial graph of the child's hearing capacity in each ear.

Jack's audiogram indicates that his hearing is within normal limits, so his teacher must search for other reasons for his inattentiveness. However, Mary's audiogram reveals that she has a profound loss of hearing in the right ear and a moderate loss of hearing in the left ear. Ms. Allen talks to Mary after the test and notes that she appears to be watching her lips very intently, a sign that the hearing loss is probably of fairly recent origin. She notes that the child has a running nose and inquires about colds and allergies. Mary tells her that she often has earaches, and sometimes has to have her ears "drained." She says she is still getting over a cold she has had for three and a half weeks, and tells Ms. Allen that her ears are beginning to hurt her again. After the child leaves, Ms. Allen writes a note to Mary's teacher and the school nurse telling them about the audiogram and suggesting that the hearing loss might be temporary, but must be analyzed and diagnosed by the child's pediatrician and outside medical and hearing specialist. If the hearing loss is found to be permanent, Mary could require the use of hearing aids, and perhaps even special remedial education.

After this, the child who needs the speech diagnosis—Jerry—enters the makeshift room. A freckled, blond eight-year-old, Jerry's greeting to Ms. Allen comes out in a lazy drawl: "Maw-nin, Miz Ayl-len." She immediately recognizes a deep Southern accent, as broad in the vowels as the words were long in emerging. Quickly she glances at the name of the referring teacher and smiles as she recognizes the only member of the faculty from Boston. No wonder they couldn't understand each other.

It is a regional dialect problem. As Ms. Allen moves through the test, asking Jerry to name the pictures to which she points, she hears the broad vowels, the lack of r's, and the colloquialisms of the rural Kentucky town from which Jerry has transferred. She knows that within a matter of weeks the class will have adapted to Jerry's "sound" and be able to understand him quite well; and his teacher will wonder why she ever referred him to the communication specialist in the first place. She writes a cheerful note to this effect for Jerry's teacher, giving it to him to take back. Another year and he'll sound just as "citified" as the rest of us, she thinks, reflecting for a moment that it is a shame; part of his intrinsic charm will have been lost in his need to fit in.

10:45 A.M.: Individual therapy time. Michael is a sixth grader who is a severe stutterer. Any attempts at spontaneous speech are accompanied by intense facial grimaces and agonizing ticlike physical mannerisms. The teacher finds him extremely difficult to understand and the other children make him an object of their jokes. Ms. Allen sees Michael in conjunction with the school psychologist, who is trying to help him with the anger and rejection he feels toward the children who ridicule him.

As Michael talks with Ms. Allen, she notes his stuttering patterns. What types of questions and answers provoke the most dramatic speech "blocks"? What happens to the stuttering behavior after ten minutes of speech? Is the stuttering pattern consistent? She finds so few improvements for which she can reward him. The problem is, and will be, a long-term handicap. Then she reads in unison with him, a technique that allows stutterers to speak without the stutter. This releases his anxieties about his ability to speak. Next, they practice speaking in rhythms, using a ticking metronome that reduces Michael's stuttering in her office but has not yet been tried outside school. She wants Michael to continue practicing the method until he is able to speak perfectly in her room before he tries it outside. He cannot afford another major speech failure before other people.

After Michael follows a child with a voice problem. Tommy comes from a large, noisy family, and has spent a good deal of his life yelling in order to be heard and "hollering" in rambunctious play with his brothers. As a result, he has developed little growths, which are called nodules, on his vocal chords. Unless he can learn to speak correctly and quietly, these nodules will become aggravated until they will require surgery or will cause ultimate loss of voice if they remain. Tommy has been chronically hoarse for the past six months.

Ms. Allen must both re-train Tommy to speak correctly and enforce a regiment of periodic vocal rest, a difficult task in an active six-year-old. Tommy brings his weekly chart of "silence periods" to the session, and Ms. Allen notes on his record that it appears to be easier now for him to have silent periods at home. After the vocal exercises and instruction, she writes a note to Tommy's parents congratulating them on increasing the periods of silences for Tommy which can be tolerated by the family.

At **10:55,** as she is finishing her notes on the day's activities and is about to leave the school, a knock on the door is followed by the entrance of the little girl with the running nose—the same one she had found there earlier in the morning. Ms. Allen sighs. "Still not feeling well?" A nod. She leaves the child with the wondering, big eyes straightening her dress to lie down on the nurse's couch in the corner of the multi-purpose room.

The Communication Specialist

11:00 A.M.: A drive across town to the J. W. Riley Intermediate School, with a ten-minute stop for a carry-out hamburger.

At 11:45 she is checking into her box in the principal's office when Ms. Hankley stops her. "Ms. Allen, Sandra Carson's lisp is no better. It's driving me crazy." She imitates Sandra's speech, substituting "th" for "s."

Ms. Allen fights off a moment of anger. Sandra has problems enough being constantly faced with her lisping speech without having to cope with an intolerant teacher. Seventh graders need acceptance, not rejection.

She sighs, swallows, then replies, "Sandra is fortunate to have a teacher like you who is interested in helping her with that annoying lisp. You know, kids her age are particularly susceptible to any form of ridicule, and that generally makes the lisp worse. Her parents lisp too, so she has trouble hearing the right 's' sound. I'm sure you're sensitive and give her some private reward when she speaks without lisping. I'll continue to help her from time to time in private sessions, but I appreciate your being on our team."

Ms. Hankley has picked up the serious tone of the speech pathologist and drops her eyes. "Yes, I'm on your team. I guess it takes time. See you later." And Ms. Allen moves on to the speech pathology office.

12:00: Noontime begins with a meeting with three teachers of learning-disabled children during the first half-hour of their lunch period. Ms. Allen has been meeting with these three teachers through the entire school year, helping them with the problem of language stimulation in their classroom.

Immature language is a problem that is particularly prevalent in children who have learning disabilities. Language development or language stimulation is the application of the educational method to help children master their own language—English. These learning-disabled children often have troubles with word sequences, vocabulary, tenses, meanings, and, particularly, the higher level of concepts and abstractions. They can read a sentence aloud, know every word, be able to define each one, and still arrive with a garbled version of the true meaning of the sentence. It becomes the responsibility of their special teachers, with the aid of the communication specialist, to help them master the rules and idiosyncrasies of the written and spoken English language with enough facility to use it in everyday school tasks.

Ms. Allen has spent the first semester working with these teachers on the principles of language stimulation and production. She has worked with them on the importance of continual language production, and had them talking to their students constantly using long and complex sentences. She helped these teachers insist upon standards for sentence production within their classroom. No student could give one-word answers; each had to answer in sentences. She helped the teachers talk about

51

words, experimenting with different meanings, and assisting students to find words for concepts with which they had trouble. Now she has reached the stage where she only has to conduct "staffings" with these teachers. Each time she meets with them, one person presents a puzzling problem from her class and the entire group discusses it. This helps Ms. Allen obtain a clear picture of the level and quality of language activities going on in the classrooms. For the teachers, these sessions give them the opportunity to apply the principles of language stimulation to the everyday activities within their classes.

It took a whole semester before the teachers could trust Ms. Allen enough to share their problems with her openly. She is proud of the growth and accomplishments of these three special education teachers. These sessions are, in fact, some of the most professionally stimulating of her week. They really make her glad to be a communication specialist.

12:45 P.M.: Three students in fifteen-minute sessions for articulation or stuttering therapy come next on Ms. Allen's agenda. Sandra is the first; she practices the "s" sound, initially by concentrating on the difference from the "th" sound, and then in the production of the "s" sound in words. Ms. Allen mentions that she gathers Ms. Hankley is interested in helping Sandra, and encourages her to ask Ms. Hankley for occasional help to find out how she is doing in class. Ms. Allen knows that Ms. Hankley is one of the students' favorite teachers. She counts on the teacher's concern about Sandra's speech problem to maintain their relationship on a professional, non-threatening classroom basis.

Jack, a young man with the stuttering problem, is always a little depressing to her. Here is a youngster with a ten-year pattern of intense stuttering accompanied by the most grotesque facial contortions. He has had a lifetime of speech help with apparently little or no success. What makes her think she can effect a modern-day miracle? Right now she is seeing him jointly with the school psychologist in an attempt to work on the near-surface anger that rages inside him. The school social worker is visiting and counselling Jack's family since there is little hope of helping him without an effective team approach. Anyway, the hope exists, though growing fainter as each year passes.

The third child, Fu Twan, is a joy and dream to treat in therapy. This Korean child was recently adopted by a family in the neighborhood and is being sent to an American school for the first time. Her English writing and reading is passable, thanks to orphanage schools in her native country; but her pronunciation of English is almost unintelligible. Ms. Allen is helping her with that pronunciation, and thoroughly enjoying the quick response; the shy smile of triumph at each correct sound hesitantly offered, and the quick, demure bow of appreciation at the teacher's compliment.

The Communication Specialist

Another month and Fu Twan will have all the skills necessary for continued growth. Ms. Allen reflects that she will be proud but full of regret when it is time to dismiss her completely.

2:00 P.M.: Ms. Allen now makes another quick dash to the Roosevelt High School for her set appointments with students in individual therapy, a few articulation problems, two voice problems—and Jeremy.

Jeremy was captain of the football squad last year. Tall, ruggedly built, quick-witted, and mature, Jeremy had been the school hero, the embodiment of the administration's hopes, a model student. Until one day his helmet slipped, and he hit the goalpost with his head. When he regained consciousness he had lost much of the control of his right side and, at the same time, the ability to say the right word. Ms. Allen is helping him with this problem of aphasia, which is the word for Jeremy's inability to use the correct word to express himself. Many times when she is working with him on familiar sentences, she realizes that in his slow and halting way he knows the word: it is a simple word, a common word. She watches him struggle as if his mind is fighting him for it. She observes his mounting frustration and sees the tears building in his eyes from anger at his failure. And she resists giving him the answer, but gently helps him seek it. Sometimes, when he finds it, his radiant grin lights up her office. Those are her gold star days. They do not come very often with Jeremy. Probably they will recur more frequently during later years, but she will not be there to witness them. Jeremy's problem has a long road to solution. She can only help him take the first steps.

3:00 P.M.: Back to the main office. This is her time for logging in the day's events, dictating a few notes on the progress of the children and teachers she has seen, and selecting materials for the next day's events, which are to include work with two other elementary schools. She takes out a few files for the preparations she must make at home that night.

Today her mail includes three new referrals from teachers in the schools she serves, and she knows she must reserve a half-hour of her precious time for each of these students in order to do a good job. She can only take on two of them, since her caseload by school regulations only has two vacancies. However, if they really need it . . .

She also has a couple of requests from parents who are worried about the speech patterns of their children. One mother says that she did not know her child had a problem until her other children pointed it out to her, and then other mothers told her. Would Ms. Allen please see Jenny? Ms. Allen writes a short but firm Yes, checks her diary, and sets a date. Another parent of a preschool child feels that her child is beginning to stutter. Ms. Allen smiles—most children have what is called "non-fluencies" around age four. It is a normal part of speech development in a growing child. She writes that she will see the child, and hopes to be able to tell the parents to ignore those non-fluencies; otherwise they could reinforce them by their overconcern.

She looks up at the document over her desk that shows she has received a Certificate of Clinical Competence from the American Speech and Hearing Association, her "license" to do communications work. She glances at her framed master's degree diploma next to it. And she thinks of the student days when she dreamed of the job she has now, when she wondered if she would ever be that accomplished, certified speech pathologist, clinical communication specialist, or speech therapist (whatever "they" were going to call her). She smiles as she remembers those early dreams and the fears that when she finally obtained the job as communication specialist in school she would find the work dull and boring.

Now the first wave of exhaustion hits her. She smiles again. Monotony is a foreign word to her.

The daily diary you have just read, a fictionalized one, encompasses the spectrum of tasks that can be performed by all communication specialists. Unless your school system is quite small, you would not expect one specialist to do all those tasks, at all those levels, with such a consistently high rate of competency. But it was presented to you that way so you, as parents of a potentially speech- or language-disordered child, would be aware of the complete range of services a communication specialist can offer to your child.

Let us review some of the kinds of problems for which you might ask the help of your school's "Ms. Allen."

1. *Articulation problems.* It is very difficult to understand your child's speech. Perhaps you understand him or her but you notice that very few other people do, and either you or his brothers or sisters have to translate. Maybe there is one annoying speech difficulty like a lisp, a substituted "w" for an "r" sound, a very juicy and noisy "s" sound, or baby talk that does not improve. When these speech problems persist to an age where you notice that few if any of your child's classmates have similar difficulties, then a call to your child's teacher or the communication specialist would be in order. Unlike many other problems, it may be realistic when you are told that your child will "grow out of it." Articulation problems are often remedied by the child himself around eight or nine years of age. However, the

call will at least serve to warn the communication specialist that there is a potential problem. If it does not appear to be improving over a period of time, your child will probably be recommended for speech therapy.

2. *Hearing problems.* Your child is prone to sinus problems or ear troubles, and you suspect that there may be some hearing loss. Perhaps you notice your child studying your lips as you speak. Is he not coming when you call, and does he "ignore" you when his head is turned away from you? In a conversation your child may interrupt you almost randomly and be slightly off the subject, suggesting that he has comprehended only part of your previous remarks. He constantly complains that his ears feel full, or his doctor may have had to puncture the eardrums frequently to relieve the pressure of accumulated fluids. All of these symptoms could point to possible hearing loss, either temporary or permanent. Let us hope that it is temporary. But only the communication specialist can make that first diagnosis that will help you discover the extent of the problem.

3. *Language problems.* These are often a difficult set of problems for parents to spot, since disorders of language are liable to be quite complex. A good first clue, however, and one which the parent is best at spotting, is a delay in talking. A late start in forming words and sentences may mean not only that your child has problems in hearing or speaking, but that he or she has been having great difficulty in making sense out of the total communication cycle— a language problem. How late is late? That varies, of course, from child to child. The first child usually speaks earlier than the second if the two are fairly close in age. The child from a large family may not be as stimulated to speak early as the only child. The quiet child may not communicate at as young an age as the active child. But if a child has no language by age three, or if you notice a great lag in words and sentences between any of your children, or your child and his friends, notify the communication specialist. It may be a false alarm, but in a problem as serious as a language disorder, it pays to be concerned early. The earlier the child receives proper corrective help, the less devastating that problem will be later. In the case of the language disorder, do not become concerned about false alarms. Use a pound of prevention instead of the proverbial ounce. Unchecked, a language problem will influence a child's entire educational career—it can put him on a track of repeated

failures and underachievement. A language disorder is one of the great "hidden handicaps."

4. *Disorders of the vocal mechanism.* Ms. Allen suspected that some of her children with articulation problems had causes for their disabilities which were based upon neurological malfunctions. Perhaps the child had had a head injury, or meningitis, or a birth anomaly affecting the brain. These kinds of conditions result in bizarre and difficult speech production. Sometimes neurological problems are subtle and hard to spot. You often will think that the child merely has minor articulation problems. However, the kind of treatment, and the length of time it must continue, will be very different for this neurological speech handicap compared to the child with a developmental articulation problem. If your child has had an illness involving the brain or nervous tissue, and if his/her speech was different after that illness, call your communication specialist immediately. Again, immediate therapy is needed.

Another set of problems, often treated in a clinic rather than the school, is that of physical disorders of the mouth area. A cleft lip or cleft palate, which used to be known as a harelip, is an "organic," physical speech problem which can be helped by a communication specialist. Indeed, the child who is now born with a cleft palate can usually expect to have full use of speech by the time he or she is an adult because of the wonders of modern plastic surgery and speech appliances. But he will have to have speech work throughout his childhood. If you have such a child, let us hope he is on a multiple-therapy regimen, including speech help. If not, run, don't walk, to the nearest speech communications clinic. Even an adult can now expect profitable help with speech if he has had a cleft palate or lip.

There are, of course, other disorders and anomalies of the mouth which will require speech work. Cerebral palsy often combines neurological and physical problems. Missing teeth and accidents of the jaw may require some speech help. Some children have difficulty manipulating their tongues or other muscles of the mouth. All of these conditions may require speech work. A search will find competent communication specialists who can help you. If such specialists are not located in your school district, one should be available nearby to the school system. Your school communication specialist can follow through on her work by supplementing your child's communication treatment in the classroom.

5. *Voice problems.* One of the most common voice problems is that

of nodules on the vocal chords. Consider your child for referral to the specialist when he has chronic hoarseness or when he loses his voice frequently without colds or after vigorous yelling (excluding boys whose voices are changing). If the quality of a child's voice is "tight" and he has to strain to talk, he may be a candidate for voice therapy. Any operation which requires vocal rest for long periods should have the attention of a communication specialist. Boys whose voices do not change after many years of puberty may also require the attention of the communication specialist. The same rule of thumb applies to voice problems as to all other communications difficulties. When in doubt, refer. Let the voice problem be ruled out. At least you will know, and then you, the teacher, and your child can all stop worrying.

6. *Stuttering.* This is another serious problem that responds best to therapy if discovered and referred early. How early? Probably at about five years of age. There are many explanations of what causes stuttering, but no explanation covers all the cases. One accepted theory does have direct relevance to parents: this states that every child, as he or she develops speech, goes through a period of stuttering at about ages three and four. This period is known as "normal non-fluency," meaning that the child doesn't use clear speech—and that is normal; his mind is running faster than his mouth. The theory states that if during this time of non-fluency, his speech pattern is accentuated, talked about, played up by the parents, the child may become fixed in that method of expression. Stuttering starts. Our advice, then, is that if you suspect your child is stuttering and he is young, refer him quietly to a speech therapist and do not attempt to correct the speech abnormality by yourself. Wait for the therapist's advice. However, if your child is older, the referral is an absolute necessity. Again, though, wait for professional advice. Stuttering therapy, like most speech therapy, should *not* be started at home without the advice of the communication specialist. She should start the therapy and direct it. You must then join her team, taking her direction. Your child's speech success is at stake.

7. *Dialectical problems.* Remember Fu Twan, the Korean girl? She is an example of a dialectical problem. The communication specialist was working with her to change her speech habits and make her more understandable to her friends. A communication specialist generally will not work with an American dialect (like Jerry from the Kentucky hills) unless the speech pattern is quite unusual or difficult

to understand. Temporary speech therapy work with a foreign dialect is usual and expected.

If you are the parent of a child with communication problems, there are also some "do's" and "don'ts" to remember:

*Unless so advised, don't continually try to correct the problem in front of the child at home. Wait for your child to finish communicating with you, hold your frustration in check, and then repeat what you think you have just heard. Don't admonish. Don't force the child to repeat the sounds correctly, which may be impossible at that point. Talk to the communication specialist about how to work with your child at home to minimize the embarrassment and maximize the sense of self.

*Don't encourage baby talk or cute mispronunciations. Use correct speech at all times with your children and hold this model up as your expectation. Because we run the risk of being considered too grumpy, we will permit you a cute word or two. A mispronunciation of "Grandpa" or "Grandma" will always be reinforced by grandparents. Let only those specifically mispronounced words become the family legend.

*Don't ridicule, reject, or criticize defective speech patterns such as a lisp or the speech of a person with a cleft palate. What would it do to your psyche if you were chided for your size, your appearance, or your speech? A child with a speech problem has enough social worries without a parent adding to these frustrations.

*Talk to your children frequently and in mature and well-pronounced English. Challenge him or her with words, sentences, thoughts, and ideas. If you believe that children should be seen and not heard, you may be prolonging their silence both verbally and intellectually. A silent voice often reflects a silent mind. Reading stories to children is a warm and verbal beginning . . . always good for children and usually a joy for parents.

*Listen to your children frequently. We mean *really* listen. Don't force them to yell at you or employ various means to make themselves heard or understood. This may be hard to do if you have many children. You may have to set aside some personal, individual time for each child. During these private moments, listen carefully. You will learn a great deal from them and about them.

6 The School Psychologist

The telephone rings in a busy office at the local bank, and the call is put through quickly. "Your wife, sir, and she sounds a little upset," briskly echoes over the intercom. "Jim? I'm glad you're in, honey. I'm going a little crazy with a problem that's just come up, and I think we have to talk about it now, before I make it worse." Phyllis Greene finally halts her hurried, muted speech.

A pause, a deep breath, an attempt to organize her thoughts, while Jim Greene tries to ask her, with studied calm, to tell him what is wrong and what is happening.

"Jim, Tony's got to see a psychologist." Jim feels the tightness in his throat, but he forces the cold, businesslike attitude he uses in crisis situations. He asks her to explain what she means. "What psychologist? Who's sending him? Why?"

Another sigh. A silence. The voice comes back on the phone with the tone that Jim knows instinctively could suddenly lead to tears—or raging anger. "I—I got a call from Mr. Burke today. You know, he's Tony's principal? Well, he said that he had just called me to tell me that they've scheduled Tony for a session with the school psychologist on Wednesday, and he wanted me to sign a permission slip that Tony would be bringing home today. Jim, I asked him why Tony had to see that . . . that person, and he told me that it was just to find out more information about Tony so the school could help him better in his classes. And that's all he'd say, Jim, although I asked him several times to be more specific, and to tell me why Tony needed psychiatric help, or what Tony's problem was. All he would say is, 'It's just to help Tony in school by finding out more information.' " She pauses and wets her lips. "He said that we'd be able to talk to the school psychologist—or psychiatrist—or whatever—about Tony when he's finished. But that doesn't help us now, Jim. I want to know more about *why* Tony's got to see him. Is there something wrong? If so, why can't *we* know too?"

She pauses, but her husband is silent, waiting for the final outburst: "And if they can't tell us, does that mean that we might be part of the problem? Is Tony sick? Is he having serious school problems? Jim, I'm really worried. Should I sign that permission slip, or force a meeting with Mr. Burke? Honey, I don't know if I can face Mr. Burke without crying, I'm so nervous about it. What should we do?" Her voice comes to a whispered halt; she feels drained but still aware of an inner fear that will not be dispelled. Jim Greene looks around his small paneled office almost searching for some way to escape. He has no answers for his distraught wife—he does not know what to say.

This call, and the thousands like it which are made every year, could have been avoided. The anguish that this couple is experiencing need never have occurred. In the daily school situation, amid the pressure of dealing with the needs of hundreds of children, scores of teachers, and innumerable problems, the school administrator sometimes forgets to be sensitive. He begins to treat all problems like administrative tasks —they become information to be conveyed and decisions to be made regardless of other people's emotions.

But it does not take great sensitivity to realize that telling a parent for the first time that his or her child needs to see a school psychologist is going to invoke concern, guilt, anxiety, or fear. A school psychologist is not readily identifiable in the school system as an instructor; he is seen as a professional from another field who comes in especially to work with "problem children." Many people accept offbeat stereotypes of the school psychologist. For instance, a nationally syndicated comic strip shows a school psychologist sitting behind a psychoanalyst's couch taking notes while a very young child lies there prone, talking about parental rejection. This common but frightening image provokes the natural anxieties of parents who have experienced the many myths associated with psychology, such as: there are no bad children, only bad parents; mental illness might be inherited (remember that Aunt Minnie was in the state hospital); parents who argue in front of children can cause serious child neuroses; psychologists only work with "crazy" kids. Every parent knows of skeletons in the family closet, and there is the distinct concern that the visit to the school psychologist will, of necessity, throw open those permanently closed doors.

The School Psychologist

That is why all school administrators are obligated always to tell you the reasons (note the plural—reasons) for the referral to the school psychologist. Preferably, the administrator should tell you *before* the child's visit in a private conversation with you—or in the presence of the other referring or responsible school personnel. If the administrator at Tony's school had taken the time with Tony's parents, he would have told them why children are usually referred to school psychologists, what the background and tasks of a school psychologist are, and what he will attempt to accomplish during his visit with Tony. The administrator is also responsible for outlining what information the parents can expect from the psychologist after his first visit with Tony.

A school psychologist is in fact part of the instructional staff of a school. He or she is usually a person who has specialized in two fields: one, the testing and counselling part of clinical psychology; and, two, the field of teaching and instruction. Whether the school psychologist is Mr., Ms., or Dr., that person has taken both kinds of coursework and field experience, and has been certified by the state department of education as either a school psychometrist (a person who only gives and interprets tests) or a school psychologist (a person who tests, counsels, and makes recommendations about improved instruction or therapy for children). The school psychologist speaks two languages—psychology and education. Do not confuse him/her (as the syndicated comic strip does) with the child psychiatrist and his two languages—medicine and psychology.

The school psychologist generally works with children on a one-at-a-time basis; he usually sees a child only when that child is referred to him by other school personnel for some specific reason. The person who refers the child needs to know more than can be detected from the classroom setting or from the group tests that are usually administered to a large number of children at one time. It is therefore safe to assume that your child is being referred to the school's psychologist because he or she has demonstrated some set of problems or learning difficulties that the teacher or other school personnel cannot fully understand. As a result, the school referral of your child to the psychologist must be taken seriously. However, this referral does not mean that your child's problems are necessarily chronic, severe, intractable, or debilitating.

A school psychologist may be asked to see a child just because the child's current level of performance in school is not what the teacher expects and the possible reasons have not been explained to his or her satisfaction. All of the tests and observations which the teacher can make do not provide her with the full picture. Tony might be a transfer in the middle of the school year from another school—another lifestyle —2,000 miles away. Or he might have scored in the mid-range of his achievement testing this year but was in the upper 10 percent two years ago. He might be an adopted Vietnamese orphan with a minimal command of English. Or he might seem to be doing a lot more day-dreaming this year and the teacher cannot uncover the basis for his inattention.

None of these are necessarily severe problems, but they do make instruction difficult for a teacher unless she knows more about the child. Therefore she seeks out another professional who can systematically uncover more information than she is able to amid the daily limitations imposed by twenty-nine other children in the class, little free time, and a minimal knowledge of the techniques required. Ideally you, as the parents of the child, would be called in to meet with the teacher before the referral is made, because you can obviously help shed some light on the overall situation. But on occasions you are neglected because the teacher really doesn't feel that you are a major part of your child's school problems. She may deduce that the problems arise out of language difficulties, changing schools, a bad testing day, or a potential need for vision testing. Therefore she doesn't "bother" you. Very likely, she does not want to alarm you. Give her the credit for this positive motivation. But do not pause an instant in finding out why she has made the referral.

The school psychologist may be given a referral to see or test your child because there is a question whether the child should be transferred to a special program, such as a gifted program, a college preparatory program, a vocational program, or a special education program. In this case, the teacher—in combination with the principal, the guidance counsellor, or the special teacher—may feel that your child would profit from some particular educational approach which is very different from the one in which he or she is presently enrolled. In most states, the only way a child can get into these other special programs is via the preliminary route of testing and recommendation, whether by the school psychologist alone or by a special team which always includes the school psychologist. Whichever "certifies" your child for a special program, you must be aware that the final decisions should always be determined both by individually administered psychological tests and clinical observations and by first-hand information provided by the teachers and other school personnel who have come into daily contact with your child.

If your child is currently enrolled in a satisfactory school system, you will always be one of the important people who contributes to the information about your child—information which will be used in recommending a placement in a different setting. You should know from the very beginning whether your child's program is the best for him or her. You should have some idea about how the proposed new program differs from the one in which he or she is currently being taught. In what ways do the objectives and teaching methods vary? A referral to another program should *not* come as a surprise to you unless it occurs only a few weeks after the child has started school. Because this change may represent a major decision in your child's education, you should insist on knowing all the reasons for the referral—the behaviors or lack of behaviors, the educational problems, the benefits of changing programs, the principles and curriculum involved, the goals and pace of the new program, and the personnel who will have a role in making and implementing the final decisions.

In most states, when a child is to be referred for a special class or a change in program, parental permission must be obtained before the school psychologist can see the child; and in all states, the child cannot be placed in a new or special class until parental consent is obtained. This is called "due process" under the law and will be talked about at greater length in a later part of the book. But you must know that you have a good deal of leverage in becoming an integral part of the decisions which may affect your child's educational and emotional future so dramatically. When the school psychologist wants to see your child and you find that the referral has been made in contemplation of a program change, you must insist that you become part of the decision-making team immediately. Talk to the teacher and to the principal—and to whoever else they recommend as part of the "team." This is your right.

You should also be well aware that you have an obligation to your child to help him or her obtain the best placement. That is *his* right. Initially, you may wish to withhold your permission to have your child tested until you know all the reasons for seeing a school psychologist; but after you have reviewed the "appropriate" reasons, you should give that permission, receive the psychologist's advice, and continue acting in the best interests of your child. You should accept the fact that the school may be in a unique position to offer you guidance from an external framework quite different from your family viewpoint. Keep in mind that the school personnel will usually feel justified in recommending a special program for your child only if they can build a factual case to justify this action. The justification which they give you must satisfy your informed idea about the conditions which are best for your child's education. State laws protect the child. Be informed about the special programs, many of which will be described in this book; but do not prescribe for your own child in direct opposition to the school team unless you have received sound advice from other qualified professionals. Your child is too important for "home remedies."

If your child is in a special program, such as special education, or if he or she has missed a number of important classroom group tests, you may find that the school psychologist's referral was for the purpose of assessing the child's progress. This is often required by state law. The purpose of this law is to make sure that your child is being taught satisfactorily and that his educational program is the best possible one for him. If this is the case, sit back and relax and make the experience as pleasurable as you can for your child by preparing him, honestly but reassuringly, for the experience. Such a "progress report" can only offer you more information than you already have, and help you reward your child by informing him where and how he has gained and grown intellectually. It will offer you and the school guidance about the areas in which both can help your child continue to grow. However, in your child's "progress report" you must remember that if he is progressing at the expected pace and level, the school personnel sometimes will feel they do not need to inform you of the results in detail—there is no longer any "problem." A gentle inquiry to the school psychologist should be made so you can obtain the reassurance and helpful knowledge needed for your child's continued educational planning.

A final important reason why your child might be referred to a school psychologist is for psychological guidance. The reasons for this referral might indicate that the school did not understand the significance of certain repeated or unusual social or classroom actions. Perhaps the child appears constantly frightened of school—a condition called "school phobia." Perhaps a child seems to be having serious problems with another student or a group of students, and his anxiety about these relationships appears to be affecting his work. Perhaps he is in an unexplained slump in school, when all his intelligence and ability tests indicate greater potential than he is exhibiting. Perhaps your child and his teacher have irreconcilable differences. Perhaps . . . The list is endless. But what we are describing here are any number of situations where tests of thinking and learning abilities are not as helpful as discovering the inner machinery that runs the world in which your child lives—or the world in which he perceives he lives. This is where the psychologist undertakes the intricate and vital task of reconstructing the fears and angers, as well as the pleasures and rewards of your child, reweaving the entire structure of his life so that the responsible adults in his home and his school can offer constructive guidance and change.

This may be a referral which is difficult for you to understand. Indeed, it is often one which proves hard for school people to explain to a parent. Sometimes your child may be acting differently in the school setting than he or she has been acting at home, and you may not understand or fully believe the explanations for referral. You may even think the whole situation is fabricated. What appears to be happening to your child may provoke fears or guilt about your own part in his problems. It is not unusual for a parent to begin asking, "Where have I gone wrong?" If you are this parent, you may feel defensive. Anger at the school may dominate your thoughts. You may feel that you can handle the behavior problems of your own child better than "those strangers" can. And you may be right, of course. But you may also be wrong. Chances are that since you care about your child deeply you are both right and wrong. You love him so intensely you want to offer him helpful change or appropriate justice—you are responsible for him, so it is natural that you want to perceive him in his best image.

When your child is referred for psychological guidance or a psychological exploration of his or her problem, try to stay cool. Find out the reasons involved. Do not try to give immediate solutions, but accept the referral as an attempt to get objective information. Ask your child to be as candid with the school psychologist as possible. After the conference, make an appointment to talk it over. And listen! Your child has had a chance to talk about things he might not have mentioned to you. Threatening as this possibility sometimes seems, you must consider it a plus. Make every effort to become part of the educational team for your child. The psychologist should give you his or her interpretation of the problems, their causes (again, the plural), and the options open for solution. Tell him which options you prefer, negotiate the immediate actions, and follow the plans—consistently. Many children have temporary problems in school which are turned into permanent educational problems when parents and school become enemies rather than allies. A compromise will usually satisfy all parties. Your child will profit by this action, sometimes survive because of it, and certainly grow as a result of it.

What we've just talked about are general reasons why children are referred to a school psychologist. Any person in the school who works with your child may ask for a psychological referral just to obtain information, to certify a child for a special program, to assess the progress of a child, or to explore "routine" problems. But did you know that you, as parents, can also make a referral to a school psychologist? Usually you have to do it through a teacher, principal, guidance counsellor, family physician, or other professional. There are two reasons for this involvement of other professionals. The first is that in most school systems, there are usually not enough school psychologists to accept all direct referrals from parents; therefore the school wants to involve other professionals who might be able to help you without using the limited time of the school psychologist. The second reason is that the school psychologist needs as much information as he can get before he sees your child; involving another professional ensures that he will obtain some of this additional information. When you feel the need to refer your child for psychological evaluation, talk to any one of the school personnel and lay out the basis of your case.

Why should you want your child to see a school psychologist? Perhaps you have the same needs in mind that have already been given as frequent causes of school referrals. But you, as the parents, are in a position to spot other problems and situations that you think might require the help of the school psychologist.

For instance, you might be worried about a child's severely negative attitudes toward school when he or she is at home—attitudes which are not yet becoming manifested in school problems. A child you have to force into the school bus every day is a later candidate for problems. A child who comes home each night with a different bruise and eyes swollen from crying is a likely candidate for ultimate social damage or terrifying fears if help is not secured quickly. Perhaps you suspect that your child is bored and understimulated in school and is receiving all of his education at home from the five books he reads every night. He might need greater challenges at school before he gives up on the place completely. All these problems, which might not show up at school or might result in classroom behavior patterns so subtle that the teacher does not suspect the underlying problems, are appropriate reasons for "parent referrals" to the school psychologist.

Other problems which only you can spot are those surrounding traumas within the inner life of your child. The death of a close grandparent, sibling, best friend, or pet will often activate intense fears, grief reactions, or denial of the death itself in a child. Separation or divorce may have an effect similar to this loss despite the best of explanations. Perhaps seeing a tragic accident or being lost on an outing will provoke disabling anxieties. And sometimes the addition of a new member of the family (a new baby or an adopted brother or sister) results in destructive behaviors. All these trauma reactions are the roots of reactions at home which, if ignored, will probably disrupt a child's education. You need a sensitive person in the school who can see what is going on with your child, help create rewarding schooltime for him or her, and perhaps provide the outlet for the expressions of hate, anger, frustration, or grief with which he or she cannot deal at home. This person would be the school psychologist.

You may recognize the need for some short-term counselling which no other professional within the school setting can do equally well. Does your fatherless child need someone with whom to talk about sexual adjustment problems? Is stealing a chronic problem? Does your child demonstrate some type of peculiar behavior which you don't understand and which appears to be hurting his/her social standing? Does your child appear to have distinctly different study habits from his peers? Possibly the school psychologist can help your child prevent this present problem from expanding into a disabling handicap in the future.

Other professionals in the life of your child may be picking up problems which you did not know existed. Your optometrist or opthalmologist tells you of a visual problem that may be affecting his or her success in school. Your family physician wants to try a long-term medication but feels that it might affect the child's learning performance. The Little League coach tells you that Johnnie has observable coordination problems and wonders if this makes a difference in school. Aunt Edna, a speech and hearing therapist, thinks that Joanne should have twice the vocabulary she now possesses, and should also use her words in a better way. These people have spoken to you in good faith. They are accustomed to dealing with many children, and could be spotting problems in advance. On the other hand, they could be unduly alarmed. But why should you take a chance when you have a professional in the school who can help you? Make your own referral to the school psychologist.

Once you understand the referral, and what it is all about, how can you help your child and the school psychologist to get the most out of the conference? What should you tell your child in advance about the meeting? What information should you be seeking when you visit the school psychologist?

Generally speaking, the school psychologist will do some testing and some talking. The testing will be an individual screening, with just the psychologist and the child present, and will probably involve paper-and-pencil tests for the child and sometimes tasks that are unique or unusual. The child may be asked to draw or to perform spelling, math, reading, or other academic types of tests. But he or she may also be asked to name colors, recall information, follow directions, arrange blocks, balance his body, trace designs, describe pictures from inkblots, make up stories, act out situations, or string beads in patterns. Whatever he is asked to do, recognize that the school psychologist is asking him for a sample of his behavior. He's trying to find out what the child will do under a variety of situations, and he will compare what your child does with what other children generally do under those same circumstances. You cannot know what behaviors the school psychologist is testing or what he has found out in comparison to other children unless you are another psychologist with similar training. Therefore it is foolhardly for a parent to speculate. The preparation you can give your child, we suggest, should go something like this: "When you see Mr. Jones tomorrow, he may ask you to do some special things for him. These things will probably be like a game to you, and they will help him get to know you better. I think you'll have fun doing them." Your child *will* have fun doing them because school psychologists reward the child, verbally, for playing such "games." Usually the school psychologist and the child emerge from a session of testing as good friends.

In the talking part of the session, the school psychologist will try to find out how your child perceives his/her world. In order to do this, he will try to have the child recreate for him what school is like, what home is like, what his friends are like—to the child himself. This is necessary in order to understand the frame of reference of the child, to learn what rewards him and what punishes him, what are his fears, his joys, what are his motivations and his vulnerabilities. This talking part sometimes can be a little frightening to parents. "Will he find that Tony is unhappy at home? Will Tony tell him about all our fights?" you may ask. He might; but the psychologist is generally not that interested in *your* adjustment problems, particularly if they fall in the category of the "usual problems of marriage and raising children." He is far more interested in the specific problems which affect Tony's immediate behavior—problems that can be found at school, home, church, on school buses, and everywhere Tony is interacting. He is interested in the fears which Tony carries with him and what activates these fears. The school psychologist is not judgmental. He probes. He realizes that all families—all parents and children—have different lifestyles and different reaction patterns. He is only interested in those patterns that appear to have the most effect on the school problem. The psychologist generally is not interested in a full-scale analysis of your child. If he becomes concerned to that degree, he will refer the child to a specialist. Rather, he is interested in the problems of your child's adjustment to the educational system. What he and your child talk about will bear on that concern. So preparation of your child for the talking part of the conference should follow this theme: ". . . and I think you'll like talking to Mr. Jones, because he's really interested in you and how he can help make school a happy place for you."

When the conference between your child and the school psychologist is over, what then? A scheduled appointment to discuss the outcome should be next on your agenda. This meeting may be just between you and the school psychologist, or it may include other relevant people, such as the teacher, the special teacher, the principal, the school nurse or doctor—whoever else made the referral. Sometimes, because of lack of time, the conference may be set up without the school psychologist, but you will be wise to insist upon his presence. As the process proceeds, the older child may well become a member of his own planning sessions. This is something to be worked for.

What questions should you ask? If the information is not volunteered, for the results of the tests. You will not need the exact scores, since those numbers are meaningless except to other psychologists. What you need is the school psychologist's *interpretation* of those scores. Ask him how they compare to those of other children. What do they predict? And how do they compare to tests given previously to your child? Which scores show strengths and which weaknesses? Which of the scores are used for entrance into special programs? What test scores will go into your child's permanent records and how will they be explained in those records? Who will receive a copy of the scores and what they will mean to those other professionals? And what will happen to those scores in the future if you exercise the options that will be suggested?

Then you can ask him to reconstruct for you the entire testing situation with your child as he found it. What has he learned about your child's world? What seems to motivate the child? What gives him/her pleasure, or pain? What is common to many children? What about your child is unique to him alone? What adults are significant to him? And in what ways? What children are helpful or harmful to him? What activity does he think is most beneficial to the child's problems? What situation gives your child the most trouble in school? He may not know all the answers to these questions because they may not all be relevant to the referral problems; but chances are that he can give you a fairly good view of the problems through your own child's eyes. That is going to be extremely helpful to you as a parent.

Finally, ask him for his recommendation. See if he has more than one option or solution. He usually will. Request that he describe what the consequences will be if you and your child follow these different options. What can you expect in six weeks; one year; five years? What should your role be in each case? What should you look for as being "progress"? When will be a good time formally to check on that progress? Who will explain the options to the other members of the team—the teacher, specialist, counsellor, school nurse, and so on? In other words, who should supervise these options? Who will "captain" your child's team?

Having asked these questions, you should automatically be recognized as a full-fledged member of the team which makes decisions about your child's education. You are in a position of responsibility to help meet your child's needs, and you have objective and current knowledge at your fingertips. However, a word of caution. When your child sees a school psychologist, it will probably be for problems or solutions that may be unfamiliar to you. You may find it difficult to relate to either the problems or their solutions. You will feel protective toward your child; and you may be unwilling to accept his or her weaknesses, particularly if they are being revealed to you for the first time. If this occurs, you may want to get professional corroboration of the school psychologist's conclusion. If you feel negatively about the findings, please seek this additional counsel. You have the same right with this professional that you have with any other professional, be it physician, teacher, or counsellor. But if corroboration occurs, settle down to final acceptance. Accept your part in the ultimate answer or you will become part of the problem. Your child's education should not be jeopardized by your insistence on unsupported principles or assumptions. Even if the conclusions are painful, accept the pain and move forward to help your child. Free your mind of dashed hopes and bitter self-recrimination. When the progress report is made about your child, you will be able to assess clearly which of the options presented by school psychologist should be selected.

If you have digested all this information, you should be able to answer your wife's question, "What should we do?" when she calls, frightened because your son (or daughter) is being referred to the school psychologist. Your answer might go something like this:

"Don't get upset, Phyllis. Tony's going to the school psychologist. Probably Mr. Jones, the one that Tom VanScoy's daughter saw last year when he had that problem with her class placement. Hey, frankly, I'm relieved because you know how worried we've been about Tony's grades. According to Tom, Mr. Jones is really a sensitive person and was able to give them a lot of very helpful information about their girl. Anyway, they worked out a special educational program for her and it seems to be working beautifully.

"Look, Phyllis, this is what we should do. When Tony brings home the permission slip tonight, don't treat it with any concern. Let's all talk about it at dinner. I'll tell Tony what goes on in the meeting with Mr. Jones. Then we'll sign the permission slip, but put on the slip that the meeting should occur only *after* we talk with Mr. Burke. I can't understand why he didn't set up that meeting in the first place. But anyway we'll ask for a time, and then we'll know what the referral is all about.

"And then, after the meeting with the school psychologist, we'll probably find out what happened and what they think is the best school plan for Tony. As his parents, we have to agree to any changes so they are going to have to tell us their findings in detail. Tom says Mr. Jones usually gives you options—and spells out what might happen in each case.

"Phyllis, I'm really pleased that we might find out more about Tony. You know how we've worried within ourselves. But now . . . "

This is the beginning of the ideal relationship between parent, child, and school psychologist—with all parties informed, willing, and open to learning the truth.

7 The School Physician

The term "school physician" has different meanings, depending upon the location and type of school in which your child is enrolled. Many schools in this country have no provision for a specific school physician; they rely on the services of community physicians. In urban areas there are often itinerant school physicians, who come into the school for a brief period on either a weekly or biweekly basis to evaluate the health needs of the children. Some are responsible for only one school, while others make a sizable part or all of their income from attending a number of schools on an intermittent but scheduled basis. There are private schools which retain the full or part-time services of a physician who cares for the broad medical problems and health education courses within that particular environment. Occasionally medical schools or teaching hospitals will include courses and practical work on the health needs of school children as an integral part of their training of the resident staff. In these areas, young pediatricians or "family medicine" trainees provide the services and fulfill the role of school physician, supervised by the senior school faculty.

Clearly the parent must question a particular school system to find out whether a physician is working in his child's school, whether he or she is a pediatrician or family practitioner, a graduate M.D. or a physician in training, and whether he will be there only one half day per week, part time, or full time.

There is also a great diversity in what the school physician is expected to do within the various systems. Job descriptions vary so dramatically that parents must determine the responsibility and duties of the individual physician so as to know what can be expected.

What are some of the tasks performed by school doctors throughout the country? A list of their responsibilities should indicate the scope of work with which these people are involved.

The School Physician

1. Physical examinations for all children entering kindergarten

Many systems require their doctor to examine every kindergarten or first grade child entering school. This examination is designed to reveal only very obvious physical abnormalities in a new schoolchild, which may not have been previously uncovered. How often is something new going to be discovered? Very rarely indeed.

First, almost every child who enters the school system has had at least one physical examination during the preceding five or six years. Such examinations may have occurred at a time of illness. Check-ups may have taken place in a busy clinic or a crowded emergency room; more likely, the child has had several or repeated check-ups, either at the well baby clinic or at the office of the family physician or pediatrician. Because there have been previous health exams, important congenital physical abnormalities should have been discovered much earlier. It is quite unusual for a serious birth defect to be detected at the school entry physical. Other serious, chronic illnesses that can affect children—such as rheumatic fever, heart disease, diabetes mellitus, chronic kidney infection, cystic fibrosis, to name but a few—are very likely to produce serious and significant symptoms which would already have alerted parents and physicians that a severe childhood illness was present.

Secondly, imagine a school doctor faced with the volume of necessary entrance physical examinations and only one half day per week to accomplish this formidable task. Obviously the examination will be perfunctory and superficial. Any subtle, previously overlooked condition most probably will remain hidden. Only when the school employs a physician on a part- or full-time basis can one expect the thoroughness and care of an office medical examination. We can recall one case in which a very serious and complicated congenital heart problem was discovered in a preschooler of four who was attending a private school nursery program and was examined by the full-time pediatrician (a devoted elderly lady) who worked there. The little girl was the daughter of a physician and was under the care of one of the city's very best pediatricians. The condition should have been discovered earlier—but it wasn't. This rare case demonstrates the unusual combination of a dedicated school physician with sufficient time and expertise to spot an obscure illness.

But it is not the norm in most schools. Therefore it is extremely wise for parents to have their children checked medically by a private physician or their dependable nearby child care clinic before they enter school.

If parents want to take action to correct problems within the school, then they should be alerted that the initial physical by the school physician is usually a waste of his or her valuable professional time. There are far more important things he can be doing, which we will discuss later. If your child is receiving that rushed initial physical, take up the cause! Free the physician for his other much more vital medical responsibilities.

2. Routine yearly check-ups for all "special education" children

There is little question that one of the prerequisites to placing a child in a "special" category—whether this involves a special class, a resource room, or merely a notation on the school record—is that the school physician should see the child to ascertain if there are any significant medical features that would help explain the "special" problem or that require fresh or continuing attention.

Some of these "special" children have significant physical handicaps which will require regular follow-up in special clinics or specialists' offices. But the school doctor can ascertain yearly progress, as well as determine the parents' compliance with the child's need for regular attention, during these annual school check-ups. In addition, he or she can note any improvement or deterioration in the child's physical, emotional, or educational condition from year to year. The teachers in the child's educational life may change; but if the school physician and/or school nurse remains relatively constant, a "checks and balances" system operates to protect the "special" child from changing for the better or the worse unnoticed.

However, the school physician has to assess something more than just the physical health of the child if these yearly physicals on the "special" child are going to have full significance. He or she must take a thorough history of the previous year's developments, question both teacher and child as to changes in classroom work and behavior, and note differences in the child's behavior, attitude, and ability to get along with others. This is extremely important information, which must be added to the physical examination if the doctor is to develop a complete picture of the overall health of the "special" child.

If you have such a "special" child within the school system who is scheduled to receive the yearly examination by the school physician, you should be aware of the broad, expanded type of information he or she needs to fully assess your child. If he is not asking the right questions, if he is not consulting with you as well as with the child's previous and current teacher, if he is ignoring information from the school nurse, then your child is not receiving the type of medical work-up necessary for regular reevaluation. Whether the problem is one of sight or hearing, orthopedic, intellectual, emotional, or chronic illness, speak up when the examination is over if you honestly feel your child has been medically shortchanged.

If you get no satisfaction, you have one of two choices. Often the school physician is employed by the local health department. Call the head of School Health there and register a complaint. Secondly, if the school physician is an employee of the school system, start with the principal and move upwards administratively until someone listens. Do not accept a routine report that "Johnny hasn't changed" unless all the facts are in and you can be certain that that medical judgment has been made on solid and complete evidence.

3. The handling of sudden temporary illnesses

This is certainly appropriate if the school doctor is on hand at least part of every school day. But to expect a doctor who comes only once or twice a week to become overwhelmed by a passing parade of sore throats and stomach aches is a gross misuse of his/her time. What does the school do on the days when the school doctor is not there if Janice has a sore throat or Steven has a stomach ache? Usually the principal calls a member of the family to inform them and asks them to take the youngster to their own doctor or the clinic. Exactly the same should apply when the school physician is there. But, you argue, he's already there, and my kid is sick; so I'm lucky that it happened on the very day he was at school. Why shouldn't he see Janice's throat? He's a doctor, isn't he? And he's right there!

Yes, he's there. But there are many other very important things that this school physician should be doing which he rarely gets a chance to do when the current school operation bombards him with sore throats, slight fevers, and twisted ankles. If your child had one of the more significant long-term health problems, wouldn't you demand that school doctor's time? Who should have the greater need for this professional's valuable knowledge and limited time within the school? Obviously the parent and child with the long-term, more serious problem need the school physician's undivided attention far more than the child with a temporary mild illness.

So be understanding if the school nurse calls to tell you that your youngster is sick or hurt and when you ask if the school doctor is there, she says: "Yes. But he's very busy with another important problem." He really is—or should be. Don't let your child's sore throat keep him from these problems.

4. Assessing long-term complaints

Often the school nurse will request that the school doctor see a child who has been worrying her for reasons of health, behavior, or appearance. She has watched the child from a distance for a while, her concern gradually building, or she may be alerted to the problem by the child's teacher. The complaints often take such forms as: "Bobby falls asleep in class every day," or, "Richard appears to be staring off into space every once in a while," or simply, "Jill just doesn't act like she feels well most of the time." The school nurse will observe the child, get as detailed a history as possible from the teacher, and present the case to the school physician. He or she will examine the child carefully and recommend any outside referrals and consultations he thinks necessary. Often he can detect a minor or short-term problem which can be managed by the parent at home. However, because of the limited diagnostic facilities within the school building, the doctor will frequently refer the child to an appropriate outside medical resource when he wants to make certain that nothing is overlooked. In this instance, the school physician is acting as a "triage" agent, screening for the obvious, easily managed problem, and referring child and parent to the proper outside medical resource when there is uncertainty or concern about a more serious health problem.

When you learn that your child is to be examined by the school physician, find out why. Then consider whether the reasons given warrant your decision to consult your own private doctor or a clinic without the preliminary intervention of the school doctor. You need not accept his/her services, but you should have a more desirable medical alternative. If you decide to let the school doctor examine your child, be present to answer questions and ask for a thorough discussion at the conclusion of the examination. Do not accept a referral to an outside specialist unless you know to whom you are going and why you are taking your child there. We are constantly amazed at the intelligent and concerned mothers who arrive at specialists' offices with their children without the foggiest notion why they are there. "He told me to come," is the usual response. A parent must never be afraid to ask a physician for full details about diagnosis, treatment, or referral. No doctor should be too busy or too "important" to finish his job, which is to inform you fully about your child.

After the referral and final diagnosis, the parent will frequently have to make repeat visits to the specialist or consult with the school physician on a regular basis about the child's health. Here is where the school physician can create a valuable link between your child and the school. The child with a long-term health problem often has attendance irregularities, special health or nutritional needs; he or she may have to be observed for the effects of medication, may need special class placement or tutoring, and even devices for special mobility such as wheelchairs, crutches, or sensory aids (glasses or hearing aids). The school physician can function in all these situations to pave the way for the satisfaction of your child's needs. Careful explanations to teacher and principal, instructions to the school nurse, regular supportive conferences with the child to help him or her to overcome the "specialness" he is feeling—all of these can be the function of the competent, caring school physician. This is an important part of his professional responsibility. Do not be afraid to ask him to perform these services for your child.

5. Developing a health education curriculum

This is another key area where the school physician can offer extremely valuable advice but is very seldom consulted. In designing courses on Family Living, the school physician can not only act as consultant on appropriate material but also serve as class lecturer and small group leader. The controversies over sex education within the school system would become less heated, and the adversaries of school-based courses in intimate human behavior for children less vocal and effective, if the school physician both planned and participated in these all-important programs.

Often elements within the biology and social science courses are directly related to the broad field of medicine. The school physician may serve as a resource person or an actual participant in these courses. In addition, he or she can bring to class other professionals who can offer the children valuable first-hand information about specific study units related to health or the human body.

A dedicated school physician will work assiduously to promote a course on personal health and hygiene within the school. Here the parents can join forces with him to convince the administration that in addition to reading, writing, and arithmetic, the young schoolchild should learn about the mechanisms for caring for his body and himself.

6. Monitoring safety within the school

Again this is an area that far too few school physicians have the time or energy to undertake because of other, less significant commitments. There is no question that in some schools the accident rate among the children is alarmingly high. Why? Someone must take the initiative to answer this question. The most logical leader would be the school physician. In one of the Baltimore public elementary schools, a young pediatrician was working for half a day every other week as school physician. He was shocked and alarmed at the broken glass and debris all over the playground; little wonder that the level of serious accidents in this particular school was extremely high. He repeatedly mentioned this problem to the somewhat disinterested, phlegmatic principal, who persisted in ignoring it. Finally, the school physician and school nurse called the sanitation department and the mayor's office. Within one week, the debris was cleared away. Because of the nature of the neighborhood, the glass and other dangerous materials quickly reappeared on the playground. However, this time when the principal was confronted with the problem, she organized a "clean-up" campaign and the playground remained free of dangerous debris for the remainder of the school year.

An interesting question comes to mind as we consider this true story, which occurred only recently. Why didn't any of the parents demand that degree of safety for their children? Why didn't they confront the principal and make the necessary phone calls to get a dangerous situation corrected? If the principal could not be roused to action, why did the parents not seek help from higher authorities, as did the young physician? What would you have done? Don't count on helpful advocates like this unusually perceptive and concerned young physician to monitor the safety of your child. True, it is part of his job; but it is also part of yours.

7. Providing the medical information required for diagnosing behavior and learning problems within the school

This is where the action should be! And this is where our school health system in this country is falling down badly. Teachers are begging for help with children who are hyperactive, who have significant learning problems, who have emotional disturbances that cause tantrums, withdrawn or antisociable behavior in the classroom. Parents are looking to the schools to help them unravel the reasons why Bobby cannot learn or Philip won't speak or Johnny is hyperactive or Janice cannot read. These are complex problems that require intricate teamwork. On that team must be a school physician who has the time, the interest, and the training to make a knowledgeable contribution to the diagnosis, the management, and the educational prescriptions for these difficult children. All too often they are shunted right past the school doctor to the nearby hospital clinic, where they are squeezed in between the child with an asthma attack and the infant desperately ill with meningitis. It should become apparent how much concentrated attention they will receive at that time.

The lucky children are referred to special clinics for those with learning and behavior problems. But such clinics are few and far between. The child may go with his or her parents to his local pediatrician, who refers him to the local psychologist, who refers him to the local child psychiatrist, who refers him back to the pediatrician after six months with a brief note suggesting that another approach might be in order. All this time, the child is not learning, is creating serious disturbances in school, or is playing truant because of repeated frustrating school failures. What these children need is a team approach that looks at all facets of their learning and behavior problems. There are professionals within the school system who can work together to form this team. Almost every school system has psychologists, speech and communication specialists, social workers, special educators, school nurses and school physicians—all the elements of the necessary team. What is needed is an organizing professional to act as a focal force and bring them together, so that they can work through the special problems. That organizing professional can be and should be the school physician.

He or she should have training in these problems. If he is not one of the younger pediatricians who has received this experience during his recent residency, then he should take a special course or workshop to familiarize himself with them. The school system or the health department should be responsible for developing these workshops for school physicians and school nurses so that they can function properly within the field of childhood learning and behavior problems. We have too few neurologists and child psychiatrists to expect each of our problem children to have such a specialized consultation. Frankly, it is not necessary. Most of the problems can be diagnosed and managed by the team of professionals mentioned above, working hand in hand with the child's parents and teacher.

The school physician should make certain that each of these problem children sees the appropriate professionals. Then the case should be discussed by the professionals involved. Diagnosis and educational advice can be developed and shared with the child's parents and teacher, each one often playing an integral role in the therapy that follows. If necessary, the school physician can prescribe medication and follow the child on a regular basis within the school. What an ideal way of managing these serious and confounding childhood problems. And what an appropriate way to utilize the talents and time of the school physician. Now do you understand why we make the plea to relieve the school doctor from the sore throats and routine entry physicals? There is a much greater job to be done. If your child has this problem of learning and behavior disability, then you are fully aware of what we mean.

You now know the seven areas in which the school physician can make an impact upon your child. As a parent, you have the right to evaluate each of these functions. Obviously, even if the doctor were in your child's school three half days a week, he could not perform all these tasks well. Which do you want him to do? If you had your choice, which job description would you write for your child's school doctor? You *do* have that choice. If the P.T.A.s and other parent organizations developed a clear, strong viewpoint on the role of the school physician, there would be change. And the change, we are sure, would be for the better. We must develop a specialty of school physicians who take care of the "school health" of our children. The most potent advocates to see that this comes about are you—the children's parents.

8 The School Nurse

Like the school physician, the school nurse has to be one and many people. Her daily work can vary from school to school. She may be employed by one of a number of different agencies, depending on the city or county in which the school is located. The amount of time she spends in your child's school will also differ from one school system to another. She may be extremely important to the total educational process of your child, or peripheral to his or her daily school activities.

The school nurse's qualifications may range from those of nurse's aide to licensed practical nurse to registered nurse; from public health nurse to nurse practitioner to doctor's assistant. How do these titles differ and what do these differences mean to your child?

A nurse's aide has had the minimal training required to practice nursing. Much of her education has been first aid and learning how to assist the graduate nurse in carrying out hospital and clinic duties. A nurse's aide may have sufficient skills to handle minor childhood emergencies such as the scraped knee or the cut finger, but the knowledge that would permit her to distinguish between a serious head injury and a minor "knock" would be beyond her scope of training. Most of these paraprofessionals (i.e., a skilled nonprofessional helper) can use the instruments of the graduate nurse such as stethoscope and blood pressure apparatus. However, it is when findings need interpretation that the graduate professional nurse is distinguished from the trained nurse's aide. If your school has hired a nurse's aide as school nurse, expect no more than an individual in a white uniform who can manage the minor cuts, bruises, and sniffles but who should not be required to go beyond offering such minimal first aid to your child. If your school's nurse is a nurse's aide, insist that the school call you or a trusted other person who will be available for any injury or physical complaint suffered by your child in school. In addition, do not accept the findings of the nurse's aide if she is delegated the authority for screening your child physically in his or her school. This paraprofessional rarely has had the depth of training to be able to perform an adequate screening examination on a schoolchild except on a supervised basis.

The licensed practical nurse has had more training than the nurse's aide. However, unless she has had extensive training within a school system or in a pediatric or family medicine clinic, she usually does not possess the skills to handle all childhood emergencies or physical complaints. She works best in recognizing emergency situations, using the referral system, and working under the direction of the school physician. Checking up on children to ensure that they are complying with a prescribed medication, diet, or rest regimen also falls within the scope of the trained licensed practical nurse. To expect more than this would again be overestimating the nurse's capabilities in caring for your child while he or she is in school.

A registered nurse has the capacity to handle many of your child's emergency problems—not only by treating the minor emergencies such as mild injuries or transient abdominal pains but also by recognizing the seriousness of other acute and long-term health problems. This professional nurse will often initiate a referral on her own to a nearby clinic or recommend a visit to the family doctor based on her observations of the schoolchild. When the school nurse is a graduate registered nurse, the parents should always heed the medical advice of this member of the medical team. Often she has been on the scene in the schools for many years, has watched hundreds of children pass by her office door, and treated a high percentage of these children at one time or another. Her advice is based upon training and experience and should not be ignored.

The public health nurse has not only received a training and license in nursing but also additional training in the prevention and management of diseases that are particularly common to special groups such as schoolchildren. She is especially well versed in the necessary immunizations, the prevention of communicable disease, health education for children and their parents, and the common athletic and other injuries suffered by schoolchildren at play. These skills are additional to her clinical talents in recognizing serious or long-term illness or injury, and to her ability in managing the minor childhood complaints.

A relatively new type of nursing professional has been receiving training within many of the progressive universities and hospitals throughout the country. The government is strongly encouraging the development of more of these special training programs for nurses. Graduates of these special nursing education programs are called by several different names: nurse practitioners, physician's assistants, or pediatric associates. They receive abbreviated but intensive courses in medicine, which provide them with the capability to diagnose and treat the minor physical and behavioral ailments of children. In addition, these nurses are trained to recognize a serious illness with speed and expertness and to refer the sick child to the appropriate specialist with equal skill. Pediatricians, family physicians, and clinics have begun employing such nurses to screen all sick children. Those who are found by the specially trained nurse to have minor treatable illnesses are treated by her, while those with more serious problems (as determined by history and physical examination) are immediately referred to the physician. These specially trained nurses are essentially medical practitioners of minor primary illness. And some of them are now finding positions in the school system. This type of school nurse would be able to diagnose and treat your child for most minor complaints. You could rely upon her medical background and training. She would be supervised by an attending school physician; but her skills would free the school physician to manage the more complex physical, emotional, and educational school problems. Our ultimate goal throughout the country should be to supply every school with nurses who have been so thoroughly trained. The saving to each child and family in time, money, and lost school days would far outweigh the cost of training and re-training the current school nurses.

The parent must be aware that the regular professional school nurse has been the front-line medic in the schools for years. School physicians are a fairly recent development, but the school nurse has been a treasured member of the school for a long time. Many of today's school nurses have the skills and experience on the job that would almost qualify them for the title of nurse practitioner. If the school nurse has been confronted with the daily problem of sick and injured children and has had little or no professional back-up, she may have had to acquire, through first-hand experience, much of the skill and knowledge taught to the special nurse practitioner. Whether she has grown with the demands of her job into a consummately skilled and informed back-up professional will depend upon the individual's dedication to her job and on her motivation to do more than just put in the hours. Many long-time school nurses have broad and extensive medical skills. If your child is in a school with a professional nurse who has been there for years, stop in, meet her, and ask her about her system of managing the everyday childhood emergencies. If it appears that she is assuming primary medical authority, it would be wise to check with the principal and the school physician to ascertain whether her qualifications and skills are equal to managing acute minor illnesses and injuries. If she receives a high rating from her educational and professional colleagues, she will likely be an excellent resource when your child takes ill or is injured in school. If she does not receive their endorsement, then your next step is to insist upon an immediate call from the school whenever an illness or injury occurs. Leave your telephone number (or that of another person who can be available) in the nurse's office.

Some children have health problems that are not severe enough to require special schooling but that will need monitoring to check on symptoms, medicine compliance, diet, and so on. It becomes important for the parents to know when the school nurse is available at their child's school. As we said, many schools only have school nurses available one half day per week; in other systems the school nurse is in school three half days per week. Only some fortunate schools have full-time medical personnel. For the child with such special health problems as diabetes, congenital heart disease, cystic fibrosis, sickle cell disease, or chronic kidney disease, this may be insufficient for either child or parent to feel secure should an acute physical emergency arise. If the school nurse is not in school at least part of every day and your child has an illness that requires the sensitive and informed medical knowledge of an adult there, then you will have to insist that either the principal, assistant principal, or guidance counsellor sits down with you, learns about the details of the illness, and assumes the responsibility for handling any sudden emergency that may arise. You are not shifting the responsibility—you are merely requesting that an informed adult assume control of the situation until you can arrive on the scene. If the school nurse *is* on the premises or within driving distance on a daily basis, your problem may be solved. A consultation with her should reassure you that your child will receive the appropriate immediate care for his or her particular problem until outside help arrives.

Often when a child is not performing well in school the question arises whether this is related to physical, emotional, or situational problems. The school nurse is a skilled observer. She is in the position of watching your child within the classroom and within the total school experience, including lunchtime, recess, and visits to the health office. The trained school nurse who has spent many of her professional years among school-age children has both an educated and an intuitive sense of the differences between the physically ill and the behaviorally maladjusted child. She should be able to take a much more objective, less emotional and interactive viewpoint than you or even your child's teacher when observing your child's overall performance. Often the classroom teacher is very much like another parent in that she or he has your child for long periods of time and feels a deep sense of responsibility for his/her learning and behavior. Much like yourself, your child's failure may be taken very personally by the teacher as a mark of her own failure. The school nurse does not have to get caught in this subjective web; she can stand back and analyze professionally what the key factors appear to be in such generally poor performance.

Johnny was intermittently inattentive and sleepy. His schoolwork was slipping badly in the fourth grade. He arrived each morning alert and attentive; but as the day progressed, he experienced periods of marked vagueness. He became easily distracted. Often he could be found dozing, his head on the desk. Johnny's teacher, trying to find a reason, began to regard the boy as primarily "lazy"; her attitude changed from one of high expectations and encouragement to anger. She became punitive in her reactions to Johnny's inability to pay attention and respond appropriately on occasion. She sent a sharp warning note home with the boy indicating that if his behavior did not change dramatically, she would seriously consider failing him in the fourth grade. Her opinions had been formed; nowhere in the note was there the suggestion that the boy should be analyzed from any other vantage point in order to determine the cause of his inattentiveness and fatigue.

Johnny's mother suspected other problems. She came to school and wisely consulted not only the teacher but also the school nurse. The nurse asked a few pertinent questions and indicated that she would spend the next few weeks observing the young boy during her three days within the school. At the end of two weeks, the school nurse called the mother and teacher into her office. She had watched Johnny closely in class, on the playground, at lunch, and when he was preparing to leave in the afternoon to go home. She had charted the following observations: Johnny arrived at school in the morning fully capable and willing to tackle the schoolwork. His performance deteriorated until immediately before lunch, when he appeared tired, distracted, and occasionally quite nervous. Immediately after lunch, the boy seemed vigorous again but quickly slid back into the increasingly lethargic state of mind that was preventing him from attending to his schoolwork. By the time he was on the school bus, he was a silent, pale, and tired boy, far beyond the expected fatigue at the end of an exciting, physically vigorous school day. The school nurse also noted that while on the playground, Johnny had a rapidly deteriorating ability to coordinate and use physical strength in sports. By the conclusion of play time, he was usually sitting quietly alone on the sidelines staring blankly at his surroundings.

The school nurse pointed out how these swings in behavior were directly related to Johnny's meals. He appeared vigorous and actively alert immediately after a meal, yet quickly began losing his physical and educational strengths as the minutes separated him from his previous food consumption. The school nurse suggested to Johnny's mother and teacher that the boy was not "lazy" at all but had a physical problem that needed immediate attention and diagnostic procedures. She called Johnny's pediatrician so she could describe her findings in detail. After an extensive work-up, Johnny was found to have a problem with his pancreas which caused him to have very low blood sugars soon after the carbohydrate and other food elements from the preceding meal were burned away. This extremely low blood sugar prevented him from demonstrating a full physical or intellectual performance since circulating blood sugar elements are directly involved in the activity of all cells, including brain cells. Treatment of Johnny's condition required a concentrated "team" approach between physician, Johnny's mother, his teacher, Johnny himself, and the school nurse, who monitored his activity and assisted his mother and teacher in their management of the delicate chemical imbalances that were seriously interfering with the boy's total behavior and learning pattern.

This actual case clearly demonstrates how the competent, well-trained, observant school nurse can be effectively used as professional consultant in the physical, emotional, and educational health of the individual child. However, unless the problems are brought directly to the attention of the school nurse by either teacher or parent, she cannot be an effective ally. Therefore if the teacher has overlooked this special resource, the parent must be sufficiently aware of the school nurse's potential to seek her out for consultation.

Only in a very few schools is the liaison between teacher and school nurse a mandated, significant one. It should be! Whenever a child is not functioning properly in the classroom (for whatever reason and in whatever specific area of schoolroom activity), the teacher should ask for a "nurse-teacher conference." This important meeting is designed to share the problems of the particular child between the educational and health professionals. The teacher often inquires about relevant information on past or present medical problems which may be known to the school nurse. The nurse also will be able to question the teacher as to visible suspect physical or emotional symptoms which will play an important role in the assessment. This conference usually results in a combined plan of action—the nurse assuming certain tasks in order to uncover the cause of the child's poor performance and the teacher attempting to gather new and valuable information. If your child has a problem in school, this nurse-teacher conference can be an extremely pertinent first step in reaching the proper conclusions as to why. Some parents take offense at their child being "discussed" by the school professionals. They should be reassured that this discussion is a professional, confidential meeting between two trained observers who are concerned about the school progress of their child. Together the two professionals will gain far more useful information than either would be capable of doing singly. There is absolutely no reason why you, as a parent, cannot be made aware of the conclusions of such a conference. All you need do is set up an appointment with one or the other, preferably both, professionals, in order to be brought up to date on their joint thinking about your child.

In fact, if a school nurse attends the school on a regular basis and your child is experiencing significant problems, you might be the person to suggest and initiate the nurse-teacher conference. The more informed the professionals who are observing your child and contributing their educated opinions, the more likely your child is to be helped. A full picture of his or her school problems will have been assembled, analyzed, and acted upon by all of the concerned authorities. These nurse-teacher conferences often stimulate the nurse to attend class and observe your child. She may bring him into the health office for a talk or a physical examination, or schedule him to see the school physician with a high priority because of her stimulated concern. She may also visit your home to chat with you about the social and family interactions which could be playing a role in your child's inability to get the most out of his school experience. These visits are not the "spying" trips suspected by too many parents. They are professional "house calls" by a medical specialist (in this case, the school nurse), who will meet you and discuss within the privacy of your home the special family and social problems that may be contributing to your child's school failure. She will observe the interactions within your home which you, as a parent, could be too close to the eye of the storm to appreciate.

Obviously the nurse-teacher conference should increase the teacher's sensitivity and knowledge about your child. She has shared her frustrations over your child's performance; in return, she has received support, information, and advice which will permit her to approach the child with renewed interest and patience as well as expanded knowledge about the causes of his problems. The school nurse will often make the teacher focus on the real problems in the classroom, so that the latter no longer experiences a diffuse feeling of anger or frustration when dealing with your child. After the conference, the teacher will often regard your child and his problem as a new challenge and a new stimulus for success. It is with these positive virtues in mind that we strongly endorse such conferences for children with significant school problems, and equally strongly recommend the establishment of these valuable meetings within your child's school if they do not already exist.

It would be incorrect to assume, however, that the school nurse only works with problem children. She is just as concerned with the *prevention* of problems. In today's schools, with today's morals, the painful and crucial problems faced by misinformed or inadequately informed children are the very problems which the school nurse is attempting to prevent. Many parents worry about the attempts to teach courses on Family Living and sex education within the schools. There is a loud outcry that the people teaching these courses to their children are "untrained." "We have the job to teach them the facts of life," they say. There is a serious flaw in this reasoning. To return sex education and Family Living exclusively back to the home environment is to place the burden of this delicate and sensitive task in the hands of the least professional individuals—the parents. Unless the next generation of parents differs quite significantly from previous generations, the children of tomorrow will receive halting, inadequate, embarrassed sex education in the homes of a large percentage of American families.

Of course the mother and father have the right to make sure that this other person has the knowledge, training, and sensitivity to implant such crucial information carefully in an impressionable and receptive young child. Many progressive school systems hold regular mandatory workshops for the teachers selected for this important assignment. Parents have every right to assess a teacher's training course and the curriculum being offered to their child in this vital area of education. However, for parents to dismiss as totally out of hand the concurrent value of school-based courses on Family Living and sex education is thoroughly inappropriate.

The School Nurse

Who should you turn to to act as a professional liaison between you and the school when the issue of Family Living and sex education arises? The two medical professionals, the school nurse and the school doctor, are your proper recourse. The school doctor may also be called upon to answer pertinent and troubling questions posed by the teachers who have been asked (or who have volunteered) to teach such courses. However, it is very likely to be the school nurse who will be approached for consistent advice and monitoring of a school's course in intimate human behavior and Family Living. Most nurses qualify as excellent health educators. They have been trained in the biological and social aspects of human sexuality. One of us recently conducted a three-month workshop for school nurses who worked in an entire school district. Their high level of interest and training enabled the group to discuss many controversial issues of human sexuality quite openly. The nurses were very capable of expressing their own biases and concerns without the sense that these personal feelings would color the health education approach of the teachers. The author finished the course with renewed conviction that one of the most important functions of the school nurse was to contribute to the health education of pupil and teacher alike. This should not be limited to the subject of intimate human behavior and sex education; the school nurse has the ability to offer much useful information in biology courses as well as courses in social science.

Does your child's school use the professional expertise of the school nurse to fill in the expected gaps in health and/or sex education? And if not, why not? If the reason is because the school nurse is not in the school a sufficient amount of time to complete all her tasks, then it may be necessary to revise her job requirements. How much time is she spending filling out duplicate forms? How much is assigned to unnecessary administrative meetings and organizing medical screening programs? The secretarial, administrative, and planning aspects of many school nurse's jobs could be handled with far better skill and use of personnel by a competent secretary-administrator. This would free more time for the school nurse, which could be spent performing many of the crucial tasks outlined in this chapter.

Can you do anything about an indiscriminate use of your school nurse's time? Of course! As parents, you have a great deal of vocal and voting power. Everyone in the school administration recognizes this fact. Obtain the necessary information, reach your conclusions objectively, organize a parent group, and then present these new proposals to the school administration, the school board, the local and state governments, and the local and state departments of health. Start with your local school administrator and move upward until you have received the satisfaction of seeing that the medical professionals within your child's school and in the other schools in your community are being asked to perform tasks which are of maximum benefit to the children in their daily school experience.

We have already stressed (in Chapter 7) that the school nurse can be a vital and integral part of the "team" of professionals who attempt to solve the problems of behavior and learning in the child with special difficulties. In significant new school health programs set up in Galveston, Baltimore, and Rochester (among other places), this team of professionals combines their skills in medical and educational diagnosis prescriptions for the child with behavior and learning difficulties. And they include the school nurse as a key member. Very often the school nurse has been asked to perform the job of "getting the child to the right people" by herself in the past when the particular child has overwhelmed the school administration (including teachers and principal) with problems in behavior and learning. Frequently she had to struggle with inflexible bureaucratic educational and medical systems in order to assemble enough professional help for a particular child. Thus the field of learning and behavior problems is not a new one for the school nurse. What we are recommending is that the school nurse should be relieved of the *total* burden of coordinating the diagnostic and treatment plans for the child with special educational problems. As a member of a team that includes school physician, school psychologist, school social worker, special educator, and communication specialist, the nurse may contribute her nursing and administrative skills without the unnecessary and inappropriate burden of coordinating "the whole show." She often cannot succeed in this—or else the process takes almost forever. Who suffers? Your child if he or she has a behavior or learning problem. Therefore, find out from the administrators in your child's school what the process will be if you are approached and told that your child has special learning or behavior problems and must have a "work-up." If the school nurse is saddled with the total task of finding the proper outside professionals, assembling their submitted data, and interpreting that data to the teacher and principal, then your child will be receiving far less than adequate diagnostic help. The school nurse is being burdened with a task that exceeds her professional capability or time. Again, a crusade by involved parents may be necessary to make accessible the professionals needed by the teacher and the school nurse so that the "team" approach to your child's special learning problems can occur in weeks rather than months. It is reasonable for the school nurse to be central in the coordination of this process; what must be assured is that the other professionals are within her immediate reach for their contributions.

Usually, the school nurse is a skilled professional. As such, she can offer much to your child when special problems arise within his or her school day. She can deal with acute physical emergencies and make the proper referrals. She can be instrumental in the observation and care of the chronically ill child. She can be a diagnostician or coordinator of diagnostic teaming for physical or learning and behavior problems. Clearly, the school nurse has the potential to act as a child health educator of the highest caliber. What she should NOT be is a secretary, a school administrator, or a total diagnostician and medical coordinator, burdened with all sorts of non-educational problems. Which of these is the nurse in your child's school? If she is not what she should be, it is up to you as a parent to give your child access to the highest professional skills the school nurse can provide.

9 The School Social Worker

A modern school represents a minor miracle in the evolution of public education—the realization that a pupil's right to education includes the remediation of home influences that hinder that education. The modern public school system now cares about keeping children, and adapts its educational and remedial programs to meet the needs of the child with a problem. It is recognized that the best education for any child occurs when the child is rewarded for learning *both* at school and at home. Recognizing this fact schools have hired people who can help to make this cooperation between school and home helpful and productive.

School social workers, sometimes known as visiting teachers, or itinerant teachers, were not a significant part of the public education scene until the last decade. Social workers have, of course, worked for a long time with children and adults, and have included schools, courts, hospitals, and institutions on their lists of contacts. But a social worker, hired by a school to focus on school-related problems, had to await two educational milestones: Education had first to declare that educational services were for *all* children; then colleges and universities had to devise ways of training people, both in social work and in education, that would give them the skills to uncover and analyze the many reasons for apparent combined educational and home problems. Such courses had to provide the approaches and the techniques needed to remedy these problems. Now state departments of education give certificates to school social workers who are properly trained, just as they do to teachers. Most states have funds to help the local school systems pay the salaries of their own social workers. What you may not know, however, is just how to find them—and what they can do for you and your child when you need them.

The School Social Worker

Ask a school social worker what she does, and she will tell you "a little of everything." Looking at samples of file documents, it appears that she covers a wide territory. Do not be misled, however. She does *not* do "everything." She does not teach your child in a classroom setting. She does not give batteries of psychological tests. She does not carry out extensive therapy with children. She does not do long-term parental therapy. She does not make administrative changes. Instead, she facilitates; she gathers information; she helps people make changes they want to make. She knows about and can get to the resources that parents need. She "talks through" minor adjustment problems with parent, child, and school personnel. She brings other professionals together to discuss a child's problem. She, in essence, advocates for the troubled schoolchild. She spots an educational problem, investigates its roots, brings her knowledge to the attention of all those—including you, the parents—who need to know about it, and then helps put the plan for remedying the problem into effect.

That means that you will probably never meet the school social worker in your system unless your child is having an educational problem that the school feels it cannot solve without more information from you about yourselves and your home.

Often these problems involve your child's attitudes. The child simply is not working to his or her capacity, and there seems to be no way that the teacher can help motivate him. He constantly hurries too fast, does sloppy work, and refuses to improve his papers when he has free time. Or he cries every day during the arithmetic period, unable to concentrate on the work and unwilling to participate in the discussion. Perhaps he spends almost all of his time interacting with—and bothering —other children around him, to the point of disrupting the lessons both for himself and for the other children. Yet he is unable to work alone when removed from the group.

When these problems last for a period of weeks, without relief, they will often cause a referral to a school social worker and then, of course, to you, his parents. The school social worker's job will be to analyze the problems from the viewpoint of the factors motivating the child at home as well as those that influence him or her at school. The social worker will ask you about the attitudes of all the family members toward school. She will seek to find out the attitudes of other people who are significant in the life of your child, such as playmates or relatives. She will try to learn how you reward—or punish—your child's behavior in school. She will investigate what happens to the child on his way to school. She will probably observe him in the classroom to document what attitudes are apparent in the teacher's behavior and in the behavior of classmates to which he may be reacting. In other words, she will try to reconstruct the child's world as he sees it in order to bring out the causes of his negative school behavior. She will expect that many of the causes of the behavior will not be malicious. For example, you may not know what subtle cues the child is taking from your sophisticated talk about the merits of your child's teacher. Or you may not be aware of the devastating effects of the nickname given to your child by his classmates. But the school social worker is trained to look for all of these things. She should be able to put all this information together and create a total picture of this puzzle for you and the teacher.

True social problems are another type of concern that usually activates a call from a social worker. Your child's teacher may be worried about the frequent fights in which your son is involved; his unpopularity may cause most of the other children to shun him. On the other hand, she may be worried only about his lack of interaction with the other children. Or perhaps he just sits and daydreams most of the time, paying little attention either to his lessons or to the others around him. In any case, the teacher cannot explain his behavior and feels that she needs to know more about it. Enter the school social worker.

A third set of problems in which a school social worker often gets involved is that broad class of behavior patterns known as attendance problems. Your contact with the school social worker may be the first time you have heard that your child has been tardy every morning for the past six weeks. Or you may find, to your horror, that he actually has not been at school for whole days when you thought he was there. "Where has he been?" and "What has he been doing?" will be your immediate questions; but they will not be as important as the question: "Why the tardiness—or absence?" In problems of attendance, what is being avoided is probably more important than what is being sought. And your school social worker will be quick to tell you that the problem may not be merely your child's attitude. It might be social—or both social and attitudinal. Whatever the causes, the school social worker will treat attendance problems in your child as a symptom, not a disease. Together, you and the school social worker will need to find out about the rest of the problem—and then the causes behind the dilemma—before you can work out the cure.

From these examples, you might deduce that a call from a school social worker is cause for great alarm. Something has been happening with your child in school that needs drastic action. He or she has severe problems. Usually, however, the contact from a school social worker does not work that way. If you know your child, you have doubtless suspected the possibility of a problem for some time. Probably the teacher has talked to you once or twice. Your child's report card is very spotty, poor grades mixed with the good. Something about the attendance figures seems unusual because you cannot recall that many instances of lateness or absence. And so, generally, the call from the school social worker is the welcome first step toward defining and remediating your child's suspected school problem.

In some cases, a contact from a school social worker might be for the purpose of *preventing* a problem. It may have been suggested by other school personnel that your child might profit from a different class placement or a special education referral. The social worker will want to talk to you about your feelings about this change, explain its significance, and work toward a smooth transition for the youngster. Or your child might be eligible to apply for an award—for example, a scholarship to college—and she wants to explain the award and the process of application to you. Perhaps the school personnel have noticed a chronic physical condition that seems to be affecting your child, and they want to know how to work with it in the future. Perhaps your son appears to be increasingly influenced by the wrong kinds of companions and the school wants to help the child work his way out of a potentially destructive social trap. Your daughter may need temporary tutoring to help her catch up with her class, and the school social worker can help obtain that tutor. There are many preventive actions which the school social worker may initiate in an effort to inform you and assist you to help your child in the future. It is as important for the school social worker to be alert to potential problems as it is for her to spot current problems. Her duty is to let you know about them.

All these are good reasons why you might be called by a school social worker. But, as you know, the telephone is a two-way instrument, and you have an equal right to call a school social worker and request her services on behalf of your child. Before you do that, however, it might help to know a bit more about how the social worker functions. What are her skills? What can you ask her to do for you and for your child?

Basically, she functions as a gatherer of information. Given a problem, either present or potential, she sets off to acquire as much information about the child involved from as many responsible parties as possible. She generally starts with the parents, often with a visit in your home at your convenience. During this meeting she will probably ask you questions covering your whole philosophy of child raising, questions about the family's medical and social history, questions about the relationship of your child to his or her friends and siblings, questions about your child's feelings on school, and questions about how your child learns best at home. Some of these questions may seem quite personal, perhaps even intrusive; but they are being asked for a purpose. They are necessary to uncover the reasons for a problem and come up with a possible solution to it. Your school social worker is strictly bound by legal and ethical rules to keep all information confidential, so you can feel free to talk about anything she requests or that you want to tell her. As a professional, she will not ask you for information she does not feel pertinent to the problem. Nor will she share any irrelevant material with other professionals. She will not be judgmental; she won't try to "blame" you for any attitude or activities you have undertaken. She is there to reconstruct the child's world in an attempt to understand the problem—its causes and its solutions. For your child's sake, do not deprive her of information that she needs to do this. But remind her that you will be asking for this reconstruction, once she has interviewed all the parties, so that you too can be a part of the solution.

Another of the school social worker's particular skills is the ability to find help and resources for those parents who need them. In her day-to-day activities, she will come into contact with various courts, welfare agencies, counselling centers, hospitals, recreation agencies, private schools, professionals in private practice, employment agencies, governmental agencies, and others who may help. Resources that she does not know personally she can often recommend through other professionals, directories, or the grapevine. She knows, or can find out, what are the requirements which must be met before an agency can help you. And she can assist you in starting to contact those agencies you might need. Although her main concern is the educational welfare of your child, she knows that the general welfare of your family will affect the progress of your child in school. Therefore she makes it her business to help any family improve itself when they ask her, generally by helping them find the right source of assistance.

If necessary, the school social worker can also do some short-term counselling. By the time she has fully investigated a school problem, she is in an excellent position to inform those who can best help the child. Sometimes she needs to do this in several sessions. She usually feels that it is her responsibility to offer information about the child to you, the parent, in whatever form she senses would prove most helpful to you. In some cases, it may be presented to you at the very same time that she interprets the information about you and your own problems as well. This type of counselling is one of the outstanding skills of the school social worker. But it should always have definite purposes in mind. Almost no school social worker will have the time to see you for a long period of therapy; and few will want to, since they must maintain a close working relationship with the child (who is, after all, their primary client). Nevertheless, the school social worker will also help you get whatever intensive or long-term counselling and/or therapy you might need, and you should not hesitate to ask her for the necessary referral if you feel that you do need extended help. The same ground rules apply when the school social worker counsels your child. A school social worker might see your child for a few periods to gather and dispense information; but generally she will not see him or her on a long-term basis. She might, however, get periodic reports on his progress from the teacher and counsel him as needed. If he appears to need long-term therapy, she will make this recommendation to you, as his parents, and in her report to her employer, the school.

Finally, the school social worker possesses one skill which is not often recognized by parents but which should be used more frequently than currently is the case: she can talk professionally to the teacher about your child. Often, in the natural quarrels between teacher and parent over their responsibility for a child's education, valuable information is lost that ought to be shared. Poor communication occurs because neither the teacher nor the pupil's parents can remain objective about that student. To the parent, the child is "his"—to the teacher, the problems are "hers." A school social worker can look squarely at the problem. She is not out to blame anyone—a fact that needs repeating. She knows the child and his or her needs; she hopes to become familiar with the parents and their needs. She knows the history of the child and his problems, what expectations surround him, and the consequences of various options taken by either teacher or parent. Therefore she can talk to both parent and teacher with the specific child in mind. This is her job. Sometimes, however, only *you* can ask her to do this.

Yes, you can make this direct request, and more. The school social worker is part of the school. She is paid out of tax funds (or tuition in private schools)—your money. She is there as an advocate of your child. She can receive requests and referrals from you just as she can receive them from school personnel. And now that you know what she can do, you know which of her services you can request for your child.

You can ask her, for example, to help you with home problems that may be affecting the child. If you are contemplating a divorce or separation and you feel that it may be a potentially severe problem to a child, ask the school social worker to help you work through this major family disruption as it affects your child and his or her progress in school. Is your Aunt Mildred—the one that hates children—coming to live with you for a year? Consult the school social worker. Is the death or serious illness of a relative or close friend causing family disturbance? Are you afraid that your child cannot handle new tragedy? Let the school social worker help you. Is your child feeling increasingly inferior because his intellectually superior sisters are outshining him in all areas? The school social worker can watch out for and help prevent future failure problems which might affect your child's schoolwork and social life.

Perhaps you have questions about the child that need explanations the teacher cannot give you. Why doesn't he have any friends—is he a bully? Why does she have "hives" every school night? Why are his grades so much worse this year than they were during the last two years? Why won't she talk about Mr. Pritchett, the art teacher? How serious is this pressure to start dating? A school social worker can help you find the answers to many problems of this kind.

Call the school social worker when you think that you need the help of a special agency. Maybe you are temporarily unemployed and need food stamps. Perhaps your child has a long-term physical illness and you wonder if there could be any financial relief from the medical bills. You might sense the possibility that your child or another member of the family is in need of psychological or psychiatric counselling and you want to find a mental health center or agency. Or perhaps you have been giving serious consideration to adopting another sibling for your only child. In any case, tap the resources of the school social worker. And keep her informed about what happens when you make that contact she recommended. If it is not successful, go to her again and she might be able to help you further.

Sometimes, when you are working through a long-range problem with a child, you will need someone at school to talk to that child occasionally—to offer a little encouragement or to determine whether you and/or the child are making progress and if what you perceive to be adverse conditions at school are changing. Don't hesitate to ask the school social worker if she could do a little "maintenance counselling"; that is, ask her to see the child as often as is needed just to check on progress or to counsel a little. Let her be a "friend away from home" for you.

You know, of course, that the school social worker is the possible key to referrals to other school personnel like the school psychologist, school physician, speech therapist, or to a special education program or the administrator. Since she will sometimes be your chief contact, do not hesitate to ask her for these referrals when and if you feel they can be helpful. Should you need to know more about these school personnel than has been outlined here, she will be your best source. Use her as your key contact with diversified educational services.

The school social worker is your ally in seeking the best educational program possible for your child. She is the embodiment of the concept that each child ought to receive an education in the best possible environment, both at home and in school. Too many parents do not know what to ask of the school social worker. The most practical referral you can make is the one that requests help in defining what is educationally best for your child. Your school social worker understands what this means and will help you to understand too.

THE CHILDREN

10 The Expelled or Excluded Child

When a child is expelled from school, the action is often a quick decision based upon some unexplained action by your child with which the administrator of the school felt helpless to cope. Generally a great deal of anger lies behind the expulsion of a child from school. The teacher is angry if she felt the action was directed toward her or disrupted her class. The principal often harbors a good bit of anger at being forced to reach the decision for expulsion sometimes demanded by the teacher. The child frequently has an overriding sense of being mistreated, misunderstood, and individually selected for punishment. Therefore, he, too, is upset. The parents may become angered at a system that refuses to care for and teach their child during hours when they must work or be away from home, usually they have no immediate alternative plans for the school hours. Thus, expelling a child from school is commonly surrounded by irrationality and fiery outbursts of temper.

Expelling a child from school should be very carefully considered by all parties involved, and everyone concerned should be quite certain that there is something to be gained by it. Children should not be expelled as a form of punishment, nor to get rid of them for a "cooling-off" period of days. This merely delays the solution to the problems that led up to the dismissal from school in the first place. A cause-and-effect principle must be brought to bear in the expulsion. Every parent has the right to request an explanation of the causes behind the expulsion, as well as the rational objectives hoped for by the administrators who carried out the child's temporary dismissal. No parents should accept the expulsion of their child from school without making certain that these two questions have been thoroughly and satisfactorily answered by the school administration.

On occasion, a child will be expelled with the provision that he or she will be readmitted if he receives outside consultation from professionals. Our experience has been that all too frequently the school officials will expel a somewhat overactive youngster with the stipulation that he may not return to school setting until he has been "cleared" by the doctor. Occasionally, the school will actually dictate the specific diagnostic and therapeutic treatments necessary before the child can be readmitted. Requests such as, "To see the neurologist and have an EEG [electroencephalogram] before readmittance," or, "Cannot come back to school until he is placed on medication," are frequent accompanying instructions when the expelled child appears at the clinic or private doctor's office. This reasoning must be viewed as totally unacceptable. By expelling the child, the school officials are relinquishing their responsibility for the diagnosis and work-up of his school problem, and forcing the parents to search for the answer alone. No parent should tolerate such behavior. It is perfectly permissible for school and parent to seek the proper diagnostic and therapeutic facilities outside the school setting, but this should not be attempted at the expense of the child's education. We have already indicated that there is little reason why such services cannot be made available to all children in need of diagnostic and therapeutic follow-up within most school systems. However, if these services are nonexistent or not immediately available, then the school has the obligation to work with the child's parents to locate and program the appropriate investigation. Expelling the child and forcing the parents to seek this work-up elsewhere is inexcusable and should not be tolerated.

Another situation which should not be tolerated is the expulsion of the child from school because the child has done poorly in his or her academic work. This is clearly an illogical action. How can a child learn unless placed in a learning environment? How can a child be taught without a teacher? This kind of action usually stems from frustration, the guilt of inadequate teaching, or from an unconscious desire to punish. Investigate it, and work at its solution calmly, rationally, objectively. Look for the aspects of the school that can reward, not punish. Look for the teacher or administrator who can view your child as a learning problem—not as a problem learner. Insist on keeping your child in school.

In simple terms, if the expulsion of your child from school is merely a substitute for the school's understanding and cooperative help in uncovering and treating the child's difficulties, then you must fight this action with vigor and determination. How do you do this? First, send your child back to school until a conference has been held to discuss the causes and effects of the expulsion. Secondly, contact the local school administration and the state school administration, if need be, to complain about the procedure. Inquire from your state school administration about the appeals mechanism which you can use to fight this unilateral action of expulsion. And, further, check up on the state or local laws which determine the limit of time a child may be temporarily expelled from the school setting.

If, on the other hand, the school officials contacted you first and held a conference during which you were informed about the reasons why the officials felt expulsion was necessary and told of the positive effects that expulsion would create for the child, then you might wish to join the school in the process. You should only join, however, if you understand and agree with their explanation and their reasoning. In addition, you should find out how they are planning to provide the subsequent help your child obviously needs if he or she is to continue in the school environment. In this way, you can become a part of the process of expulsion and the subsequent gains which can result from the temporary dismissal of your child.

As a parent, you must be aware of what expulsion may mean to the child. It usually singles him or her out as a person with a special problem which is far more serious than any other child's behavior and learning problems. He may begin to view himself differently, with a lessened sense of social "belonging"—more of an outsider. This must be prevented at all costs. The ultimate result of a gradually increasing sense of being different—the "special problem," the outsider—can be the eventual assumption of the outside role in its extreme. Jean Genêt writes in his autobiography, "I became a thief because they told me I was a thief." He was a child at the time. Children play the roles we give them. If the expelled child is not informed why the expulsion was necessary, what positive steps will be taken to correct the problem, and that the learning process must continue, even though temporarily out of the school setting, he may begin to become a "lost" student, one of the external people in our world, extrinsic to our laws, our customs, our lives.

The expelled child must have a structured work schedule while at home. Lessons must be obtained from his or her teacher. He should be expected to keep pace with his classmates, and his work should receive the scrutiny and criticism of both his parents and his teacher.

His time should be carefully predetermined, with schoolwork first, followed by help around the house, outlined in meticulous detail. Expulsion time should not be a vacation period. It is not to be rewarded by playtime or the lessening of responsibility. The child must view this period as one of investigation and consultation relative to finding help for him. His role is to continue his studies and maintain his responsibilities both at school and at home. The teacher must work with the parent in preparing home lessons and grading them. The school cannot be permitted to ignore this child during the period of his dismissal. If the period is to be a positive and instructive one for the child as well as for teacher and parent, then the youngster must be given an appropriate awareness of a continued sense of responsibility on the part of the school, despite the unfortunate need for expulsion.

Parents should be alerted to the dangers of "permanent expulsion," which means exclusion. There are very few children who should ever need permanent expulsion from the public school setting. In the past, certain school systems used the mechanism of exclusion to force the parents of handicapped children to seek private school placement for their disabled children. This still exists to some degree today—often as an illegal act. Parents must be aware that all public schools are required by law to provide a suitable and appropriate education for *all* children, no matter what the disability. If your child has a physical or emotional handicap, do not permit your local school district to exclude him or to force you to look for external educational resources. The responsibility is theirs, not yours alone.

In addition, if your child has been expelled and the causes are such that a prolonged therapeutic period will be needed to correct the problems that caused the dismissal, the schools are responsible for finding alternative methods of educating him or her. In some areas, the emotionally disturbed child is forced into continuous homebound teaching because the local resources for teaching emotionally disturbed youngsters are extremely limited. This is a national disgrace which needs strong parental action to pressure for change. If you yourself are the parent of such a child, or are interested in helping the parents of such children, you should begin a serious planned campaign through your state or federal congressional delegation to lobby for proper legislation. Often, however, the laws are in place, the school is just "dragging its feet."

Occasionally, a child with severe physically disabling handicaps will be excluded from the public school system and assigned homebound teaching on a temporary basis. This is done in order to give the local special education division sufficient time to locate the appropriate special school, either locally or elsewhere, where the child can receive a proper equivalent education. This exclusion from school should always be temporary only. Any prolonged delay should cause the parent to demand action for an alternative placement for the physically handicapped child.

There is a natural tendency for some school systems to exclude the special child or the disabled child from many curricular and extracurricular activities; in most cases, however, this is improper and counterproductive to the child's physical and emotional well-being. Physical education teachers are now being trained in college for "adaptive physical education," which deals directly with the problems of how to keep the physically and mentally disabled child in the important physical activities of the school. Certainly some of the programmed activities may need modification, but these youngsters need both the physical exercise and the mental therapy of participation without exclusion. The more enlightened schools create specific functions for their disabled youngsters on varsity athletic teams so that the experience of teamplay and grouping which sports engender will not be denied to these special children. Recently, both of us watched a mutual patient diagnosed as having severe hyperactivity with neurological dysfunctioning play a featured role in the school play. Casting him took great courage, and coaching him and waiting patiently for him to learn his lines infinite tolerance on the director's part. However, the play came off well. Despite an obvious effort at remembering his lines, the young man did a creditable job and earned the congratulations of friends. There is little doubt in our minds that his inclusion in this experience and the recognition he gained are key factors in his current improved showing in the scholastic area. This is his first "good" year. He is seventeen years old and represents a fine example of the value of including the special child in extracurricular activities.

We have watched the blind play football. The Theater for the Deaf is a brilliant example of the way handicapped young people can expand their lives without fear of failure or embarrassment. Wheelchair basketball now has national leagues. There are few curricular or extracurricular activities that cannot be adapted for the special child. The physical education teacher may need "encouragement" from a cadre of parents to accomplish this. The drama coach, the music teacher, and so on, may need additional help and financial support to coach special children and to buy the necessary equipment for modifying activities that would permit the handicapped child to participate and perform. The school which claims to offer equal educational opportunities "to all children" *as required by law* must find these resources. Do not accept No as an answer when you ask!

Parents must protect their children from exclusion—whether as a result of physical handicaps, poor scholastic performance, or problem behavior. The mother and father are frequently intimidated by the power of the schools to expel their child. As a result, parents beg, plead, and agree to just about anything to facilitate getting their child back into school.

But parents should remind the school that the expelling of the child was a beginning and not a conclusion . . . a beginning of the process to ameliorate the conditions that precipitated the dismissal, and not a termination of the school's responsibilities to the child. Exclusion or explusion must only be a genuine "last resort."

11 The Child Who Is Failing—"Failure Factors"

Your child has taken his hand from behind his back where a tight fist was clutching a brown envelope with his name written on the front. He extends his hand toward you. You watch his ashen and frightened face as you reach for the trembling piece of paper. As you remove the contents of the envelope and begin reading, the full impact of the message comes across very clearly in the long vertical line of Fs or Unsatisfactorys which makes the strong and painful declaration of failure. On the bottom of the report card is a statement penned in a small but blunt handwriting asking you to come to school for a conference as soon as possible. You immediately begin to feel the chill of fright and embarrassment that will linger until the day of that difficult visit when you must confront this stranger who holds your child's future within his or her hands and ask, "Why is my child failing?"

This is a very appropriate question for a parent to ask a child's teacher. However, the parent must be aware that he or she is going to receive nothing more than an educated guess as a response unless the teacher has undertaken an extensive series of testing procedures on the child before the ultimate failure. Usually this is not the case. Unfortunately, all too frequently the testing and the investigation follow the child's humiliation and pain *after* he has failed. The teacher, the principal, the guidance counsellor has each in his own way observed your child's school activity and come to his own or a consensus opinion about the reasons behind the failure. But they do not have all the pieces of the puzzle. You possess some of these reasons, while other professionals may contribute key bits of information on the rest. What are the issues that parents must investigate and question when approaching a school system that is failing their child?

A great deal will depend upon the age of your child and his or her past history. Each age period has specific qualities that should be examined before entering the school office to discuss your child's failure with his teacher.

Let us assume that your failing child is in one of the first three grades in school. He has not done well since school began and now you are faced with a totally unsatisfactory performance. What are the primary factors that deserve your and the teacher's careful consideration at this time? What are the "failure factors" in this situation?

1. Could your child have entered school at too early an age? This is not an uncommon problem in the very early grades. The child whose birthday is in November or December but who is registered for school with other children born six to nine months earlier may be less prepared for the pace, or the social and educational demands, of a system geared for children at a slightly more advanced level of age and maturity. Each child develops educational skills at his own pace; some move very quickly, others more slowly. The result is usually the same—each ultimately reaching a satisfactory range of assimilating and adapting information during the first few years of school. If a youngster has entered school at an early age and has sluggish but normal learning skills, he or she will find the class breezing by and leaving him far behind in the race for knowledge. This child could easily fail despite his serious and earnest efforts to succeed. If this is your child, he will often demonstrate signs of frustration and anger, first at the teacher and the school, then at his peers and friends. Possibly he will direct this anger and exasperation back upon himself. He wants to be like the others, do well in school, not be the slowest in the class; but he cannot "put it all together" at quite the same rate as his slightly older peers.

Often this youngster has not only failed in the academic areas but has begun to daydream or act out physically or verbally so that his behavior and attentiveness are quite poor as well. These deficiences are a direct result of immaturity and his subsequent frustration at the slowly developing nature of his learning skills when compared to his somewhat more sophisticated classmates.

One of the first things you must insist upon is that your child be tested. There can be no confusion or error relative to his mental capacity or learning abilities. If he tests within the normal range, then observation of his behavior and performance within the classroom should confirm for you and the teacher that he is not functioning at the same level of maturity as his older classmates.

What do you do in this situation? Do you insist that the school move him ahead because you strongly suspect that the emergence of his learning capacities is just around the corner? Many parents take this inflexible stand because they fear the impact of failure upon the emotional state of their child. However, what these parents resist recognizing is the tremendously negative force that continual failure and below-par performance can have even on the normal youngster.

If social and learning maturity are the key factors in your young child's early grade failure, then holding the child back in order that he or she may repeat the early grade successfully may have several positive features. Instead of facing the prospect of running to try to keep up with the others in the class, the child will have experienced the material and will taste success and esteem during the repeated year. These two senses of accomplishment can go a long way in softening the discomfort of being held back. In addition, his age will be more in keeping with that of the older youngsters in the new group; in terms of social maturity, peer acceptance, and coordination in games and sports, the child may have much easier sailing with this second group than he ever would have had with the older classmates. The child would clearly benefit from repeating the year in the very early grade. This must not be viewed as a failure on the teacher's, parent's, or child's part; it is merely a delay and reassignment to a more appropriate group according to age and level of learning maturity.

Parent and teacher must work together to reach this conclusion after they have ruled out a number of the more serious delays in learning, such as mental retardation, specific learning disability, and emotional disability (among others). Once the diagnosis of "educational immaturity" has been made and agreed upon by all, then the decision for delay or progression must be made mutually by school and parent. Each must view the child and the future environment realistically to estimate whether the child will be able to adjust to the same peer group in the next few years without educational or emotional repercussions. Often the decision is that the wiser choice is to allow the youngster to find his or her own social and educational level by holding him back.

The child, however, will need some help in seeking that social adjustment. By being retained one year, a child faces the taunts of his or her peers, who are all too ready to label other children "dummy" or "slow" as a way of bolstering their own budding egos. Parents should help their child to learn a vocabulary to overcome this potential loss of status. The retained child must be made to feel positive about the decision: to know that it will provide more time to learn; to realize that there will be more playmates closer to his own age; to experience the sense of being ahead of the class for a short time (and possibly the first time). Parents can point out the many benefits of this action to the child, and should then help him to rephrase these positive aspects. "My parents chose to help me get a good start in school by letting me spend more time in one class," or, "I'm young for my age so my parents are helping me get younger friends," or, "I really want to learn everything very well so I can be very good when I get older," are the sort of sentences that parents can help their children remember to use when questioned about remaining in the same grade. A vital rule of communication between parent and the failing child is optimism. To protect his or her self-esteem, the child will have to learn—and frequently repeat—"what it means for *me.*"

2. Some children fail in the early grades because of very poor class adjustment known as "school phobia." These are often only children, first children, or the last child from a large family. School phobia generally results from the child's reluctance to leave the familiarity of home and attempt the strange, regimented, and integrated milieu of school. Here the child must blend into the whole, must share and wait his turn, must obey the commands of a new and foreign authoritarian figure, and must be judged as a success or failure on performance rather than merely on existence. For the immature child, the pampered child, the unprepared child . . . these are difficult adjustments to make. As a result, the young child will cry openly, throw temper tantrums, or retreat into the nearest corner refusing, with face averted and head shaking, to take part in the flow of daily classroom activities.

There are various degrees of school phobia. The most serious includes those children who resist going to school in the morning with all the emotional stops pulled out: the tears, the tantrums, the physical balking. Other youngsters suddenly develop strange and exotic maladies on Monday mornings which last mysteriously until the following Friday afternoon and seem to ebb after the ringing of the first school bells. These faked illnesses are another manifestation of the school-phobic child, who will miss sufficient amounts of schoolwork to warrant a failing report card. Other less severe school-phobic children will refuse to participate in school activities once they have been coerced into the classroom. Some daydream; some slip out to the bathroom far too frequently. In some manner, this child is detaching himself (or herself) from the school experience. And this child will fail.

What can you and the school do for the failing child with a school phobia? You must act first: the results of your initial actions may determine the ultimate success of turning this failing school-phobic child into an adjusted schoolchild. Your first vital move is to get the child back into school. You must not reinforce the negative behavior toward school by allowing it or encouraging it. Permitting the school-phobic child to remain at home away from school, even for one single day, reinforces the negative. He must be in class so that the teacher may do her part. Once you have gotten the child back into the class, do not usurp the teacher's role by lingering too long within the child's view. The child with a school phobia will very often feel the need to perform for the observing parent, and the performance will not be a pretty one to behold: tantrums, tears, running and clutching at the parent's clothes. The school phobia can be handled best by the school personnel when the parent has managed to get out of range of the manipulative child.

The teacher must then play her very important role in this special problem. If the aversion to coming to school is based on a real fear of being bullied or abused by other children, the teacher and principal must correct the antisocial group behavior or remove those children from the class who pose a genuine threat to the others. If the school phobia is rooted in a teacher-pupil conflict, the teacher must reassess her approach to this over-sensitive child and possibly soften her approach to the entire class. For if this child is visibly demonstrating overt signs of teacher-induced school phobia, there are probably a half dozen other children within the classroom who have been doing work far below their potential as the result of the distraction and worry caused by the same overly strict, punitive teacher.

If the school phobia is caused by the fear of separation from the family because of the recent illness or death of a close member, the teacher must understand that the fear is related to the child's deep and terrifying concern that something serious and dangerous could be happening while he or she is separated and forced to remain within the classroom. In this situation, the perceptive teacher will permit the young child to call the parent at appropriate intervals until the overriding fear that a disaster is occurring will lessen and finally be swallowed up in the excitement and confusion of rewarded work and play.

The child who is phobic about school merely because of over-solicitous and involved parenting that has prepared the child poorly for separation must be dealt with on two levels by two different individuals. The parent must step back and reevaluate the entire parenting process

113

occurring within the home. How much of this phobic behavior on the child's part has been suggested to him or her by the mother's or the father's attitude or conversation? How much does the child feel that a quiet separation from these two doting individuals is, in actuality, an act of family treason, that only a visible display of reluctance can indicate the depth of the parent-child attachment, and thereby fix the parenting process in a set pattern of continued overindulgence? You may ask how such a young child can be so sophisticated in his thought processes and so manipulative in his actions? We continually underestimate the cleverness and perceptivity of our children, younger and older. The school-phobic child is delivering a message to parent and to teacher. The teacher is the other person who must act with sensitivity to this phobic child. A calm insistence on social play, with the use of positive rewards for tasks done well, will often go far in replacing the "lost" positive supportive atmosphere of home. The clever teacher will often find tasks for the phobic child to perform which will earn him or her honest and sincere praise. Obviously the teacher cannot devote her entire teaching time to such a child. This he must learn to accept as well. Parent and teacher must work as a team to help the young child whose lack of accomplishment is based on school phobia.

Other reasons for poor school adjustment which rest within the child's home include the child who has no structured discipline at home and does not understand how to adjust to the authority of the teacher in school. The child who has never learned to deal with peer group situations will find the school experience frightening and will often retreat into a shell and fail to learn. The child who has been understimulated at home may find school like a suddenly opened door, and will flit excitedly from activity to activity, learning nothing but tasting every new and unfamiliar sensory stimulus. These children will often fail the lower grades because they come to school "home-handicapped." The teacher must help the parent understand the significance of the interrelationships between home and school. Other professionls such as the social worker, the psychologist, the school nurse, and doctor may become part of the team that helps the parent see the impact of the child's home life upon school performance. If you have seen your child mirrored in any of these descriptions, your task lies clearly before you. Communicate with the school, the teacher, the other professionals, and begin a combined effort to readjust and redesign your child's home and school experience so that he or she will no longer be a school failure.

The Child Who Is Failing—"Failure Factors"

3. Occasionally, a young child will fail in school because he or she believes that the experience is not a very important one. Where does he get that message? He learns it in one of three places: the home, the street, or the school itself. Parents are at times alarmed to learn that their own indifference toward education and learning has rubbed off onto their young children. The young who are reared in homes where no books are read, no letters written, no social subjects discussed, and where the educated are accused of "putting on airs," should not be expected to give education a high priority in their everyday lives. Very often, parents never contemplate that this is the underlying message of their lifestyle which is being delivered daily to their children. No teacher or school system can overcome this negative influence. Can such parents change in order to help their child? It is difficult; but unless a dramatic reversal of educational values is reached in this home, the child will truly become the product of his or her parents, and the failure to absorb the educational possibilities which surround him will pass from one generation to the next.

The young child, as well as his older counterpart, can fall in with a "bad crowd" when it comes to education. The street children who perpetuate the myth that education is an unnecessary evil may be your child's companions. Children are influenced greatly by the words of their peers. As Pinocchio grew donkey's ears and a long nose, so the deluded youngster who dismisses education because of peer contempt can become deformed intellectually and end up a school failure. Here the parent must play the role of authority and the "heavy." The solution is a new set of friends . . . and a renewal of an old set of ideals and concepts delivered in a gentle, persuasive way by the parents.

We know of cases where young children have "failed" in school because the teaching is so incredibly bad as to make the subject matter indecipherable or the atmosphere is so low-keyed as to make the school day an impossible bore. Even a gifted child may fail in this environment. You cannot expect a young child to overcome an incompetent school system which does not teach. As we said before, it is vital for every parent whose young child is "failing" to sit in on a random day or two of instruction to make quite certain that the "turn off" to the child's educational growth is not occurring right there within the classroom.

4. Some youngsters fail because they simply cannot learn in a particular teacher's classroom. She/he may be competent and organized, but an emotional barrier to learning has developed between teacher and

child. Often it is not solely the fault of one or the other; however, the parent cannot expect either person to change suddenly and alleviate the problem. When it becomes rather obvious that your child is failing because of serious, uncorrected friction with a teacher, every possible effort should be made to have that child transferred into another classroom. A word of warning must be put forward here. If this continues to happen, the parents must search their own child's behavior and adjustment patterns more closely. A realistic analysis of what the child may be doing to antagonize or alienate the teachers may prove the key to helping this child adapt to the classroom and avoid repeated conflicts and subsequent failure.

5. The other causes for failure in the young child will be discussed in detail in subsequent chapters, but are worth mentioning here because each will precipitate an ominous report card. They require the special approaches by parent, teacher, and school system that have been elucidated in earlier chapters. These conditions are:

(a) specific learning disability
(b) hyperactivity due to neurological causes
(c) mental retardation
(d) sensory impairment (visual or auditory)
(e) acute or chronic emotional illness
(f) acute or chronic physical illness

The main message that must be gleaned from this chapter is that parents must never quietly accept the school failure of their child. They must never allow the shift of their child from an academic school track to a vocationally oriented school track without explanation. They must never tacitly and passively accept any of these consequences of failure without requesting—no, demanding—a full investigation into why their child has failed in school. The mere anecdotal description by the teacher of a child's daily performance, or the combined assumptions of teacher, principal, and guidance counsellor, are insufficient evidence to condemn a "failing" child to an inferior education. Every parent has the right and should insist upon the results of tests and investigations that will confirm the assumptions behind the failure.

Often school professionals are correct in an "off-the-cuff" diagnosis because of their daily observations of the child and their years of experience in the school system. But equally often they may be incorrect or incomplete in their overall assessment of the failing child. What must be remembered by both parent and teacher alike is that no two children are quite the same. Even though another child who failed looked exactly like your child in performance and behavior, this does *not* mean that the causes for failure in the two children are in any way the same. Therefore, it becomes essential that the parent follow a unique quest after this failure. He cannot be satisfied with half-answered questions or undocumented diagnoses. Parents should ask to see the tests and the results, requesting full explanations, outside professional assistance if needed, and those adjustments and changes that the test results suggest would benefit their child.

Failure paralyzes the intellectual and often the emotional growth of children. You cannot wake up every morning knowing that you are and will be a failure and still feel good about yourself. Therefore, parents must leave no stone unturned in attempting to uncover the reasons behind their child's school failure. And they should expect the complete cooperation of the school in this investigation. If there is a reluctance, a dragging of the feet, the parents should not hesitate to approach the local school board, the state education division, and, if necessary, the governor's staff and the local congressman or congresswoman and senators. We are mandated by law to provide every child with an education—not a misdiagnosed or misdirected education but the best education possible. Parents must be the advocates for their failing children to see that this does occur.

The older child who has previously done reasonably or rather well in school and suddenly brings home a failing report card may be delivering a very different message in that envelope. Youngsters in junior and senior high school must put forth increasingly more effort to receive passing grades in our current school system. Home study and even more difficult examinations are the progressive landmarks in the educational process. Most parents watch their child demonstrate increasing responsibilities year after year within the local school system. This ascending responsibility for study and learning is the basis of the development of that self-discipline and sense of pacing which are such valuable attributes in later life, whether the future is academic or vocational. Both authors are highly suspicious of any school system that does not require some degree of study on one's own, self-pacing, and the demonstration of skills and learned materials. The "totally free" educational environment prepares the child for a world which does not exist and in which he/she will either fail quickly or fight upstream to learn the habits that were previously underemphasized. The older child who fails is often making a conscious effort *not* to study and not to do well. The key to success is so obvious that the reasons behind the "failure" may be more important to uncover.

If the young person had any of the problems mentioned before, it is highly likely that he or she would have experienced problems in school in earlier years. Occasionally the young adult with mild problems in processing information (e.g., specific learning difficulties) will do satisfactorily until the volume and complexity of information reaches the level found in upper grades. The gradual inability of the motivated young person to master material should prompt the parents to seek psychological and educational help in order to rule out a learning disability as the basis of their older child's school failure.

What are some of the other discrete reasons for the sudden unexpected failure of an older child? What can a parent do to detect and help the problem? What are the "failure factors" in this age group?

1. Adolescence is the time of rebellion. It is during this period that a young person feels the strongest need to break away from the influence and control of the parent figures. Adolescents feel that they cannot form their own individual identity without tearing away that part of their personality identified with the parents. Often the rebellion is a minor revolution so small in noise and intensity that the parents notice only a "difference," a "phase," a "coming-of-age." But frequently too the rebellion against the parental figures can be strong and forceful, transiently bitter and painful, often focusing upon the key areas which the parents have stressed during the child's upbringing. In many families, education is one of these key areas. Education means upward mobility and assured success within many American households. Where better to rebel and demonstrate one's individuality than in the area of education? How else could you more emphatically declare your independence than by bringing home a failing report card?

This is a relatively frequent cause of failure in older children. The "good" child simply stops studying and fails. How can the parent and the school deal with this problem so that it does not get out of hand and persist into a prolonged, self-destructive period? Here is a good example of where the parent and the school can work together to attempt to reverse the negative trend of rebellion. Very often the young person is not performing well in school as a direct rebellion *against* someone, usually a parent. The school can offer alternative individuals who become important in the young person's life, for whom the young man or woman will want to succeed in school. The sports coach, the editor of the school newspaper, the adviser to the debating club, the drama coach, the director of the school choir . . . these are some of the people who can assume very significant roles in the lives of the adolescent and stimulate the rebellious youngster to achieve passing grades as a subtle but realized prerequisite for continued association with extracurricular activities. A large number of young men and women have shrugged off their passive failing to achieve a level of "passing" standards as a direct result of the stimulation, example, and urging of the "other adult" in their adolescent lives. This "other adult" may come from outside the school, as in the case of a priest, relative, family friend, or family physician. More likely and more accessible are the "other adult" figures within the school environment. Join forces with your child's school and attempt to discover which activity will be most acceptable. Estimate as accurately as possible the positive impact of the director of this particular activity on your child. If it looks as if there might be a valuable match between adult and young person, then encourage the school and adviser to invite your child to participate in that activity. A personal invitation, based on genuine potential talent, may be the first necessary step toward motivating the rebellious, adolescent into more positive behavior. The negative rebellion can be rechanneled into positive creative activity. He can pass!

2. The teen-age years are the "lazy" years. The level of motivation often sinks to the lowest level of the person's entire life span. This lack of responsible drive is probably most severely felt within the classroom, where the need to perform, work, and participate are consistent requirements for school success. The result of this low motivation level will be failing grades in subjects where the young person need only make a minor effort to succeed. How can the parent and the school deal with this transient problem so that whole segments of education are not lost and the young person's record is not permanently blemished by the stigma of failures?

Usually the young adult will have interests that transcend the normal learning patterns of books, studying, and examinations. Some children draw and paint; others have a dramatic flair; some carve, while others may sew. These talents can be employed creatively by teacher and parent alike to stimulate learning. What difference if the method is unusual so long as the outcome is the gain in knowledge? If a young person can learn history or social science by acting it out before the class rather than studying the material, memorizing dates and names, and taking multiple-choice examinations, why not? Any alternative method that stimulates and motivates him or her to learn and participate in the classroom deserves first priority rather than endlessly futile attempts each day at force-feeding the information into an unreceptive, poorly motivated mind. Teachers must be willing to be thoroughly unorthodox with these adolescent children, bearing in mind that remembering a date or a person because you made a poster or composed a song about it is as valuable as memorizing the same information from the text—and possibly more long-lasting. Parents must not permit teachers to hide behind the oft-quoted phrase, "I'm too busy. There are too many children in my class for me to give individual attention to one child." This is an educational cop-out. The creative and stimulating aspects of teaching that should be behind this teacher's daily activities are the challenges of the special child and how they can be met and conquered. Open up the poorly motivated child by an alternative route and he will gradually begin to rekindle fires of interest in the learning process. Without this innovative educational approach to a recalcitrant young person, the cold ashes of his education will be all that are left of his potential. If you are his parent and this is his problem, work with the school to solve it. If necessary, show the school the way: lead them to the creative solution and reinforce the process within your home; help him with his special projects; praise and discuss them and give them as much importance as high grades in examinations. Together the school and the home will subtly overcome adolescent intellectual lethargy.

3. Not every young person is a scholar. Many can pass with dignity but few with honors. And yet the parents often have unrealistic college and professional plans for their child. The young person feels an increasing pressure to succeed far beyond his capabilities. Finally, in abject desperation, he or she simply gives up entirely, announcing tacitly and silently to his overexpectant parents that he is a failure. He will never live up to the goals they have set for him.

This young person could pass the school subjects but not with the excellence that he intuitively knows his parents expect of him. Their overly high expectations have made him a failure. Here is where the school can be of great help to these aspiring parents. Almost every child has taken group psychological tests during his school career; his folder is full of anecdotal observations from the myriad of teachers who have worked with him. Additional, extensive testing is possible to help the parents understand the limits and the possibilities in their child's educational and vocational future. Often, the news that they have an "average" child comes as a painful blow to the parents. The school may need to give them assistance via the social worker, school psychologist, or school doctor, who can sit and advise these parents that there is a nobility and social value in the skills of various vocational fields equal to the skills of professionals. These parents must be helped to realize that it is far better to have a happy, "passing," successful child who fits into the field that best matches his potential than a frustrated, "failing," very miserable child who cannot live up to the unrealistically high hopes of his parents.

If you suddenly feel a twinge of recognition in reading these words about the overly ambitious and unrealistic parent, it is time for you to find out what your child does best, what his virtues and talents truly are, what his vocational drives and inclinations might be, *not* what you have been programming him for all of these bemused, over-optimistic years. Work together with the school to create a socially contributing and self-satisfied human being.

4. We can both remember a number of cases of school failure in the upper grade child which stemmed directly from the problem of sibling rivalry and jealousy. The younger child is faced daily with an older paragon of excellence who is a very high achiever. Intuitively, the younger child feels or knows that the same performance is expected of him (or her). He realizes that he cannot hope to measure up to the older sibling's high performance level; or, if he did, he would still be traveling a well-worn pathway. He would be breaking no new, individualistic ground. This message is conveyed within the home and also within the school. Youngsters have told us with some bitterness the stories of arriving in class on the first day of school and meeting the teacher for the first time who announces in front of the class, "Well, if you're John's brother, I certainly will be expecting fine things from you. He was one of my very best students." This child faces a model so difficult to match that a common response is "giving up."

Each child is an individual with his or her own identity. Every child must be carefully investigated to find the sources of his excellence, his talent, and his interest. There is *no* child without something special and unique to contribute. To condemn a child to repeat the excellence of an older sibling is to bury the special qualities and talents of that younger child. The teacher and the parent must understand the problem of being the "second child" to a high-achieving sibling. Both parent and teacher should make an effort to underscore the individuality and separate identity of the younger child. The message at home and in school must be: "You are your own person. You will succeed or fail as yourself. What I see and value is what *you* are." If the message is distorted into a sibling competition with an older, highly successful brother or sister, the result may be failure on the part of the younger child.

5. Peer group influence can have a very marked effect upon the school performance of the somewhat older adolescent (usually more so than with the child). All too often, the youngster will become involved with a group of friends whose motivation and inclination for school success is at a minimum. To belong to the "group" is so important at this age that the youth will relinquish his educational goals to be accepted as a member. This is a serious and very difficult problem for both parent and school.

When there is reasonable communication between parent and child, the parent can attempt subtly to point out the discrepancy between the child's family style and the "group style" by inviting members of the peer group to the home for dinner and long weekends. Here the young person watches the family educational and intellectual patterns contrasted with the peer group's approach to the intellectual and social challenges of life. Not infrequently, the young person will sense the marked differences and gradually separate from the unacceptable grouping. Parents can also invite members of the group to join them in cultural visits or family discussions on social or academic matters. One of two things may ensue: the group member will become interested and act as a positive influence; or he/she will refuse to participate and force the child of the family to reassess the model offered by his friend. Either of these outcomes is desirable. What the parent does *not* want to do is forbid the young person to see or associate with this undesirable peer group. Such a demand will usually be made in vain during the adolescent period and will often only stimulate a greater desire to "belong" to this group because it fulfills the need for rebellion and also has the exquisite taste of forbidden fruit.

However, the school can assist by separating members of the group, placing those youngsters with the highest possibility of making progress in classes that will stimulate and provoke thought. Also, attempting to involve these youngsters with other groups of young people in extracurricular activities as noted above will often open new doors for self-expression and the development of new friendships.

6. The adolescent who has experienced failure in one area may carry this phenomenon over into other areas. The young man who has been "cut" from the football squad may suddenly begin to do poor work although he had been a very good student. The young girl who has not been selected for the high school play may stop working due to a seething sense of anger and rejection. Americans live in a highly competitive world. Rejection looms around every corner. It is true that every child must learn to adjust to being turned down or rejected; but the wise parent and the alert school system should have alternative areas of creative or athletic outlets available to act as a viable substitute. Intramural class teams or neighborhood teams may help heal the wounds of the rejection from the varsity squad. Church plays or behind-the-scenes work on the main production may minimize the feeling of being left out that so often precipitates more failure, particularly in the academic area.

When your child is entering the highly competitive arena of sports, dramatics, music, and so on, and stands a fair chance of not being selected, you should have thought through these possibilities and investigated alternative options to lessen the blow and keep the creative or athletic energies flowing. If not, all activity may come to a halt, including school work, with failure in school the ultimate complication.

7. Parents may discover that the child they considered intelligent and creative is doing very poorly because of the school environment. Upon investigating that environment, they might find that the school is so rigid, so mainstreamed, so focused upon discipline and grinding studiousness that the child's creativity, freedom of thought, and self-expression have been stifled and suppressed. As a result, the young person makes a minimal effort in a silent message of discontent and frustration. This is seen on occasion within some of the so-called best private schools, which pride themselves on their "academic products." These schools essentially are not dealing with expanding the minds and spirits of children but are obsessed with filling the vessels of their minds with the greatest quantity of information possible. Many children respond positively to this regimented, "overkill" type of education; they become the obsessive-compulsive workers of tomorrow. But there are a number of children who cannot tolerate this atmosphere; it simply dries up their energies and their spirit.

One of us recently experienced such a school in Baltimore. After attempting to explain and underscore the many problems noted in the students from that school, it became obvious that the school was deliberately structured and would not change or demonstrate any flexibility toward the children. There is only one solution for the parent faced with this impossible situation: remove the child from the school as swiftly as possible, or he will end up an academic automaton like all the other graduates. This is fine for those who choose it. But if it is not academically compatible with your child's personality, get him or her out of there as quickly as possible. At another school, the young man whom one of us transferred went from below-par grades (and failing a math course) to A's and B's (with an A in Geometry).

Children fail for a variety of reasons. Commonly, failure is due to intellectual restrictions. Learning problems prevent the potentially successful child from ever learning the proper information. Emotional factors often play a role, as do the social factors of stimulation and priorities for education. This chapter has mentioned these but has attempted to expand on the "failure factors" that may be causing your child to fail in school. All too often, these additional important problems are overlooked and children are labeled as failures due to academic difficulties and learning problems.

Now again you are about to approach the teacher and the entire school system with the report card in your hand that announces your child is failing in school. What are the steps you must take to uncover and solve the problems outlined earlier?

1. Analyze the failures. Are there more than one? In what subjects?
2. What indications did you have in the past that there were problems in these areas? Is this the first "bad" report card?
3. What could be happening at home that might be adversely influencing your child's performance in school? What can you and what can the school do to help overcome this problem if it exists?
4. How do you view your child? Are you surprised at the grades? Has he/she changed in behavior at home?
5. What does the child have to say about the grades? The young child may have precise insight into his problems. The older child's attitude toward the report card may be the key to the causes of the failures.
6. What does the teacher feel is the basis for the failure(s)? What

tests or documentation does she have to substantiate her impressions?

7. What does the school plan to do further to investigate the source of the problems that have led to your child's failures?

8. What are the immediate options for your child in school considering these failures? Can he repeat the course or could he take remedial work? Will he be promoted with his class? If not, why not? Is this decision compatible between parent and teacher?

9. Once the causes are known, how can you and the school work together to correct or adjust the situation to prevent future failures?

10. Is your child in the right school? the right class? the correct curriculum? What is the best long-range plan for your "failing" child?

These are the ten key steps that a parent must go through systematically when faced with a child who is failing in school. Each must be answered and investigated. Only when all ten have been assiduously answered can a parent feel that nothing has been omitted in assuring that the "failure factors" have been thoroughly assessed and analyzed.

This is a long and detailed chapter because the problem of school failure is a complex and difficult one for parent and school. In addition, it touches the lives of more families than any of the other special problems in this book. We suspect it is also handled with the least sophistication and expertise by the parents involved. As a result, the failed child all too frequently becomes the failed adult. To prevent this from happening in your family, reread this chapter again.

12 The Child with Learning Disabilities

There can be little doubt that you have heard of children with learning disabilities. Someone may have given your own child such a label. Famous people have learning disabilities—Nelson Rockefeller is one of them. Large national organizations are devoted to finding further causes and "cures" of learning disabilities. "Why, the field of learning disabilities must be one of the last of the great unconquered diseases," you may be thinking. And, like most people, you will likely add this silent postscript, "With all that literature and research backing up the scientists, I wonder why they haven't found a way to cure it by now."

Be prepared for a surprise. The common use of the term "learning disability" by scientists and parents is a practice which is less than twenty years old. To be sure, the field of learning disabilities is a young field—the youngest in the whole area of educating handicapped children. And because the field is so new, it is beset by lack of clarity, insufficient coordinated research, fuzzy and inadequate definitions, early trials at treatment, and "territorial" problems for those professionals who work with it, each of whom thinks the problem belongs in his particular area.

This educational problem is often described by parents of learning-disabled children as a maze. They picture their child in the center of this maze, with its confusing pathways of different diagnoses and facts that must be carefully traveled and understood by the parents and the teachers before the child's problems can be reached. Only then can the child find his or her way out of this maze of contradictions into the calmness of the directed, purposeful education which is required to help this special child with his/her learning disabilities.

To illustrate how bewildering the pathways of the maze can be, you should analyze the most commonly used federal definition of learning disabilities:

Children with special learning disabilities exhibit a disorder in one or more of the basic psychological processes involved in understanding or in using spoken or written language. These may be manifested in disorders of listening, thinking, talking, reading, writing, spelling, or arithmetic. They include conditions which have been referred to as perceptual handicaps, brain injury, minimal brain dysfunction, dyslexia, developmental aphasia, etc. They do not include learning problems which are due primarily to visual, hearing or motor handicaps, to mental retardation, emotional disturbance, or to environmental disadvantage.

Having read that long definition, where are you in that maze—trying to find out what "learning disabilities" are or are not? After pondering its complexities for a time, you may have to create your own definition —one that you understand. You know that your child cannot achieve in school, even though he or she has a good mind and appears motivated. You know there is *something* blocking his learning. It has become sidetracked; sidelined; disabled. If you are a wise parent, *that* simple statement of fact will have to be your definition. You must hold to it despite all the other terms for learning disability which you will hear from the various "helpers" of your child.

But even when you have come through the pathway of definition, you often will reach a dead end in treatment. Your pediatrician may tell you that he can treat your child's learning disability with medication. The psychologist may suggest psychotherapy. The educator could affirm that the problem is an educational one, to which the other professionals will nod their assent—and quietly continue to insist on medication, psychotherapy, visual training, changed diet, allergy tests, and the multitude of other proven and unproven theories of causes and treatments. Your task becomes the major one. You will have to find the one educational treatment that works with your child. It probably will turn out to be a combination of many treatments, some of which are mentioned above.

The maze of learning disabilities also contains other dangerous detours. These are the emotional detours surrounding your child. You may find yourself fearful of this strange and unknown problem. The future may loom terrifying, particularly when you consider the kind of training that must be decided upon in order to help your child make an appropriate vocational choice. Your child may also be angry, lonely, negative, and socially aggressive because he or she does not understand the problems any better than you do. The fact that he has so few rewards for his efforts only compounds his emotional negativism toward his problem. Together you face the irrational with uncertainty—a difficult method of finding your way out of that maze.

But the direct pathway within that maze *can* be found. It requires a search by the parents for a *single* learning-disabled child rather than a composite of many. The search requires the parents to look for the definition, the professionals, the educational process, the "treatments" that fit their specific child—not all learning-disabled children. It requires a search for an individualized plan for the child, a plan that the parent has a right to expect, a plan that the parent can and should demand of the school and of all of the professionals who work for the educational system, a plan that can be understood by all, a method to assure your learning-disabled child the "correct" education.

How can you, the parent, seek and find this plan? Here are some steps to consider:

1. Take charge. Remember that the field of learning disabilities is an evolving one. You will receive different information and different impressions from the various professionals with whom you and your child have contact. And you will have to sort out much of this material to determine what is best for your child. Be prepared for this confusion in advance. Put your thoughts in focus and set your sights on determining what preparation for later life you want the school to give your child. Then you can obtain a reasonable and realistic "educational prescription." The admonition to take charge does not mean that you should have to make all the decisions about your child. Taking charge means that you should sort all the advice and information you receive and refuse to approve an educational plan until you know what it will attempt to teach and to what long-range effect. In the field of learning disabilities, so crowded with the jargon of professional opinion, a child needs a single, clear-thinking advocate—you, his parent.
2. Insist upon a multidisciplinary diagnostic examination. Your solution to the confusion of definitions is an effective interdisciplinary, multi-professional approach. All professionals need to see the child and confer. Some children are best treated by the use of an educational process alone; some may need medication to control the hyperactivity which is preventing them from concentrating (see Chapter 13). Other children may need visual training; still others

motor exercises. As in any other generalized disability, the handicap is not as important as the child himself and his inherent strengths and weaknesses. Therefore any diagnostic work-up must include as many perspectives on these strengths and weaknesses as possible. At a minimum, a child with suspected learning disabilities should be seen by an educational specialist or school psychologist and a pediatrician. You should expect the school to furnish the school psychologist; you may have to furnish the pediatrician, or the school doctor may be available and trained in this area. This would be ideal. *But Make Sure All the Professionals Confer!* Professionals who work independently with your child and never bring their expert but differing points of view together must be compared to giving the blind men an elephant. Is this how the professionals have been analyzing your learning-disabled child?

After the thorough evaluation and interchange by the various experts about your child, the diagnostic journey may not yet be over. Ask each professional if he recommends further diagnostic tests. If so, ask the school to refer your child to the appropriate person or agency, and then see if the school system will also pick up the bill. Under today's liberal education laws, the chances are quite good that the schools will be required to do so.

What is the next step? Following this evaluation, you *must* ask for a report from the school which synthesizes the findings of all the professionals. Don't let the school say to you, "We found this, Dr. Peabody found that, and Mr. Jenson found something else." The language which should reach you when you finally sit down to learn about your learning-disabled child should sound like this: "Well, the three of us who saw your child have gotten together, and this is how we see Jane right now." Don't accept mumbo-jumbo or disagreement. Demand a careful, clearly expressed interpretation.

3. Develop an educational plan. This is something you must do in conjunction with the school. Actually, the school will put together the educational plan; but you must insist upon final approval, because schools often develop the expedient habit of fitting a child into an existing program, rather than vice versa. In the case of a learning-disabled child, the program must fit the complex child's needs. This is absolutely essential for your child, and you must assure it. Ask for an interview with either the special education coordinator, the school psychologist, the special learning disabilities teacher, or the principal. Be bold enough to suggest a special conference of all of

them to talk about your child's plan. And as you talk to these school personnel insist on two frames of reference. First, you must insist upon knowing all of your learning-disabled child's strengths and weaknesses, not only in the academic areas but also in the social and vocational areas. Secondly, insist that any recommended school placement be based upon what they think the child will gain from that placement in terms of his/her future adjustment and job or career opportunities. In other words, you must refuse to accept the summary that says: "Jane is learning-disabled and therefore she should go into a learning disability class," or: "Jane is hyperactive and therefore should be placed on drugs, probably Ritalin." Instead, you must ask these professionals to explain very carefully and thoroughly what skills and information they want Jane to learn and master. Can she do this by being in Mrs. Jacobsen's class? And when do they anticipate Jane's success in reaching these goals? If drugs are suggested, you should find out what behavior changes should be noted if placed on drugs, how you will know that these behaviors have changed, and how long Jane will be on medication. When you walk away from that meeting, what you want to know is how Jane is currently functioning in school, what the professionals estimate she needs and can attain in her later life, and how her schooling is going to help her reach her highest potential. Naturally, if you have this information, you will have some idea of how you can help her with these aims outside the school.

4. You have worked out what appears to be a reasonable educational plan for your child; now you must make certain that your child's school placement is accomplishing the plan put together by you and the school. Any placement of a learning-disabled child has to be experimental at first. A child has to develop a trust in his or her teachers, a method of working in the classroom, and a feeling of positive reward for his work. This often takes a good deal of time. Sometimes the plan fails. Often the school cannot and should not be blamed if these objectives cannot be obtained quickly or easily. But as your child's advocate, you must find out if the plan can be fully realized and if the goals are being obtained after a reasonable amount of time. If not, insist on a reevaluation of your child's placement. Since you know the general plan and the periodic goals you can talk to your child's teacher(s) at regular intervals with an informed agenda. "How is he doing in his language skills [for every-day social communication], his writing skills [for correspondence],

and his math skills [for independent living]?" These may well be the crucial questions for your learning-disabled child. Ask, too, whether your child has a sense of reward in school. How well is he getting along with the teacher and his peers? How comfortable is he with accepting new work? How much of her schoolwork is she avoiding discussing at home? How is she handling stress? You should be acutely sensitive to the fact that many children with learning disabilities develop serious social problems because of the consistently recurring frustrations they encounter in school. Therefore parents have to be alert to their emotional responses. In other words, it is up to you to find out how your child is perceived in school, how far along he has progressed on his plan, and how far he has yet to go. If you are satisfied and pleased with the information you uncover, tell the school personnel. If you are dissatisfied, let the professionals know exactly why you are unhappy and what you were led to expect. Demand an explanation as to why there has been a slowdown on the previously agreed pacing of your child's educational plan. These school professionals are employed to help your child.

5. In your opening conference with the school psychologist, he informed you that your learning disabled child would be re-diagnosed periodically. Well, is your child receiving these regular assessments? If not, you have a right to insist on it. Learning-disabled children often experience changes in their whole mental and physical make-up, particularly around the age of puberty. At this time, they may make tremendous growth strides both physically and educationally. Because all children are dynamically changing human beings, learning-disabled children, particularly, should be reassessed formally by an interdisciplinary team at least every other year, during the early years, and *every year* from ages eleven to thirteen. Federal laws now require this child's reevaluation, but many schools are slow in complying with this ruling because there are not enough personnel to do the necessary testing and conferencing. Insist upon the regular reevaluation. Repeat step number 1 by taking charge. You and the school may discover a completely different picture of your child the second, third, or fourth time around.

6. Stay out of the actual educational process unless you are invited inside. We are aware that we have urged you to advocate your child's diagnosis, placement, and reevaluation. You fully understand his/her educational goals. But education of a learning-disabled child

is a highly specialized task. The teachers of children with these very special learning problems generally have advanced educational degrees. As we stated before, such children generally have been frustrated and "burned" by bad teaching in the past. Don't compound the teaching problems if you don't know what you're doing. It will be a natural impulse to assist the teacher in your child's education. But as a parent, you have now reached the crucial stage of separation and observation. Stay apart from the teacher's methods of educating your child. Just watch to ensure that this relationship to his teacher is a positive adventure in learning for your special child.

Parents often have difficulty with the separation at this point. They have worked so hard to advocate and become a "team" member that it is very difficult to fade out of the picture. But impeding, disagreeing, or interfering with the "right" learning disability teacher only confuses your child and significantly harms his or her education.

Many educational games and books for parents are sold over the counter in toy and variety stores. Avoid them unless you know (by first talking to the child's teacher) that they are appropriate for your child's educational plan. Be content to let the school do the educating once you have helped to structure and design the blueprint.

7. Consider joining a parents' organization. The Association for Children with Learning Disabilities (ACLD) is the largest organization in the country for parents with learning-disabled children. There are chapters throughout the nation, and your school will know how to get in touch with them. But there are also other relevant organizations, and almost all of them exist for the purpose of bringing information about learning disabilities directly to parents. Such information—ranging from discussions about the latest "fads" such as megavitamin therapy, learning disabilities caused by food additives, or learning disabilities as an allergic reaction, to lists of colleges and universities which have special programs for young people with learning disabilities—can be obtained from these groups. In addition, parents in these groups or in the local school's P.T.A. with children whose problems are similar to your child's can give you helpful information on which pediatricians are best versed in the subject of learning disabilities, what private schools have to offer, and the strengths and weaknesses of the local public schools. You'll have to sift the information you get from these national organizations and from other parents; however, you will probably find shar-

ing a similar child's problems with other parents both rewarding and helpful. If, in your journey through this confusing maze, you discover that there are dramatic changes needed for your children to receive the best education possible, remember the practical truth that there is unquestionable strength in numbers.

Until the maze of learning disabilities becomes an orderly and clearly marked country—and it will—your child will be fortunate to have an informed and active advocate like you.

15 The Hyperactive Child

You've always known that your son moved around a lot, that he was constantly "on the go." There were days when he was growing up that you felt like you were chasing a roller coaster moving at top speed. But it never worried you to a serious degree. You felt that he would eventually slow down, calm down, as he got older. Everyone told you that boys were wilder than girls, so you've been patient and tried to understand your unsettled, restless son.

Now the school has called you and told you that you need an immediate conference with your son's teacher and the guidance counsellor. He's only been in school one week and already you've received a call that he's in trouble. How can a five-and-a-half-year-old boy in kindergarten be in trouble? They gave him a name over the phone. They said he was a "hyperactive" child. What does that mean? Is it different from what you already know? If you can manage him, why can't they? What is going to happen to your little boy? "Hyperactive" sounded so serious when the teacher said it over the phone.

The term "hyperactive child" is used much too freely and without careful definition by many professionals today. The teacher, the psychologist, the pediatrician, the child psychiatrist, all use this term to describe children.* Yet each of these people may be referring to a completely different person when they label a child with that broad and overwhelming word.

There is no question that something called hyperactivity certainly exists in many schoolchildren today. Constant uncontrolled motion can be extremely disruptive within the classroom, causing the teacher to look for an instant solution so that she can return the chaotic classroom

---

*Boys predominate in numbers over girls in this condition. Various studies have indicated ratios ranging from two to one to five to one.

to a state of order and organization. However, unless the overly active child is carefully appraised, he may receive a series of potentially inappropriate attempts at treatment for his excessive motion, including drugs, special classrooms, and child and parent counselling.

What causes a child to be hyperactive? There are many reasons, but the key ones often lie within the following possibilities. First, a child may be over-active when he has never learned the true meaning of restrictions and restraints. If your child has never been taught to "slow down" and respond to your requests and commands to "stop," there is little doubt that he could become totally uncontrollable when faced with the problem of classroom regimentation. Imagine a child who has been allowed to run totally free within the home environment without many rules or regulations. Then place this uninhibited and unrestrained child in a class full of other children where he must sit still, obey commands, raise his hand for requests, and hold back his impulses to shout, run, and play. We would classify this "hyperactive" child as an "untrained" child, who is unprepared for dealing with the restrictions and rules of an outside world.

Another cause of over-active children in the kindergarten classroom is the "spoiled" child. Here is a youngster who has always received what he has wanted upon request. He has never been challenged or denied. Suddenly he is faced by another adult, known as teacher, who indicates that he must conform and cannot move and run at will. In addition, he must share and often cannot have the toy or crayon or book being held in the other child's hand. It is easy to see how this youngster could erupt into uncontrollable movement and begin thrashing about the classroom in a frenzy of petulant anger.

Occasionally a young child who has lived in a very sheltered, unstimulating environment can enter the wonderful world of kindergarten and be bombarded by the constant stimuli around him. This child, whose home life is very quiet and deprived of exciting stimuli, suddenly is confronted by so much that maintaining control becomes impossible. He runs excitedly, uncontrollably, from new experience to new adventure. He is a hungry child let loose in the candy store known as school. Sometimes this behavior can be observed in children who have grown up in a completely adult society or a society virtually devoid of other children. The sudden association with other youngsters their own age triggers a chain reaction of excitement and restlessness.

All too often, the so-called hyperactive child is a normally inquisitive youngster who has an under-active teacher. The bright youngster is constantly seeking out the answers to questions, the secrets behind closed doors, the explanations as to how his world works. These children are never satisfied to sit by quietly while the exciting flow of life's mysteries moves by them. They are constantly reaching out to grab the ring of the daily merry-go-round. When the teacher demands total conformity to the rules, when she refuses the explanations and explorations so necessary at this inquisitive age, when the whole atmosphere of her classroom is one of adult complacency rather than youthful exuberance, the normally active youngster will appear "hyperactive."

Not all explanations of a child's hyperactivity are this simple and relatively easy to diagnose and treat. Some of the causes are truly significant in the physical, emotional, or educational sense. Some cross all three areas, in equal combinations, or one cause occurs as a result of the other. A parent cannot dismiss the speculation of "hyperactivity" too lightly once it has been made. Because of the potentially serious causes, the parent is obligated to follow through and work with the appropriate professionals within the school to find the proper internal and external diagnostic help.

One of the emotional causes for the hyperactive child can be directly traced in some children to short-term upsetting incidents in their lives. We remember quite clearly a case of a seven-year-old boy who was referred from the second grade teacher for "uncontrollable hyperactivity." It took a great deal of time while obtaining the history to discover, finally, a key factor which had suddenly precipitated this previously normal seven-year-old into over-active classroom behavior. Two weeks before the start of school, this young boy's grandfather had died unexpectedly. There had been a silent but devoted attachment between the elderly man and this young boy. The family had not been sensitive to the implications of the grandfather's death upon the boy; they had dismissed it to the intelligent boy by simply stating that the grandfather had "gone away for a while." Sensing that his grandfather had died and not having a counsellor or adviser in whom he could confide his fears and grief, the little boy became very anxious. His anxiety produced a picture of restless mobility, constant motion, and frequent temper tantrums. There was a very painful, highly emotional reason for this boy's hyperactivity. Once the parents understood the cause and were helped to provide the boy with the proper support and comfort, his so-called hyperactivity disappeared. What are some of the other short-term social or emotional factors that cover an internal problem? Divorcing parents, sudden illness in parents or siblings, separation from a parent as in the case of a military father being sent overseas, even the death of a beloved pet—all of these are examples which one or the other of us have seen as precipitating factors in short-term hyperactivity.

Hyperactivity may also be one of the signs of a more serious, long-term underlying emotional problem. If the history of the child's current life does not suggest an immediate cause, an attempt must be made to try to uncover a more serious emotional basis for the constant motion. Usually these children will have many other features of significant emotional illness to alert the teacher, physician, or psychologist that the child is on a dangerous emotional course. These children often are distinguished by a "trapped bird" syndrome; they flutter about the cage of their lives relentlessly with a dazed, frightened expression, almost pleading visually to be set free from their emotional entrapment. They will need long-term help.

The last form of hyperactivity to be considered here may well be the most significant from the standpoint of combined parent-school intervention. This is the "organic" or physical hyperactivity. It is disquieting for us to have to report that little is known about the causes or the location of the physical problems which trigger this syndrome of neurological hyperactivity. Studies are continually in progress to isolate the causes; but as of this writing, the answer still lies outside our scientific grasp. Because of the lack of information about the causes of this syndrome, many "fad" cures have been suggested by physicians and educators. Parents who have a neurologically hyperactive child must beware of these. Being hyperactive is somewhat like being overweight —there are far too many inappropriate and useless suggestions on how to solve the problem.

These neurologically hyperactive children present themselves as distractible, over-active children with a markedly shortened attention span. They have great difficulty concentrating on single tasks. They often careen around rooms, sometimes running into walls to stop themselves when in motion. They lack fine control over their muscles and their impulses. They have great difficulty sitting still long enough to learn. They look normal externally. Most of these youngsters have intelligence levels that range from low normal to bright so that they can usually gain from a planned education. Yet they are like a new Porsche without brakes. They look great, but they can't stop! Education becomes a problem in many ways, one of the primary difficulties being in settling the youngsters down long enough to teach them.

Many of these children have other serious educational problems which we will discuss when we focus upon what the parent of this child should be expecting from the child's school. Emotional problems also become a significant part of the picture in their make-up. This is quite understandable if you consider the rejection, anger, and scorn that these constantly moving, impulse-driven youngsters elicit from the people who live with them and around them but who probably do not fully understand them.

Considering overactive children as a total group, let us pause for a moment to list the problems that these children create within the school for themselves and for others:

1. Extremely disruptive behavior, which prevents classroom organization and group work.
2. Inability of the child to learn because of the constant motion.
3. Inability to control anger as well as happy reactions so that all responses are taken to the extreme. With anger, this could mean physical harm to classmates. With rejection or denial, it could mean temper tantrums. With excitement, hysteria. With joy, explosive uncontrollable laughter and raucous outbursts.
4. The emotionally disturbed overactive child may also have periods of retreat and withdrawn behavior.
5. The neurologically overactive child very commonly has other significant learning disabilities which impede the learning process even when the activity is brought under control.

Let us pose a problem situation to you. Play the role of parent and try to solve the problem using your own and the school's resources:

Tommy is your five-year-old. He has been in kindergarten for two weeks when you are called to school because he has been diagnosed by the classroom teacher as being "hyperactive." He was always on the go at your home but since he was an only child and there was a great deal of playing room, you never felt that it was necessary to restrain or regulate him. He was very reluctant to go to school and had to be "dragged" there for the first week. When he comes home from school, he quietly watches television for a while and then goes out into the back yard to play with several of the neighborhood children. You don't see him again until dinner when he rushes in, gulps down dinner, and hurries back outside to play until dark. His father does not come home until much later, just in time to kiss him good night. Tommy is exhausted and goes to bed willingly. He sleeps well and awakens easily in the morning but complains constantly about having to go to school.

The teacher describes his restless, disruptive behavior. She asks if you know of anything which could be playing a role in his over-active school performance.

You can relate any of the following. Which do you think will be helpful to the teacher and to Tommy?

1. Tommy is an only child.
2. Tommy has been allowed to run "free" at home.
3. Tommy has been reluctant to go to school.
4. Tommy rushes in, gulps dinner without father at home, then goes to play again.
5. Tommy watches television for long periods.
6. Tommy plays with the neighborhood children without incident.

Look at these six facts. Are they important to the teacher and to you in explaining Tommy's behavior? Which ones should you discuss with the teacher? Why?

The answer: *All* these responses are very important to be able to understand Tommy and his school performance:

1. Being an only child may have conditioned Tommy to expect a great deal of individual, undivided attention. This could be the basis for his acting out in school.
2. "Running free" at home may have a direct extension in "running free" at school.
3. Fear of separation from mother or anger at school's interruption of his freedom may be the precipitating factor in Tommy's over-activity.
4. Again no rules, no regimentation—and also no father figure. Who does the disciplining? Or does no one?
5. Tommy's ability to concentrate without being easily distracted suggests but does not prove that his over-activity is not likely to be an organic problem.
6. Tommy's ability to play with other children without problems helps in eliminating two factors: understimulation at home and an antisocial problem.

The teacher now has all of the above information. What would you expect from her?

1. Punish Tommy for not wanting to come to school.
2. Allow Tommy the same "freedom" he has at home so he can adapt.
3. Set realistic limits for Tommy and suggest that you do the same.
4. Offer Tommy rewards for good behavior.
5. Expel Tommy if he continues to misbehave.
6. Send Tommy to the school psychologist.

This may be more difficult. But here you are playing the important role of parent and trying to decide where your responsibility starts and ends and where the school's responsibility for Tommy's management lies.

Let us consider the possible responses as solutions for Tommy's hyperactivity:

1. Punishment is not the teacher's task. Convincing Tommy that school is an important, necessary place for him to be is your responsibility as a parent. The teacher can reinforce this by actually making school an exciting, stimulating environment for Tommy.
2. Absolutely not. The school cannot adapt to Tommy's parents' lack of discipline. Tommy must be able to meet the teacher's need for a degree of self-control on his part. This must be begun at home, where Tommy must be taught the meaning of authority and rules so that this understanding can be carried into school. The teacher can help by being patient with Tommy until you are successful in inculcating within him the concept that there are times and places for freedom and times and places for conformity.
3. Here is the secret formula—the setting of realistic limits. With the bar on the hurdle at the proper height, Tommy will quiet down and emerge from this teacher's class a winner rather than a loser.
4. A really superb teacher will have the flexibility and the imagination to bury her anger and resentment toward Tommy's disruptiveness so that she can give him small tasks for which he will receive her positive rewards of appreciation in front of his classmates. This says to Tommy very simply: "It pays to slow down and behave."
5. No. Under no circumstances should Tommy be expelled for his hyperactivity. Patience with Tommy and cooperative work with you are the rules.

The Hyperactive Child

6. No. The pyschologist cannot add much more than you and the teacher have already figured out. Tommy is not "slow" or emotionally unstable. His problem is a situational one that requires the combined teamwork of a good teacher and an awakening parent to solve his problem of hyperactivity.

What would you do if you were the parent of a bright, curious six-year-old son who was labeled as "hyperactive" by a lethargic, disinterested teacher whose classroom had the dangerous sterility of silence? Could you be sure that your child was not overly active? What would you do first? First you should schedule an all-day visit to observe your child in the classroom setting. This should not be on an "open-house" day but another day when regular classroom activities are in progress. Observe the stimulation level in this classroom. Listen for the sounds of excited, responsive children's voices. If you hear these sounds, notice the teacher's response. Is she encouraging this creative, exuberant learning or is she discouraging any overt demonstration of the joys of discovery? As you watch the daily flow of classroom activities, how does your son's activity and behavior compare with that of his classmates? Does this teacher have a dozen "hyperactive" children who are all trying desperately to satisfy their curiosity in a vacuum? Or is your son truly over-active in a classroom where normal investigative six-year-old activity and play are permitted? Be honest about your son. Watch him. Compare him. Obtain a complete idea of the classroom atmosphere— the level of stimulation and the level of learning. Is he really over-active after this has all been personally analyzed? Your next step is a teacher's conference.

If you have observed your son and it becomes blatantly clear that he is the victim of an oppressively rigid and constraining authority in the classroom, which is causing his normal curiosity to be misinterpreted as hyperactivity, what do you do next?

Wait a minute! you cry. Suppose I can't get in to see him? Suppose I'm not permitted to observe a "day in class" because there are no special privileges allowed? The answer is quite simple. Demand your rights. Demand the privilege of observing your child in the situation in which he is being labeled as abnormal. If the teacher refuses, go to the principal. If the principal refuses, go higher. Were it one of our own sons, we would insist upon class observation if the label of "hyperactive" was quite contrary to the home behavior or to our own concept of the child. If one of us had to appeal to the school board, we would not hesitate to do so. It is understandable that the school system could not survive constant visits from parents. However, when a specific child is being labeled as abnormal for any reason, the parent has a right, a need, an obligation to view that "abnormality" at first hand before blindly accepting another person's assessment of his child's deviant school behavior.

You've watched for a day and you are convinced that there is no actual hyperactivity but a reaction to repression of his ability to express himself reasonably. What do you do now? The next step is an appointment with the principal to request a class change. In the small school, this is occasionally impossible. If so a conference between parent, teacher, and principal should be held in which the issues are clearly discussed and alternative methods of independent learning can be created for the child—or hopefully all of the other curious, intelligent children in the class. It is unrealistic to expect the somnolent teacher to be dismissed. Remember there is a union; school has already started; the principal must live with the other teachers. However, if the principal could be encouraged to "sit in" on occasion, then the classroom level of interaction may increase.

If you feel you are up against a brick wall with teacher and principal, it becomes your word against theirs. Here is where another professional, namely, the family pediatrician or school psychologist, may prove a very helpful ally. By observing and testing your son, they will discern the appropriateness of his behavior. Without allies, you have a more difficult battle. In addition, it is important to validate your feelings and your findings. Remember you are your son's parent. Parents are not always seen as being totally objective about their own children.

After consultation, if you have professional concurrence on your assessment of the non-hyperactivity of your child and are armed with this information, fight the labeling of your child and press for a better class placement at the highest administrative level necessary.

Since hyperactivity is often but one of the many manifestations of emotional problems in childhood, the interaction between parent, teacher, and school in the case of the emotionally disturbed child will be discussed more fully in Chapter 15.

Let us turn now to the complex and important subject of the hyperactive child with neurological disorders. This youngster is usually male and often has been a problem to his parents long before the school showed concern. Neurological hyperactivity lasts for extended periods of time. Recent studies suggest that instead of diminishing at puberty as was previously thought to occur in most cases, there may be a continuation of the distractibility and impulsiveness, with added emotional depression or acting out during adolescence. The parents of this hyperactive child may have long-range school problems. What is extremely important for the parents, dealing with their neurologically hyperactive child and his school, is to ask:

1. What diagnostic support can I expect from the school?
2. What therapy is available within the school?
3. What is the extent of the problem?
4. What parts are my responsibility? What parts are the school's responsibility?

In the case of the young child in the early grades of elementary school who is suspected of neurological hyperactivity, it is useful to approach this complicated problem in a way that makes it possible to assign roles and responsibilities.

1. A complete history of the child must be taken, usually by the school nurse or social worker. This includes family history, birth history, subsequent illnesses, and physical-social-emotional history prior to entry to school. In addition, a carefully detailed description of the child's behavior and learning performance in the school situation will be necessary. This should be documented from the very first day of school entry and should include observations by teachers and principal about the child's level of activity, ability to learn, and relationships with other children in the school.

   Obviously the first part of this step must be the parent's sole responsibility. The importance of an accurate history in substantiating the physical nature of the hyperactivity cannot be stressed strongly enough. The second part of the work-up requires the full cooperation of the school staff. Their continual recording of this child's activities will be of immeasurable help in fleshing out the entire portrait of the hyperactive child.
2. There are two procedures which are the common next steps in the assessment of these children. They are *not* useful procedures. Often it is the misinformed teacher who initiates the specific request. Occasionally it is the parent who immediately moves in this mis-

directed way. The two things which are not necessary at this point are: (i) an electroencephalogram, and (ii) an examination by a neurologist. The brain wave test (electroencephalogram) is of very little help in diagnosing these children. It is the test in which electrodes are placed on the child's head to record the electrical waves. In children with seizure tendencies, this is extremely important and valuable. But hyperactivity, in general, must not be confused with a seizure tendency disease. Putting a child through this somewhat disquieting test is totally unnecessary and not helpful for diagnosing neurological hyperactivity. It is far too premature to call in the neurologist at this point; several other professionals are needed before even considering such a specialized referral.

Parent and teacher should agree to avoid the unnecessary referral for either of these examinations.

3. The school psychologist can provide some extremely valuable information at this point. A series of psychological tests can pinpoint the organic-neurologic nature of the child's problems. An assessment of the child's intellectual potential as well as an evaluation of his learning weaknesses can be deduced from careful and thorough psychological evaluation.

The school should be prepared and equipped to provide this important information. Almost all school systems should have school psychologists. The parents have the right to request this examination. Parents should make it known that they want to learn three things from the testing: evidence of the existence or absence of neurological impairment, level of intellectual potential, and weaknesses and strengths in the learning processes. As we mentioned earlier, a high percentage of these children possess significant impediments in their ability to perceive and process information; a condition which gives them serious learning problems in addition to their hyperactivity. The psychologist may also be able to focus upon any emotional problems that the hyperactivity has created. Again this is a common secondary complication and one that interferes with the solution of the problem.

4. The next step is a complete physical examination by a competent pediatrician or family physician who is familiar with the "soft" neurological signs and features that often mark these children. The absence of these physical findings by no means rules out organic hyperactivity; but the presence of a significant number of these signs can be helpful in making the diagnosis.

The Hyperactive Child

Does your school have a school physician? Is he a qualified pediatrician or a family physician who is informed about this new and complex field of neurologically hyperactive children? If a school physician is available, ask the pertinent and acceptable question as to whether he is "up" on the latest findings in this field. This is not a sign of disrespect. You are not questioning another person's professional competence; you are asking for an honest professional answer regarding a serious possible health problem in your child. If you went to your family practitioner to perform surgery, you likely would ask him if he performed such operative work. What is the difference in the question? None. So ask; your child's future is at stake.

If there is no school M.D. or the school physician admits to inexperience in this field, seek out a pediatrician who can perform the appropriate physical examination, which will include the search for the "soft" signs of neurological hyperactivity.

5. Many of these children have communication problems. A thorough speech and hearing assessment plus a testing of communication skills is indicated.

Again the school should have a "speech specialist or communication expert" on call or a permanent one who moves from school to school as an itinerant consultant. Request a screening by this specialist to be sure your child has a complete assessment.

6. An education specialist now should see the child to determine what the classroom teacher can do on a daily basis to deal with his educational disability. The decision as to special placement for the hyperactive child should be made at this point in diagnostic process.

The diagnostic and prescriptive education specialist is not yet a common professional to all schools. However, if he or she is not available, the combined professional knowledge of the school psychologist, communication specialist, and physician may provide what is needed for your child.

7. Now for the really controversial question. Many of these children will respond very dramatically to certain medications and their hyperactive behavior will be markedly diminished. What a paradox that medicines like Dexedrine result in "quieting down" these children while the barbiturates like Phenobarbitol excite them! Your child goes back to the physician. He checks all of the previous findings to make absolutely certain that there is no neurological hyperactivity. If he is convinced, then the drugs are prescribed.

You may have to share the responsibility for giving your child

145

these drugs with the school. The most successful of these medications, Ritalin, does not have a long-acting form. If given to the hyperactive child in the morning, it will be gone by the time of the afternoon classes. It would be helpful, when the child is young, if the principal or school nurse can give your child the drug at lunchtime. Try to negotiate an arrangement to accomplish this. It may not be as easy as you think; some school systems have outdated rules that prevent their personnel from giving drugs to the children. If such a rule exists, do two things: try to work around it in your child's school and fight the ruling at the school board level. Let the community know that you want to raise the issue. There probably will be enough parents whose children are on necessary medication that you can raise a collective voice loud enough to be heard and listened to.

To monitor the medication, it will be necessary for you and the teacher to work together. The teacher must record the child's behavior, paying particular attention to changes during the day or overall changes during the long course of therapy. These observations added to your own notations will serve the physician well in his attempt to regulate the medication to achieve the best level of activity control.

If your child has additional emotional problems, you should ask for help through the school system. Unfortunately, most school systems are very short on help for emotionally upset children. However, the principal or guidance counsellor may be able to refer you to a clinic or suggest consulting your physician for a private psychiatric referral.

Beware of medication without anything else for your child! These children need a multidisciplinary approach that focuses *not* just on their muscular hyperactivity but on their learning and their concept of self as well. Don't settle for a quiet child. Do not be content until your child is learning, has tasted success, thinks better of himself, and has his impulsive behavior under control. He will need counselling, special teaching—and understanding.

We mentioned previously that there are very significant problems when these children reach the adolescent period. Schools are even less tolerant of acting-out behavior at that time. Again, sensitivity to the signs of emotional unrest within these adolescents becomes the joint responsibility of parent and school staff. Once noted, every effort must be made to obtain help for these young people or their acting out will worsen and the end of the road could be institutionalization (in prison or hospital). Here more than at any other time in their lives, these children need rewards for what they do well. They should have someone within the school system who is interested in their future. If they have the ability, there is no reason why they cannot attend college and move into work which is personally rewarding. However, because of their many educational and emotional problems, these children often will not be prepared for college careers but will need counsel and guidance in setting realistic goals. Some may require a carefully selected vocational education. Whatever information is felt appropriate for the hyperactive child approaching adolescence must be conveyed to him in the most positive terms. This is where parent and high school guidance counsellor must work as a team to instill the sense of self-importance in the emerging adult. These youngsters have far too many reasons to think poorly about themselves; mismanaged and poorly expressed career guidance can be the ultimate defeat in their lives.

One of us saw Wayne after his first grade teacher had met his parents and expressed concern over his "hyperactive" behavior. She kept a log of daily activities, and there was a consistent pattern of hyperactivity. His mother admitted to deep concern over her inability to "manage" him when he was a toddler and preschooler. He had been asked to leave nursery school the previous year because of impulsive hyperactivity.

His birth, family, and past health history were quite normal. His teacher had asked the school psychologist to test Wayne. He scored in the high–normal range for intelligence but there were signs in all tests that there was organic difficulty. He appeared also to have a very real problem in coordinating his eye-hand-speech patterns, which showed up on the testing too. The school psychologist commented: ". . . constantly in motion but seemed relatively happy about himself and his situation. No real emotional problems noted." The school communication specialist had given him a battery of tests confirming the findings of the psychologist and suggesting that learning by flash cards and with special individual assistance appeared necessary for the best results.

On Wayne's physical examination, it was discovered that his coordination was disturbed. He had a number of the tell-tale signs of neurological imbalance; his muscles moved like worms in a can, constantly, inappropriately, with impulsive muscular activity. The remainder of his physical was negative. Wayne was diagnosed as "having neurologic dysfunctioning with hyperactivity," and was prescribed medication. His mother was given some daily work sheets upon which she could monitor his behavior; she sent some to his classroom teacher.

In the meantime, his classroom teacher asked her supervisor to observe Wayne and advise on special teaching techniques that could be used in the classroom. Wayne was also taken to a special room for two hours during the day where a trained teacher's aide worked with him alone to help him overcome his visual-motor learning problem.

The medication reduced his hyperactivity dramatically. The daily work sheets from his mother and teacher permitted the physician to adjust his medication at regular intervals.

Three years later, upon testing, Wayne scored well within the normal range. He was a contributing, active member of his class. His hyperactivity was under control. He enjoyed school and was described by his parents as "a very happy little boy."

Instead of having to ask, "What went wrong?" let us ask, "What went right?" here. The answer is, "Everything!" Parent, school, and community came together as an effective functioning unit to assure Wayne of a normal, successful school experience and, because of this vital fact, a normal and successful adult life.

If you have a hyperactive child, be sure you work to get exactly the same informed teamwork for your child.

14. The Child Abused — By Teacher or Peer

"My teacher hit me today." The little six-year-old is standing in his kitchen discussing the day's happenings with his mother. She turns toward him, startled, disbelief in her eyes. "Now, Philip, don't exaggerate. Teachers don't hit the children in their class." She speaks authoritatively to the young boy. His eyes fill with tears as he nods his head vigorously. "She did. She hit me," he insists. His mother sits him down at the kitchen table and gently asks him to tell her all about the incident. After about twenty minutes of listening and questioning, Philip's mother is convinced that her son is not lying. His teacher did strike him in the classroom that afternoon. She becomes furious and agitated, pacing the kitchen floor. Finally, she dials her husband at the office and relates the story to him. Then follows the fateful question: "Well, what are we going to do about it?"

Fortunately this problem faces very few parents in today's society. But when the situation arises, the parent is often so enraged and vengeful that reason, fact, and legality become lost in the flashing turmoil of the moment. It is extremely important for parents to know their rights and their child's rights when forced to cope with a teacher who physically disciplines the children entrusted to his/her care within the classroom.

The first action that the rational parent must attempt is to ascertain a lucid and accurate picture of what actually happened within the classroom. Young children may often misinterpret a physical action by a teacher, for example, a tap on the child's shoulder when passing is called being "beaten." We have experienced the child who has to be restrained from physically harming another child. The only possible method is to separate the two children and restrain the angry, provocative child with firm but not painful force until his anger cools and he

149

can be reasoned with to stop fighting. Such firm restraint is often inaccurately reported by the dismayed and embarrassed child as physical abuse. On the other hand, teachers sometimes strike the knuckles, backs, buttocks, and so on, of children as part of their classroom discipline. The parents must be certain of the events that led up to the "beating" and know the actual nature of the physical contact before they take the matter any further. This will save them a degree of embarrassment and resentment from the teacher if he or she is unjustly accused.

If, however, the parent is reasonably sure that physical abuse has occurred in the classroom, the next action must be to ascertain the scope of the local laws. In certain states the legislatures have allowed minimal physical "management" of classroom discipline; in New York, for example, the teacher is permitted to use physical means of controlling the classroom as long as no harm is inflicted on the child. If your child comes from a locality where such legislation exists, you may have difficulty in confronting and accusing the teacher of physical child abuse, particularly if the physical action was mild and the child's actions were such that there was risk to him or to others. Again, before approaching the teacher and the school, check into your rights in this matter.

Most schools that function under the law which allows teachers to use minimal physical control have instituted the policy of requesting permission from the parents before embarking on that control with any particular child. This should always be the case. The parent should be part of the decision making that permits the use of physical discipline by others outside the home. If the teacher has not asked for this permission and has forcefully applied physical punishment to your child, your complaint to the local school administration will very likely receive a favorable hearing because of the lack of prior parental approval. If you honestly feel that the teacher has overstepped her/his bounds in the physical disciplining of your child, and conferences with this teacher suggest that such discipline will continue, a direct complaint and appeal to the local school authorities is in order.

Often the teacher has merely been overzealous in his or her attempts at controlling the class and trying to teach. There is probably nothing more frustrating to the enthusiastic and inspired teacher than a rowdy, chaotic classroom; this often leads the teacher to attempt physical controls of the disruptive elements that are destroying the educational atmosphere. The teacher is resorting to the method that he/she feels will most expediently bring "authority" back into the classroom. Although this type of control is not appropriate unless it is negotiated with the parents beforehand, such a teacher usually meant no physical harm to the child and merely needs a reminder that, as parents, you do not want physical means used to control your child within the school. It may surprise you to realize that many parents not only condone but encourage physical punishment in the classroom. This method is viewed as a direct extension of the physical spankings the child receives at home as the major disciplinary means of parental control. Unfortunately, it is very true that children reared in homes where physical violence and physical authority are part of the daily existence usually respond very poorly to other methods of control. This situation is often what the teacher faces in the classroom daily; and it prompts him or her spontaneously and sometimes desperately to resort to physical acts for control when children are continually disruptive. This must be borne in mind before you rush to school to condemn the teacher. Search your own disciplinary methods. Take a good, hard look at your own child. If you have handed over a child who is well behaved, mindful, and responsive to verbal commands, then you have every right to expect the teacher to abide by those rules and continue the proper disciplinary management of your child. But if you use the belt and the slap as your method of control, and use it frequently, then a second thought should be given to blaming and accusing the teacher of applying the same methods which you have unknowingly forced upon him or her. If you are a physical punisher, the therapy must begin at home —not in the school. Both you and the teacher should give up the physical controls simultaneously and substitute effective verbal and other disciplinary devices.

Occasionally, the child's teacher develops emotional problems that begin manifesting themselves by physical abuse of the children in the classroom. This behavior could escalate into a serious situation. When the physical punishments are repeated and seem to be focused on one or more children, the parents must take immediate action to prevent more serious harm to their children. This disturbed teacher may use physical force far beyond what would appear necessary. She or he flails out without cause or warning. The teacher's demeanor is agitated, angry, and unreceptive to discussion, and she/he will eventually impress even the least sophisticated of parents as a "sick person." When this is the case, the parents must move quickly to draw the proper attention of the appropriate authorities to this serious problem. Do not take platitudes and promises as satisfactory solutions—fight for your child's protection. Start a lawsuit if necessary and join with the other parents to demand immediate action if none appears forthcoming after tactful, confidential discussions have proven fruitless. Here again you must become the advocate for your child's safety. Be sure you have distinguished between the innocent physical discipline of the first example and the serious pathological physical abuse of the second. If the second appears to be the situation you and your child are confronting, then *immediate action* is called for.

A problem that confronts parents much more frequently than teacher abuse is that of physical abuse by peers. Every schoolchild has probably, at some time or other, run up against the "bully" who harasses, threatens, and occasionally attacks physically. However, some children face the prospect of this type of physical abuse on a daily basis. This can become so serious that the youngster actually fears going to school, makes up excuses not to go, and may be honestly described as having a serious "school phobia" which is intrinsically based on the fear of being beaten up by one or a gang of these bullies.

What can the parents do to help solve this perplexing problem? Some will turn away and mutter, "Let him fight it out like a man. He shouldn't want to hide behind his mother's skirts." This "stand up for yourself" attitude is quite reasonable if the pair of opponents are matched in age, size, and fighting experience. Then the youngsters can usually settle their own differences without the unnecessary intervention of parents or teachers. However, reasonable parents value teaching their children *not* to settle all disputes by physical violence but by negotiation and compromise. The use of the physical solution will follow the young person into his later years and may have a very unfortunate influence on the outcome of his life.

The usual situation is that the child being physically beaten is smaller and younger or is being attacked by a number of other youngsters; he or she often has little chance at reasonable self-defense. How far can a parent go to help in this area? What is the school's responsibility? Suppose this was happening to your child. What should and could you do?

The school is responsible. The school is liable for your child from the moment he leaves your home to go to school until the moment he reenters your front door having finished his day in class. Very often, the principal will shrug and indicate that the incidents are happening "away from school"; therefore the school cannot be held accountable. In most situations, this is simply not true. The school is liable and actually can be sued if something happens to your child going to or coming from school. With this in mind, it becomes the parent's responsibility to enlist the school's aid in locating the other children responsible and attempting to stop the physical harassment of his child. Usually the children who are the abusers go to the same school as the child being physically beaten, so that the school has a good degree of control in locating and monitoring these offenders. The school administration should be encouraged to deal with them effectively by means of school-based discipline and parent conferences. The parent of the child being molested would be wise to allow the school to deal with the matter appropriately since the authority and responsibility lie within the school's domain. However, if the school proves to be lax or ineffective, then you must take the situation into your own hands. A meeting with the parents of the youngsters who are causing the difficulty has a fair chance of solving the problem. If these parents are responsible citizens, then home disciplinary action should alleviate the immediate problem. Unfortunately, all too often these parents prefer to ignore the antisocial actions of their children and little is accomplished by rational discussion between both sets of parents. When both school officials and other parents refuse to take action against the juvenile abusers, the next step must, by necessity, be the law.

Parents facing a peer abuse dilemma are advised to hire a lawyer or seek free Legal Aid advice to initiate action against the parents and the children through due process of law. The mere act of turning to the law for help may motivate both the parents and the juvenile offenders to reconsider and stop the physical harassment of your child. Do not be afraid to go to the law for help in this dead-end situation. Remember it is your child who is being hurt. It is your child who is afraid to go to school. It is your child who will suffer from the missed days and the emotional anxiety, with the resultant loss of learning. Confronted by these possibilities and a school and parenting system that appear unresponsive, the law is your next and proper step.

In addition, make certain that you have registered an official complaint with the local school administration about the unresponsiveness of the school in this matter, reminding them of their legal responsibility for your child's welfare while under their care. Put your complaint on record. Expect an appropriate and meaningful response. If you do not get one, go to the state school officials with the same complaint. Do not stop until your voice has been heard, recognized, and given proper attention.

Obviously, parents must be very cautious not to overreact to the complaints that their children bring home with them. Stories of "beatings" must be distilled, analyzed, and carefully evaluated before a parent launches into a frontal attack on the school, the community, or other children in defense of his child. However if, after due consideration, you are convinced that your child is being physically abused, you not only have the right but the need to go further in order to eliminate any more episodes happening to your or any other child in the same environment.

15 The Emotionally Disturbed Child

Take a test—an important test—one that tells you something about what you know and feel about mental illness (also called emotional disturbance) in children. Why is that important? Because what you know about mental illness in children affects those children.

Mental illness in children is often referred to as an adjustment disease; it reflects an improper adjustment to life. But it also reflects an adjustment to inadequate life. That is, mental illness is sometimes defined relatively. Is a child sick in a sane society or sane in a sick society?

The answer, of course, lies not at either of these extremes but somewhere in the middle. A child is the product both of his/her actions toward others and his/her reactions to how others approach him/her. Mental illness is a disease of the interpersonal areas as well as the deeply personal areas within the single individual. Therefore, how you think and feel about mental illness in children is important. If you have daily contact with an emotionally upset child, these feelings become vital. If you are the parent of an emotionally ill child, it is imperative that you realize where you stand and what must be known. Otherwise you could be more of the problem than a part of the solution.

So, take this test, a "true-or-false" test. Then read the chapter and take the test again. Do you have preconceived attitudes or lack of information about what could maintain or worsen the emotional illness of your child? Do you lack the skills or perspective to help your child? Think about your answers after you have read this chapter.

Between Parent and School

What Do You Think?

1. "Mental illness" in children is a term that means the same to all mental health personnel, including the professionals in the school.
   _____true, _____false

2. An emotionally disturbed child should not be held responsible for his/her actions.
   _____true, _____false

3. Emotionally disturbed children are usually identifiable in the classroom by their hostile behaviors.
   _____true, _____false

4. Parents have to take a large share of the blame when it comes to creating an emotionally ill child.
   _____true, _____false

5. A parent can be the best therapist for his/her emotionally disturbed child.
   _____true, _____false

6. The family of an emotionally disturbed child needs therapy.
   _____true, _____false

7. When an interdisciplinary team is working with an emotionally disturbed child, the doctor is always in charge.
   _____true, _____false

8. The best educational program for an emotionally disturbed child is a special class containing a small number of other emotionally ill children with an experienced teacher.
   _____true, _____false

9. The usual, or average, time of special class placement for an emotionally ill child is two years.
   _____true, _____false.

10. If a child has severe emotional illness, often he/she should be taught at home.
    _____true, _____false

11. Parents often have difficulty being objective about their emotionally disturbed child and need the advice or support of a third party.
    _____true, _____false

12. An emotionally disturbed child can be "cured."
    _____true, _____false.

Remember to check your answers, again, when you have finished this chapter.

The Emotionally Disturbed Child

Let us suppose that you have a school-age child named Timmy Brown. You have been worried for a long time about Timmy's behavior, wondering if there could be something wrong, perhaps even mental illness. Finally you get a letter from the principal. This is what it says:

Dear Ms. Brown:

> I am grateful that you sent me that note two weeks ago expressing your concern for Timmy. We, too, have had concerns about him these last two years and have wondered what his outbursts have meant. With your note as a stimulus, I referred Timmy to the school psychologist, who felt the need to refer him to the school's consulting psychiatrist. Dr. Radcliff, the Chief of School Psychological Services, met with me, Timmy's teacher and Dr. Andrews, the psychiatrist, in a staff meeting which was set up to discuss Timmy. I'm sorry that you could not attend this meeting because of your need to be at your cousin's wedding, but we were helped by your hour-long talk with Dr. Radcliff the week before. Let me use this letter to bring you up to date on our thinking about Timmy. Essentially it is this. We feel that Timmy needs some special help in school because of his emotional problems.
>
> Because of these opinions, we are going to seek special placement for Timmy. Notifications of his class change will reach you shortly. You are invited to discuss our decision with us at any time in the future.

The letter was carefully signed by the principal and you note that copies have been sent to the Special Education Division of your local school system.

At this point, you are totally panic-stricken. The thoughts that echo in your mind are, "Does that mean Timmy is mentally ill?" "Crazy?" Often the only answer you will receive from the experts is: "Timmy needs some kind of special help."

Are these school people "copping out," as the children would say, by not simply calling Timmy "emotionally disturbed," "mentally ill," "socially maladjusted," or some of the other terms used to describe children with serious personal problems? Actually he will be designated by one of those terms, because that is what the principal of the school *must* do. He must call him one of those names when he submits a letter to the state department of education to ask for the money for Timmy's special class.

We would counsel against *labeling* Timmy, or any child, by any such term. All too often you have heard people commenting that certain forms of behavior are "sick" behaviors. When people do things negatively to other people, their victims often call them "crazy" or "pathological." Because of these facts, the term "emotional illness" has frequently become a brand of insult to many people. It has become a way of explaining any behavior which runs contrary to their personal code of beliefs, against values or actions which they cannot easily explain or interpret. If you and your spouse continually refer to your child as being emotionally ill, or "sick," this quick excuse could become a too easy way of explaining away, and failing to correct, his or her behaviors. You must refrain from saying, "He cannot help it because he is sick," or, "There's no reason for those actions; they're just the products of a sick mind."

The parent attitude of accepting and using mental illness in this way is usually only a crutch against a crippled school pattern. It tends to "blame" a child, not his or her surroundings. The problem, however, lies with both the child *and* his world. There are probably many reasons why your child displays inappropriate behaviors. Often in the early part of the child's diagnostic examinations, these reasons are deeply buried and will take time and expert care to unearth. However, once they have been uncovered and analyzed, then the school professional, with your cooperation, can help your child modify these behaviors—changing them into actions and reactions that your family and the school will consider more acceptable and less painful to him and to his environment. If he is labeled by a term that automatically assumes he cannot help or modify these behaviors, you can see that those school personnel who must put forth effort to help him could feel the task was futile and give up.

Very often the reason that the school personnel use the term "emotional disturbance," other than to receive the state money, is because this term specifically includes the behavior of those children who could do harm to themselves or other children if left unchecked. There should indeed be a "red flag" term to focus attention upon these children. But this term excludes a large number of children who are *mildly* disruptive to their class or their family because of excess energy, obvious hostilities to teachers, parents, or classmates, or their manipulative attraction of the class's attention. The term "emotional disturbance" usually includes children who continually disrupt the class at unpredictable times; who cannot change this type of behavior even when their class or social situation is changed; and who will eventually hurt the other children, either physically or psychologically, by their abusive and annoying actions. Less frequently, but just as important, the term "emotional disturbance" should include the overly quiet child —the child withdrawn from others, focused on a secret, painful self, and capable of hurting that aching, turbulent inner soul. Whether overly aggressive or overly submissive, the emotionally disturbed child is capable of destruction—intended or not—of himself and/or others.

Let us analyze the boy discussed in the letter from the principal. He might be your child.

Timmy falls under the category of a child who has the potentiality of hurting himself. His angry antisocial outbursts are not hurting others in the class—unless they care about his welfare. These acts seem to be more related to himself. Not only has he been destroying his ability to receive and mentally process the instruction in the classroom, but he appears to be almost systematically cutting off his potential for friendly relationships with any of his classmates. These acts of alienation are also noted within the family. He appears to be caught in aggressive, antisocial behavior, the reasons behind which he cannot fully explain nor understand. He apparently refuses to attempt to control himself or to accept help in searching for the reasons why he behaves as he does in school. Without further insight, he will continue to cut off his friends unless someone can help him find those reasons and then help him to resolve his problems by other, less disturbed and less disturbing ways.

"Are there many children like Timmy?" you will ask, seeking for some comfort. We must make it very clear to you that there is no other person like Timmy, no matter what labels or diagnostic terms are similar. Timmy is a unique individual. There are other children who, unintentionally, as a result of emotional problems, can hurt others or themselves. These childhood emotional problems run the gamut from lack of contact with reality to making one's own reality through the habitual use of drugs. Timmy is a combination of Timmy's experiences, Timmy's genes, and Timmy's perceptions. The only label the authors would prefer to use with this child is "Timmy." The psychologist, the teacher, and the others who work with Timmy will have their technical short-cut words and diagnostic terms, but when these are assembled and processed, they spell out only one label—Timmy.

Again let us assume that Timmy is your child. One of the things you will find yourself bringing up in those serious conversations with your spouse will be the recurrent, haunting doubts—"Where did we go wrong?"

Doubts hurt and sting the ego because all of us can find several actions and wrong turns we have made in the pathways of parenting. It is so easy for the parent to shoulder all the blame. If you have read any of the older books on child psychology, you have undoubtedly seen the references in the cases of emotionally disturbed children to the "problems" of parents. These books have exposed you to the old adage: "There are no bad kids, just bad parents." The authors would like to lift part of this very heavy cloak of guilt off the shoulders of parents already burdened with the stigma of having a child with mental illness. It is unreasonable to assume that the parents are usually "to blame" for the emotionally ill child. This assumption should join all the other unproven myths surrounding modern education. Where there is an emotionally ill child in a family, there will be unrest and raw emotions in that family. Whether this is a cause or an effect, the basis or the result of the emotional illness of one of the family members, is generally an unanswerable question. It is usually the cause *and* effect, the basis *and* result of the emotional illness. Emotional illness is a condition born out of an unfortunate and destructive relationship of a child with his or her environment—an environment which primarily includes parents but also siblings, neighbors, relatives, and other significant people. Research has shown, in fact, that the parents of emotionally disturbed children can be their child's best therapist or educator if they are relieved primarily of the guilt which they feel about their ill child. We strongly suggest that parents need *not* be locked into the feeling that they are the cause of their child's emotional problems.

But what does occur is that parents often are involved in the spin-offs of the child's emotional illness. If Timmy were your child, he would cause you deep consternation and recurrent frustration at home, resulting in an increased level of anxiety among the other family members. This would, in turn, result in more confrontations than usual, more fights, more withdrawals, and more strained conversations.

What can be done for Timmy at home and in school?

1. The clashes with the family are destructive and counterproductive to his adjustment and his learning. You must analyze what percentage of these conflicts actually are started by Timmy and what percentage have a basis in the actions of those around him over which

he has little or no control. You know that constant unrest cannot help Timmy to make the necessary positive change toward good mental health. So you must curb your part of his problem. Why? Unless you can do so, Timmy will be spending most of his creative and "changing" time fighting his internal battles with the family; and the causes and resolutions of his aberrant behavior will not receive his or the family's full attention.

Some way of neutralizing those family pressures must be found. This will most probably occur through counselling. Timmy's parents are going to need time to bounce off their feelings about Timmy onto an objective third person. They are going to have to be able to talk to someone about their anxiety over Timmy and what is happening to him before their concern builds into unmanageable proportions. Someone knowledgeable will have to be consulted about Timmy, who can help his parents recognize change in the child when it occurs. Positive change can be as imperceptible as the light, cool wind after a rainstorm. But parents must sense this lessening tension and refreshing change. The school social worker will often be able to help them locate that proper "someone." This consultant may be the social worker herself or someone the parents locate in a social agency familiar to the school social worker. Or this professional to whom the parent is referred may be a child psychologist, behavioral pediatrician, or child psychiatrist. The choice depends on the severity of Timmy's problems.

The school has a responsibility, also, in working with this outside "someone": it must be willing to share with the outside consultants the preliminary observations and test materials which are in the child's chart. The outside professional must know why this child has been diagnosed as being emotionally ill by the school personnel. This information is precious first-hand data; it can save weeks and months of time and money and ensure greater and quicker success in helping the child.

2. What can the school do for Timmy during this time? The answer lies in the key methods suggested so often in this book—explore and modify. Timmy may be tried in a special class for a while after the parent's permission has been obtained. In this special setting, Timmy will receive his academic courses and other school projects in a noncompetitive atmosphere where he receives consistent positive rewards for his progress. The school should also be making repeated observations as to which subjects and which teaching ap-

proaches seem to turn Timmy "off" and which appear to stimulate him. This will provide the school with the proper insight into how to teach Timmy properly and uncover clues for the psychiatrist about possible reasons and causes for his inappropriate behavior.

3. In addition to the special classroom, the administrator and the teacher must join forces with the mental health professional and present an effective two-pronged approach: concern for the personal *and* the educational part of the child. The school personnel must always consider you a partner in this search for Timmy's problems.

   In addition, the school should be alert in attempting to encourage Timmy into social situations—at first very structured situations, later more normal, looser ones. Timmy should not lose contact with those children with whom he will someday be laughing and playing once again. This flexible school social environment will give him a chance to practice new ways of meeting and interacting with people and possibly testing out friendships. Once he begins the process of change, Timmy's parents must follow suit and do the same at home.

4. There is no time limit or "sentence" which condemns Timmy to a special class or therapy for any specific period of time. So much depends upon the following factors: the degree of his illness, his relationship with the mental health professional, the parents' cooperation, and the school's full participation in his evaluation and treatment. Children with emotional problems should be allowed to heal and progress at their own speed. Thus, Timmy will be in that special class or program as long as he needs it—hopefully neither more nor less. When he is ready to leave, there will be some transitional activities between the special classroom and his other teachers. As he indicates improvement, Timmy may be programmed to leave the special classroom or special program and return to his regular classroom for only a few hours a day at first, or perhaps he may return all at once. Whatever patterns are offered Timmy during his treatment, his school and his therapy should be programmed on his own schedule and to meet his own needs. Parents must make certain that it is Timmy's needs, and not the needs of the school, that are being met.

The letter which began this chapter was fiction. However, you could conceivably receive a short typed bomb just like that, because no parent is immune to the possibility of emotional illness being suspected in his child. The suspicion is often a serious trigger. The parent must make quite certain that the concerns are real. Too much is at stake for your child. In truth, many of the attitudes that this chapter warns about—stereotyping, labeling in frustration, blaming the parents, pigeon-holing—are attitudes that exist in any school; they exist throughout society. The purpose of this chapter, however, is to give the parents of an emotionally ill child a standard to shoot for, not only in what can be expected in the school but what should be looked for in society and within themselves. One of the most difficult battles the parents will have to fight is that against the unhelpful attitudes which will surround their child and themselves. They will continually have to remind themselves that their child is Timmy—not "some sick kid."

The provisions which most schools have for children who are emotionally ill are far from ideal, but changes toward helping these children are finally beginning to come about as the need for these resources has become more glaringly obvious. Most schools *should* have a range of educational opportunities open to any child with emotional problems. At times an emotionally ill child is going to need a teacher or a therapist to himself. This should be provided for him by the school. At other times, that child will need a small group in which to work and interact on a full-time basis. That, also, should be provided by the school. Finally, as the child begins to be assimilated back into his regular society, his teachers ought to have the advantage of special guidance to ease him over the rough spots of coming back into his classroom. That, also, is a function of the school system. And, since his family unit is an integral part of the emotionally ill child, the school should help to provide these parents with the counselling that will assist them in understanding and dealing with themselves and with the child. Finally, the school should work to find the proper therapeutic help for this mentally upset youngster. If your school does not have this flexibility, this expanded attitude, and the proper staff, then you must find out why there is this deficiency—and how you can help the school and your child obtain the necessary implements for his ultimate mental health.

A word of warning. One of the old-fashioned ways of treating emotionally ill children—perhaps stemming from the primitive attitudes about relationships between mental illness and "possession" by evil—was to exclude them from school. The usual rationalization was, "Well, we just don't have the staff to help them here." In later years, to lessen the guilt of the excluding official, this practice was changed so that these children were offered a "homebound teacher"—a teacher who taught the child in the home. Unfortunately, this situation is still practiced in some areas where the parents and the school systems are unenlightened or nonprogressive. Now, if you confront school systems with this inadequacy, the explanations will usually be much more sophisticated, such as, "The economics of the situation will not allow us to hire the necessary personnel." It all adds up to the same—your child is about to get inferior educational service because he has been labeled as emotionally ill. He will be taught only part time in a home situation where he will not be permitted the needed socialization of other children. Do not let that happen. Simply refuse this option and ask the principal for alternatives. Try to keep your child within the system— the school and the societal system—and let education adapt to his needs.

Assuming that the school system can accommodate your Timmy, there are other actions that you can take that will be helpful to you and to him. One is to become part of the fact-finding and decision-making team guiding Timmy's future school life. In the letter, the principal indicated he had invited Ms. Brown to join the professional staff when they discussed Timmy. This is becoming a more common practice, but, unfortunately, is far from universal. In public schools where the personnel have been trained in traditional fashion to allow one person, usually a psychiatrist, to make all final decisions regarding the diagnosis and treatment of an emotionally upset child, you will find resistance to having a parent on the professional team. However, many public schools are moving into the enlightened seventies and recognizing the function of teachers, social workers, school nurses, *and parents* in this evaluation and treatment. Explore the possibility with your school; in your most gentle, persuasive, and informed way, you may even help them to change their minds and form the necessary school-parent team.

You should consider talking to someone outside the family unit about your child's problems to find that clear and unbiased objectivity you are going to need to start helping him. If you have been "brainwashed" into believing that you are totally to blame and carry a heavy burden of guilt, as many parents do, you might do well to talk to your minister, priest, or rabbi first. But eventually you will want to talk to someone with whom you can share raw and painful feelings, concerns, and memories about Timmy. You need the calm professional person with whom you can sit back from the problem and plumb the deep effect upon the family and the ripples of anxiety and frustration caused by Timmy's actions and reactions. Take up the principal's offer to seek this counsellor through the school's advisory system, or do it on your own. But sign all releases of information between the school and your professional mental health counsellor. Remember that you will be focusing on Timmy's illness and his progress toward emotional and educational well-being. Your attention and the school's should be concentrated upon that.

One of the first things a counsellor may do is ask you to imagine how your family would normally function if Timmy were not a part of it. This may frighten and alarm you. What he or she is trying to do is help you obtain a hold on reality once again. He will be trying to help you see a reference point of normality that can be passed on to Timmy by your actions. Chances are that your family has become different because of your emotionally ill child, and perhaps you will need to make a dramatic change as a family before Timmy can make his progress.

Unlike many other types of handicaps, the emotionally ill child can change. He can return to a normal existence in time—sometimes a long time, sometimes a short time. But he can. All he needs is the proper parental, school, and professional help blended in the right amounts, kept going for the proper length of time, and checked frequently to adjust the level of education and personal involvement.

The main supervisor should be you, the parent. You must act as child advocate in the school, counsellor in the home, and patient parent in the professional's office. It is a serious job.

Are you armed with the right tools for this job? Do you have the right knowledge and attitudes about emotional disturbance in children as it would be grossly measured by the test at the beginning of this chapter? Let us review this test, and in so doing, reveal the inherent "Catch-22" —some of the answers are relevant *only* to your child. Not all emotionally disturbed children are alike. That statement and that philosophy make the answer to question number 1 "false."

Is an emotionally disturbed child responsible for his/her actions? As much as any other child is responsible, so is he. There may be, of course, uncontrollable impulses and behavior; the degree of uncontrollability depends upon the child and upon both his physical and mental make-up. Therapy is helping the child become responsible for all his actions. Nothing can be explained away by saying, "He cannot help himself— he's emotionally disturbed." The answer to number 2 then depends upon the behaviors, the child, and the therapy.

We said that emotionally disturbed behaviors were characterized by the child's potential to hurt himself or others. Accompanying behavior could be either aggressive or withdrawn. Most people think of emotionally disturbed children as being hostile, but that is often only their interpretation. "Hostile" emotionally disturbed children usually think of themselves as just "active." Thus, question number 3 represents a stereotype that is more often "true" than it should be.

Question number 4 asks if parents are to blame in "creating" an emotionally disturbed child? Which parents? What child? What emotional disturbance? Again, we have quoted a stereotype. Parents must take a major share of the blame of a child's emotional illness in *very few* situations. Emotional disturbance has to be the result of many forces, many distortions, and many improper reinforcements to inadequate behavior. Parents may be seen equally as often being victims as victimizing. The enlightened answer to number 4 is "false."

Can a parent be the best therapist for his/her emotionally disturbed child? The answer to number 5 is a resounding "true." However, this works best when (1) the parent is helped by an objective third party; (2) the parent has been helped to see the nature of the illness and can view it with some objectivity; and (3) the child is able to establish some communication of a rewarding nature with the parent. When these systems are "go," therapy will accelerate dramatically.

Question number 6 asks if the family of an emotionally disturbed child needs therapy. The answer almost always is "true." But therapy is needed not because the family has "caused" the emotional illness, but because that illness is bound to be having an effect upon the total family. The emotionally disturbed child becomes the center of the family's problems, embarrassments, frustrations, and decisions. The family needs objectivity. And it needs therapy, if no more than occasional counselling, in order to develop this necessary objectivity.

Should the doctor always be in charge of the interdisciplinary team that works with an emotionally disturbed child? The word "always" in that statement makes the answer to question number 7 "false." The leading professional in the team that works with your child is the person who sees the child the most, or who has the most control over his/her environment, or who has the most contact with you, or who is the child's therapist, or . . . The point to this question is that the leading person on the interdisciplinary team working with your child should be (1) well trained, and (2) chosen as a result of the nature of your child's problems and prescription. Remember that you, the parent, should help in the selection.

What is the best educational program for an emotionally disturbed child? Anything that fits his or her needs. You could select one or more activities from ten columns of offerings. There is no single prescription for an emotionally disturbed child. The answer to number 8, then, is "false."

If there is no single best educational program for "the emotionally disturbed child," how can there be a set period of time that is best for that mythical class of child? Mark number 9 as "false."

Should a child be taught at home if he/she is emotionally disturbed? Only in rare instances should this occur. Remember that it is usually an administrative "cop-out." Score number 10 as "false."

Question number 11 states that parents often have difficulty being objective about their emotionally disturbed child and need the advice and support of a third party. Of course this is "true." This is your child. There should be no stigma attached to being subjective and needing help in becoming objective.

Question number 12 asks if emotionally disturbed children can be "cured."

With proper educational, psychological, and parental advocacy, emotionally disturbed children can indeed be cured.

16 The Child with Sensory Losses— Auditory and Visual

For people who have the ability to see and hear, the loss of part or all of these vital sensory functions is something beyond full comprehension. Even if we are the parents of a child afflicted with this type of sensory loss, we cannot fully appreciate the extent of the accommodation that this special child must make to the noisy, bright, active world around him or her. Part of this exciting experience is excluded from his life. The adjustment is a mammoth one; the child must continually deal with the effects on his social and educational life. It is a daily challenge, at times exhausting and often defeating for the child. As parents and educators, we must help fight this emotional fatigue which leads to childhood retreat and failure.

There are all levels to the silent world of deafness and the dark world of blindness. Children may have various degrees and various types of losses. They may not appear "blind" or "deaf" to the outside world. It becomes extremely important that, as parents and teachers, we examine the sensory equipment of our children. We have to find the "hidden defects" that may be sapping the educational and emotional strength of our young child.

An overly clumsy child who walks with unusual care is one whose eyesight must be carefully assessed. A child may listen intently to the story being read, and then when asked to "read," will recite the story from a highly developed memory while inappropriately turning the pages of the book. This, too, may be the mark of a partially sightless child. The boy who constantly has difficulty "fielding" the ball during recess should have his eyesight checked. An eye examination is in order for the girl who holds the pencil too tightly, leans into the paper, writes

168

almost illegibly or scribbles with fierce and rigid determination, and has great difficulty keeping the letters on the pale blue lines of the paper. If your child states simply that he or she is doing poorly because he "has trouble seeing the blackboard," he is a candidate for referral for an eye examination.

A basic screening eye examination ordinarily can be done by the school nurse or the nurse's aide using the various eye charts, including the common Snellen Chart. This should be routine at your child's school, if it is not find out why. If the school is depending on your pediatrician or local health department clinic to fulfill this important task, make quite certain that someone qualified is doing the job. Don't let your child's vision testing be neglected. Don't accept "Someone else is doing it," when no one is truly responsible. If your child demonstrates any defects on the initial eye screening, then an appointment with an eye specialist is the next important step. This eye specialist may be an optometrist, whose training has been in the techniques of eye examination and treatment with glasses when indicated, or you may want a medical specialist, an ophthalmologist, who has specialized in both the physical and optical diagnosis and treatment of the eye. The extent and nature of the problem must be clearly delineated so that the child can receive the type of help that will improve his vision to a point where he can function with as much sight as possible. If no sight is possible, the earlier the parent and educational system become aware of the special educational needs of this visually handicapped child, the better will be the future planning for his education and emotional adjustment. Once the eye specialist has analyzed the visual problems and made suggestions as to treatment, the parent and the school system must meet, analyze the doctor's findings, and make proper plans for the child's future.

If this partial handicap can be corrected by glasses or by surgery, the future looks quite promising. Then the main burden of the parent-teacher team is in making certain that the youngster wears his or her glasses when needed. Both must also be on the alert for the occasional hurtful remarks and actions by the young child's classmates in response to the thick, awkward glasses. Remember that for a boy, these glasses may limit participation in recess; for a girl, heavy glasses may make her feel "ugly" and "different." These can be very real emotional problems to a child with a partial visual handicap, and the teacher must watch continually for signs that they are developing so that gentle but sensitive intervention between child and classmates can be made. A lesson in "Why do we see?" might help immeasurably in informing all of the children about the magic of vision, as well as heightening their sensitivity and understanding of a child in their midst with sight problems. This must be a carefully prepared and thoughtfully delivered class session, which will test the consummate skill of the teacher.

There is always the possibility that your child's sight problem may only be partially solved by optics or surgery. In this case, the youngster may need a part-time special class, often called a "sight saving" class or "vision resource room." These classes allow the child to deal with special texts in larger print. The teachers who instruct these children schedule physical activities that do not exceed their capacities; the entire educational experience is geared to fortifying the limited sight that is present but also focusing a great deal upon the other senses so as to enrich the child's educational and emotional life. For the visually impaired, the teacher should be developing his or her hearing to the maximum, using the record player, the spoken word, the tape recorder, the musical instrument to add an extra dimension to a young life with one slightly impaired sensory perimeter. It is also possible that in this class your child will be taught to use a "low vision aid"—an optical instrument like a large magnifying glass or special television set designed to enlarge the image and enhance partial sight. You will have to learn about this device, reassure your child, and help him or her use the instrument at home as well as at school.

It is particularly important that special resources for the partially sighted child be within the regular school environment and not in a separate building removed from the "sighted" children. Children with sensory losses, by necessity, feel quite "different." Part of their world has been shut off. They are not seeing or hearing everything that other children are experiencing. This sense of being different may cripple the young person far more than the partial or even complete loss of a sensory function. The ultimate goal of all educational programs for the sensory impaired is not merely to assure them the equivalent education of their "sensory intact" friends but also to prepare them to enter the sensory intact world that surrounds them. These programs must be geared to assist the youngsters in making a success of their lives from the social, emotional, and career vantage points. Therefore, it becomes extremely important for children with partial sensory impairments to share part of their school day with their sighted friends. This has a positive effect on both the impaired and the non-impaired child. An impaired child can learn to adjust to the highly stimulating world from which he or she is receiving only partial signals; he learns to work around the missing parts of his sensory being. The sighted child at an early age should develop an understanding, a tolerance, a sense of reaching out, an acceptance of the "different"—the physically impaired companion. Both children will grow as people from a continuous and supervised association.

How do you spot the youngster with partial hearing loss? This may be a much more difficult child for the parent and the teacher to pick out of the crowd. Why? Because the child may deliberately attempt to blend with the other children to hide what he or she recognizes as his limited ability to hear. The child with a partial hearing loss may be extremely difficult to screen out of the classroom: an intelligent, motivated child with a partial hearing loss can become a rather expert lip reader and, when facing the parent or teacher, can respond quickly and appropriately. It is only when the child's eyes are turned away from the speaker that the responses are not forthcoming. The child does not hear; he also does not see your speech by reading your lips. All too often he is diagnosed as a "daydreamer" because of the inconsistency of his performance. He is chastised, coaxed, punished. But the pattern continues. The teacher may find the youngster staring intently at her when she speaks, quickly turning his head in desperation in a futile attempt to catch the lip movements of his neighbors so that he may continue to be part of the interaction in class. Often he gives up in exhausted despair. Parent and teacher must watch for these children. This is a shadow child, a child who lingers in the corners, whose voice is seldom heard in the verbal classroom; this is the unusually "quiet" child. The child with a partial hearing loss often *does* become the class daydreamer, staring out of the window into the bright sun or the trickling raindrops as the muted sounds of learning pass unnoticed and unheard around his head. The child with a partial hearing impairment may only hear slivers and pieces of other people's questions. Therefore, these children often make inappropriate replies that seem to come from another lesson, another time. The child simply has not fully heard what was asked. His response is his frustrated attempt to reply. As these children continue to respond inappropriately, creating negative reactions from their teacher, their classmates, and even their parents, they will retreat even further into themselves and often become electively mute, refusing to talk at all when questioned or spoken to.

Here we should mention children who have auditory perception problems and who often seem hard of hearing, as discussed in the chapter on learning disabilities. There is *no* partial hearing loss in these children; their problem is in the processing by the brain of the sounds they hear. These youngsters know essentially what they want to reply but their ability to bring their responses together in a meaningful, intelligible way is sometimes defective. The result is a jumbled, inarticulate, inappropriate response—not too dissimilar to the child with the partial hearing loss. The parents must make certain that their child has had the full benefit of a complete and comprehensive hearing test. A routine testing of a child's hearing is too perfunctory and superficial when we are dealing with the complex problem of hearing loss versus the perceptual-processing disorder of a communication defect. The parents must insist on an accurate, thorough evaluation of their child by a qualified specialist in hearing tests when the problem has been assessed as "auditory," that is, related to the child's hearing.

One of us saw a nine-year-old girl who was referred to a team of professionals for an evaluation of her inconsistent school performance. She was labeled a "daydreamer." She stood in front of the examiner and answered his questions in a quiet but composed voice. She seemed a charming, relaxed, somewhat introverted child. Her mother claimed that she paid very little attention to her at home; and said she seemed to be "in a fog" most of the time. During the interview, her mother called her "a sweet child but a little lazy." Past history revealed only a very mild case of diarrhea as an infant and an episode with the "ten-day measles" with high fever when she was four years old. Otherwise, the girl's mother offered little else in the way of clues or observations as to why her daughter was performing so erratically in school.

During the physical examination, she answered all questions while the physician checked her chest and stood in front of her. However, when he moved behind her to examine her back, the room became dramatically silent as his questions went unanswered. He stepped in front of her and asked the same questions. The answers were returned promptly and clearly. Several more such tests repeated the same experience. The physician was amazed. It was hard for him to admit that he had been fooled by one of the most adept lip readers he had ever met . . . and she was only nine years old. Her mother could not believe it. Testing proved that she had lost almost 85 percent of her hearing acuity, probably secondary to her severe case of measles. Not only was the doctor unaware early in his examination of the girl's profound hearing loss, but the girl's mother and teacher were not aware that a hearing problem of significant degree was the basis of her school and home problems.

This young girl brings another point to mind. Parents and teachers must remember that not all children are born with their sensory defect. They may develop these defects as complications to illness or trauma sometime later during their childhood years. Therefore the initial assessment of normal sight and hearing made during infancy will not be sufficient throughout all of childhood. Children should have regular hearing and sight evaluations. These can be scheduled by the schools through an active program of child health screening by the school nurse and school physician or can be accomplished by the child's parents through regular visits to the pediatrician or local health department clinic. Either method is satisfactory; the main point is that one or the other must be available to safeguard the child's sensory education.

The usual way of approaching the problem of partial hearing loss in children is first to attempt to ascertain its causes. The child should visit an otolaryngologist (the ear, nose, and throat doctor); in addition, he or she may have to be tested by a qualified audiologist. Every school system should have such an audiologist on tap for the purpose of evaluating the complex hearing problems of the children in that system. If there is not such a professional, the school should be prepared to provide the child with the services of qualified audiologists retained as consultants by the system. This is essentially a school-based diagnostic responsibility. The school cannot offer an appropriate education for this specially handicapped child without the advice and consultation of such a professional.

The ENT doctor may find that there are problems correctable by surgery. For example, very swollen adenoids may block the tubes that lead to the middle ear and produce obstructions severe enough to cause blockage, immobility of the eardrum, and diminished hearing. In these cases, the removal of the adenoids may restore a very high percentage of hearing. Chronic ear infections, with persistent retention of infected material behind the eardrum, or the chronically ruptured eardrum due to persistent infection, are very common causes of hearing loss in children. Operative procedures to remove the source of infection, plus the placement of tubes into the middle ear for drainage, may gradually restore the hearing to such partially deaf children. They may be able to reenter their regular classroom, catch up, and succeed.

The audiologist and physician may determine that a child would benefit from wearing a hearing aid in the ears to intensify the transmitted sounds and propel the spoken words more accurately toward the brain. In some children with hearing losses from birth and/or from subsequent injury to the hearing processes, this may restore the reception of sound sufficiently to allow the child to return to the regular classroom with only an auxiliary hearing aid. If the hearing level has become adequate, the child could function to his or her full potential in the regular classroom setting.

Again the parent and the teacher have a dual responsibility to this child. First, we should stress that it is not easy to get used to having a hearing aid attached to one's ear. Although the sudden return of sound to the child may be a very strong motivating factor, the sense of discomfort caused by the foreign apparatus may cause the child, particularly the young child, to pull the uncomfortable, occasionally noisily buzzing aid from the ear and return to the world of half-sounds. Both the teacher and the parent must encourage, reinforce, understand, and reward the continuous use of the hearing aid in school. The more the child uses the aid, the more he or she will get used to it. Eventually, the child will routinely take full responsibility for the management of his hearing aid just as the diabetic child gradually learns to regulate his insulin and the child with bleeding tendencies learns to curb his physical activity.

But it will always be an uphill struggle. Why? The parent and the teacher must work together to make certain that the hearing aid is functioning properly. The batteries in the hearing aid should be checked by parent and by teacher every day. The parent should keep the teacher supplied with fresh batteries. A sudden loss of interest or look of confusion from the child may be quickly remedied by replacing a dead battery.

The teacher and the parent must be aware that this child returns to the classroom looking different: he has a strange and unnatural instrument attached to his ear. Not only will the other children be curious, but a few will be cruel, sometimes without realizing the painfulness of their reactions to the child. Here the teacher must intervene because she knows how destructive this can be. She should not wait until the child has been teased and hurt before she begins to act to establish the youngster as part of the normal everyday functioning of the class. As with the child with sight problems and thick glasses, the sensitive teacher may schedule a lesson or discussion on the subject of hearing. As a part of this discussion, she may offer the child an opportunity to explain what the hearing aid is all about. If he is too shy or too embarrassed, which is quite often the case, the teacher should be prepared to explain the function and use of the aid. Specially prepared records that demonstrate to hearing children what a hearing loss "sounds" like can be found in most public libraries. This will both inform the children about their classmate and start them on the road to tolerance through learning more about the unusual or the unknown.

But what can be done if you find out that your child is almost totally blind or almost totally deaf and that neither surgery nor aids can improve the youngster's sensory abilities? What educational future lies ahead for this totally handicapped child? What should you know and how should you act? Will your child be forced to leave home and placed in a state or private residential school for the blind or the deaf?

In this fortunate time in our development for deaf or blind students, your child's handicap hopefully will have been discovered before he or she enters school. You will be helped to work with him at home. He will be taught words, sentences, body mobility, exploration; and most importantly, he will sense acceptance and confidence—by you and by his teachers. If he progresses well, he can enter a very special program in your school system. If he does not progress well or if he has many serious handicaps, then he may be recommended for a residential school. In either case, your doctor and the other significant personnel will do everything to keep your child at home and among his friends for as long as possible without endangering his necessarily highly specialized education.

The blind child and the deaf child must have these intensive specialized programs. This is an education designed both physically and intellectually to care best for the complete losses of sensory deprived children. It is quite rare in most school systems, especially at the elementary level, that totally blind or deaf children can be *completely* absorbed into the regular school situation. These children need a special pacing to their education; in addition, they must acquire special skills in order to become effective learners. The blind child must learn Braille to be able to read. The senses of touch and hearing must be intensified and refined so that they can become the primary instruments of the sightless child's learning. The deaf child must learn to read lips and understand the spoken-visual world. If the child has been deaf from birth and has not heard speech, he or she often will require special intensive instruction on the ability to see and then form words in speech. Today there is a marked preference for teaching the deaf child usable speech as well as the sign language which we so commonly see practiced as communication between the deaf. These special programs give the blind child and the deaf child the opportunity to socialize and empathize with other children who share the burden of the same sensory loss. They do not have to feel so isolated and so alone. Younger children quickly learn through the courage and dexterity of older ones with the same defect that there is a way toward the future, even though it may initially appear ominously dark or silent.

The teaching in these specialized educational programs is carefully paced to the gradual acquisition of learning skills. Other sensory skills are stressed but the absent sensory function must not be ignored. The blind youngster must be taught to "see" with his hands, his ears, his imagination. The deaf child must be taught to learn by the vibrations he feels, the lips he reads, the reactions he sees, the colors, the sensations, the visual images of life. These sensations form the foundations of learning. Because of the intense quality and intricate nature of the educational process for these children, which is often so diametrically opposed to that of children without sensory deficits, the concept of very early education must be acknowledged and accepted. In fact, if your community does not offer these early specialized programs for the education of the blind and the deaf, then there is a serious deficiency in the special education facilities in your area which requires *immediate* attention and remediation. If you have a child with a serious hearing or sight deficiency, you should expect the local or state school system to provide a special school situation for your child either on a daytime or residential basis. If this does not exist, consult your legislative representative as well as the state superintendent for special education to request an explanation and possible expedient action. Do not be put off or postponed. Your child needs this help desperately—now!

As blind children grow, their sense of isolation and "differentness" must be overcome. The best way to handle this very delicate problem is for the special program to arrange for them to spend part of their school day within the regular local schools, where they can mature and develop improved social and educational skills. Many of these youngsters go on to higher education independently, realizing the full potential of their lives though sightless. They have received something even more than their outer vision; they have been given an inner vision of themselves as worthwhile, potentially successful, functional members of the total society. This inner sight more than compensates for the mystery of the darkened outer world for many of these bright and well-educated children. If you are the parents of a totally blind child, your goal must be to see that you and the school help your youngster realize the full glow of that inner vision of self . . . that positive sense that, despite the disability, the world can be conquered. Integration into the regular school goes a long way toward this goal. Blind children can play basketball, swim, learn to play musical instruments, act and paint with skill and feeling. Blind children can also date during school activities. If your child is sightless, make certain that he or she has the opportunity to sample all of these important gifts that life offers. Carefully examine the school environment to make very sure that your child is not being pampered, coddled, or made to feel helpless and "different" to a debilitating degree.

The deaf child often finds himself feeling a great deal more isolated from the world around him than other children—even those who are blind. Too often, schools for the deaf provide a superb and supportive educational environment but do not permit much social experimentation on the child's part. It is our feeling that these young people need the same degree and intensity of integration with their normal peers as any other child. If your child has a profound hearing loss, join the school in a combined effort to introduce this child into "normal" society after he or she has learned the minimal social and interrelating skills sufficient to feel comfortable with his peers. It will be in this "mainstreamed," daily society that the deaf child will be attempting to find employment; it is with these "normal" people that the deaf child must learn to cope, to relate, to communicate. This is the outer world of this inner-directed child. He must be introduced to that world before his graduation from the special program where he receives his education. As he learns to get along in a hearing and speaking world, although the lessons may be slow and painful, he will respond with great emotional strength from the rewards of his social success. This strength may encourage him to reach just a little bit higher in the expectations and goals he holds for himself. The key to the rearing and education of these sensory defective children is to give them the fortitude to reach the highest possible rung on their ladder of their accomplishment. Settling for less is too often the legacy of educational and social stigma.

As the parent of a blind child or a deaf child, do not accept anything less than the highest possible rung on the ladder. If the innate intelligence is there, expect the special program to tap it and bring forth the well-spring of your child's potential. You must join the school by encouraging your child. You must never take the negative way out of expecting far less from this child than the other children in the house or neighborhood. Do not accept excuses based on the sensory defect; do not reinforce self-pity. As much as it hurts and causes you inner anguish, insist that your sightless or deaf child reach high in everything he or she does. Give him the faith, the confidence, and the courage. And make certain that the schools in your area are giving him the education, the skills, the social stimulation, and integration . . . and the sense that he can be what his brain and his hopes want him to be if it fits within the minor limitations of his sensory defect. The blind child may not see the world around him but he will feel your pride, your confidence, and your strivings to get him the best education possible. The deaf child may not hear your praises but he can see your smile, watch your interest, and know your drive to open up life's educational treasures for him.

Four people must never give up on these children: the teacher, the parents, and the child.

17 The Child with Physical Handicaps

As you watch your infant in his crib, it soon becomes very clear that he is not moving around as much as you had expected. He seems taut and tight. When you wash him, his body arches like a bowstring. Your sense of anxiety increases; intuitively, you know that something very serious lies behind the unusual things that you have been seeing and fearing. You make an appointment to see your doctor. After a long and seemingly endless examination, he turns to you, his face ashen gray, despite the surface of professional control. Before he can utter a word, you clutch at the arms of the chair preparing yourself to hear the sentence that condemns your child to a life outside the normal world of children. Vaguely you hear the doctor use terms like "spastic muscles" and "abnormal muscle movements." Finally, you can focus on his grim and pained face long enough to make out his request that you seek the additional advice of a neurologist. You ask quietly if the problem seems serious to him. He does not answer, he merely nods his head. You lift your child from the examining table, suddenly exquisitely aware of the years that lie ahead, wondering how many of those years you will be holding this growing child in your arms.

The following week, you are seated in the neurologist's office next to your husband or wife watching the neurologist repeat the same examination very carefully and thoroughly, moving very slowly from test to test. Your child lies, disinterested but uncomplaining, while his tightly stretched muscles are tapped, pulled, moved in every possible direction. Finally the neurologist picks up the baby, gently lays him in the crook of your arm, and slowly lowers himself into his chair. As he raises his eyes to face the two of you, he begins speaking in a solemn, deep, consoling voice. Both of you are ready this time. You listen carefully, absorbing each word like a parched sponge. But his words do not fill you—they are barren, arid words that leave you feeling empty inside. "Your child has cerebral palsy." You can barely listen. "He may never walk. His legs are more damaged than his arms. He will need physical therapy which must begin as soon as possible."

Finally you look at the neurologist and ask the vital question: "Will he be normal as far as his intelligence is concerned?" The air hangs heavily with the silence. This is the moment both of you have been dreading. Finally, the neurologist smiles a wan but reassuring grin. "I think so." To nobody's surprise, both of you begin to cry very softly. You were prepared for the "cerebral palsy" by this time. But you had not even dared to hope that your child could have a useful intelligence. Now a ray of hope streaks across the dark corners of your current thoughts. Suddenly you are facing a new and complex set of problems. If he is at least average intellectually, you must start thinking about his schooling. You turn to the doctor and ask in a grateful but concerned voice, "But what kind of school should we be looking for? What can we expect from the schools around here that will be right for him?"

You have just asked the $64,000 question. What is available for the intellectually average child with significant physical handicaps? This is a question that plagues hundreds of thousands of parents every year across our nation. What should they expect from the local school system when it has to deal with their physically handicapped child?

Parents with children who are burdened with this problem first must learn which questions to ask. And they must become able to formulate their own answers, with the assistance of the child's various doctors, physical therapists, and psychologists. The child with physical disabilities will have many professionals working with him who will know his potentials, his capabilities as well as or better than his parents. The parents must ask the following questions of themselves and of these professionals before they approach the local school system to negotiate an arrangement for educating their handicapped youngster.

What are these questions?

1. Will my child be able to attend the regular school or will he/she require a special school setting designed for the handicapped child?
2. Will my child require special arrangements for transportation back and forth to school?
3. Where along the spectrum of training possibilities does my child lie after considering his/her disability? Should we encourage him to "think big" and go for the professional future or is it more realistic

to begin planning for vocational training? Maybe his potential lies somewhere in between—but where?

4. In what type of extracurricular activities will my child be able to participate?

5. How can I give my child a sense of self—a realization that he/she is an important, significant member of our society, his own peer group, and his family despite his deformity? How can I work with the educational system so that my very special child can get the most out of his education and, as a result, reach his full potential as a human being?

Such questions are neither simple nor easy. But each requires careful consideration by parent and professional when the future of one of these physically handicapped youngsters is placed in front of us so that it can be considered, planned, and structured. The parents must be aware of the whole spectrum of possibilities so that they approach the school system with intelligent and appropriate requests. And, if the school system is unable to fulfill their requests or offer acceptable alternative options, the parents of the physically handicapped child must fight to gain the best possible program from the educational system for that child.

Let us consider each of the questions in turn. As parents, let us honestly look at the options and realistically place the particular child in the proper category as each possibility is reviewed. The most destructive attitude toward a physically handicapped child is one that denies a handicap exists. To avoid obvious limits while searching blindly for impossible goals will only cause continual disappointment and disillusionment for the parents. For the child, the result is a series of failures which will undermine his self-image so effectively that he will be far more emotionally handicapped than physically limited. The physically handicapped youngster himself may want a too-distant star. However, the finite success of one's life is touching a reachable star and causing it to shine with brilliance and a continual glow. The same must be true for the physically disabled child. Overreaching only leads to tragedy. Parents must be ever on the alert for this possibility in themselves, in their child, and in the school and the professionals working there.

The first question is to determine what type of school would be most appropriate for your physically disabled child. If the physical handicap does not seriously limit the youngster's movements, then there is a very real possibility that he or she may be able to function in the regular school environment. Parents must remember, however, that the normal school setting is constructed for the agile, physically competent child, who can maneuver stairways, sharp corners, and hurried changes of classes from one floor to another. If your child's physical deformity will impede his keeping pace with his classmates, then the decision is a major one. Can the value of continued association and ultimate acceptance by the peer group outweigh the strain of "trying to keep up" physically in the normal school setting? Will the sense of being with everyone else compensate for the reality of being significantly different physically?

Often school officials will make special concessions to the mildly handicapped youngster with physical problems so that he/she can remain within the regular school environment. These are possibilities that every parent should investigate when contemplating retaining the physically handicapped youngster within the regular school. The scheduling of classes may be arranged so that all the child's classes are on the same floor, preferably the ground floor. The handicapped youngster's curriculum may be so designed that the essential courses are programmed with an hour between each so that he can slowly and carefully make his way from class to class with the dignity of independence but without the strain and embarrassment of constantly entering late. He can be assigned a student helper. Physical education classes and recess, depending upon the child's age, can be painful hours. Exclusion because of a physical handicap often kindles a bitter self-resentment directed against one's own body, which is viewed as the braking force preventing group participation. This should be avoided at all costs. If the physically disabled child remains within the regular school, then these special times should be scheduled in advance with activities that are more sedentary but equally important to school functioning and classmate esteem. Special projects, office work, library assignments, artistic contributions to the school such as posters, signs, and so on, can fill those "left-out" hours with work that will gain recognition from others and satisfy the inner need for the bright but handicapped child for positive accomplishment. Another good way to raise his self-esteem and fill up non-mobile hours within the school day is to tutor other, usually younger, children, who are experiencing academic difficulty. All of these adjustments will help the physically impaired child to adapt to the regular school environment, with acceptance by his peers and himself the primary target.

Some children's physical deformities simply rule out maneuvering in the regular school. Many children live with wheelchairs or cumbersome leg braces. They will need the added protection of a specially constructed setting that has been architecturally designed with the handicapped child in mind. Each community *must* have such a school within driving distance from all residential locales. No severely handicapped child can be allowed to vegetate at home with intermittent home teaching on a permanent basis because there is no specifically structured school setting that is safe and maneuverable for him/her. Special schools are often constructed with elevators and ramps. Corners are rounded. Classes may be on one floor. Hand rails line each wall, announcing the immediate support to a possible fall. Classrooms are designed for wheelchairs and may contain equipment such as backrests for children who must stand because of muscular contractures or spinal deformities. Excellent examples of these specially constructed schools can be seen throughout the land and serve as fine examples for those communities who are belatedly preparing to correct an intolerable deficiency within their own area.

The decision whether to choose a "regular" or a "special" school placement is often a very difficult one for parents to have to make. But it is here that honesty about the youngster's physical problem is so essential. Attempting to force a seriously or multiply handicapped youngster into a regular school setting often will lead to severe social and personal frustrations for the child. The parents must assess the extent of the physical handicap, estimate the degree of success or difficulty that young person will experience in the regular school setting, approach the physicians and physical therapists for additional opinions, and then consult the regular school personnel to ascertain exactly what the structural problems and scheduling conflicts are that might confront the particular child. By bringing together personal, professional, and educational assessments in this way, parents can ultimately arrive at the appropriate school placement for their physically handicapped child.

It may be possible to send your child with physical problems to the regular school. But how is he or she to get there? He usually cannot walk to school with the other children. The exhaustion he might experience after attempting to "go the distance" even by leaving the house a long time before the other children could prevent him from participating fully in the day's activities. If you succeed in negotiating a special curriculum and special assignments, then the next step may be arranging for special transportation that will take your child to school and bring him home. If you can drive the child back and forth yourself, your problem obviously is solved—except for the cost. Many schools reimburse parents for this. Not all parents are quite so fortunate. Father and mother work; or there may be only one car in the family which the father must use early in the morning to get to work. When these problems exist, the parent must bargain with the central school administration about transportation. Some school systems have special bus services for the physically handicapped children, whether they are registered in the regular or the special school. Others provide transportation only for those severely handicapped youngsters who must attend a special school—a situation that too often forces the parent to accept placement in the special school because transportation has become an insurmountable problem. Here the school system is being penny-wise and dollar foolish, and may also be acting illegally. It is far more cost effective to retain these physically handicapped young people within the regular school environment; it is also a positive boost for their psychological image of themselves and their future social growth. If you have managed to negotiate a satisfactory school arrangement for a handicapped child but come up against the problem of transportation, you must take up this issue with fervor. Your child is suffering from the short-sighted reasoning of a school system that is in urgent need of "parent power" to facilitate change.

Johnny had a quick and intelligent mind, but he was so crippled with severe cerebral palsy that he had to attend a special school a distance from his suburban home. Because of the distance and the wide dispersion of children needing transportation, Johnny was picked up at 6:30 A.M. He rode the bus for two hours, was dismissed from school at three in the afternoon, and arrived home at five in the evening too exhausted to eat a decent meal. He would usually fall asleep soon after dinner unable to do his homework, dreading the next day's long, dull, fatiguing bus ride. There was hardly any wonder that Johnny was doing poorly in school, learning little, usually arriving unprepared, often falling asleep in class. How can this situation be corrected? There are several solutions. The quickest, most effective, yet most expensive is the use of more buses. Or school could be scheduled in shifts, half-day segments with concentrated curriculum assignments. This again would halve the busload and permit more time at home for preparation without significantly diminishing the amount of schooling. But another important aspect of the long bus ride was being overlooked. If someone had been assigned to the bus to stimulate, orally instruct, lead the children in song or story; the ride would have seemed shorter and would have been a profitable, exciting learning experience. Imagination is the first ingredient in solving problems. If we just accept the status quo, whether as parents, educators, or administrators, we will never solve the problems facing the schoolchildren for whom each of us has a share of the responsibility.

When you look at your disabled child and begin thinking about his or her future, are you being realistic or do you fantasize about what you would like him to be? This decision-making process is so crucial for the parent of the physically handicapped child. How should he be encouraged to attempt to overcome the hurdles of his handicap? What is a realistic vocational goal? What are his future possibilities in society? Because as parents our feelings for our children are a natural blend of reality and fantasy, of wishes and facts, yearnings and truth, we badly need the objectivity of external advisers to guide us. Consultation with the school doctor, the family doctor, or physical therapist will give you some idea of the degree of improvement possible in the physical deformities that currently limit the youngster's performance. Does surgery or any type of therapy hold out hope of significant muscular and activity improvement? All this is important for the child's choice of career in the future.

What is the child's potential intellectually? Is he or she bright enough to warrant hopes of a college or university degree? Does he have the emotional stamina and reserve to withstand the double stresses of physical handicap and graduate school demands? A consultation with the school or a private psychologist or guidance counsellor will give you objective, unbiased information about your disabled child's intelligence, aptitude, and emotional maturity, so that you can be realistic in evaluating the appropriateness of those high aspirations you harbor privately but passionately.

The child's daily achievement within the classroom is the best test of performance level. And no one can evaluate the caliber of his or her educational progress and pacing (as well as giving insights into the future) as cogently and perceptively as the sensitive, concerned, and talented teacher. If your child is fortunate enough to have such a teacher, ask for her or his opinion. It will provide you with the essential day-by-day information of your handicapped child's current learning style and educational speed. It should be stressed here that most teachers who are involved with the physically handicapped child have been extensively trained in this field or have indicated a particular interest in teaching and supporting these special children. Therefore the physically handicapped child has a high likelihood of having a superior teacher. He or she needs one. He must have someone who understands his physical, his emotional, and his educational problems. If your handicapped youngster is being taught by someone whose disinterest and lack of experience in the field of the physically disabled schoolchild is all too evident, complain with enough force and fervor to be heard as far as City Hall. Again, marshall your parent forces to create a collective voice that will bring about change and prevent a recurrence. Often the group should be pressuring for the future—for proper college training for the upcoming teachers who will teach your special children. If this is not done, there is little likelihood that expert teachers will become immediately available in this unique teaching field. Sometimes, the parent group will have to request that the teachers of the physically handicapped be given extra incentive pay, sufficient to attract the very best staff and reward a teacher whose day is occupied with the double task of teaching and administering to the special needs of these very special children.

Having consulted with the physician, the physical therapist, the psychologist, and the teacher, you still have one more essential person to consult—the child! He or she must be offered the same privilege every other young person should be given in this life. He must have a significant part in shaping and determining his own destiny. What does he want to do with his life? What are his pleasures and his talents; what are her own dreams for herself? All of us have dreams. Without them, we are like barren trees, our dry, cracking, days falling as dead leaves into nothingness. The child without dreams for himself worries us more than any other—he has no sense of self, no ego, no identity. Don't let this happen to your handicapped child. He is *somebody*. Let him know this by including him in designing his own future . . . and get him the schooling necessary to take him there.

The vocational possibilities for handicapped people today cover a wide range. The young person whose future lies in a nonskilled area must be made to understand that any future work possesses the same dignity, the same esteem that the more skilled professions presume. The truth is that our world could not function with any degree of coherence or order without the contributions of *all* workers. Consider for one moment how any of us would survive without the skills of the plumber, the carpenter, the electrician, the secretary, the television repairman, the farmer, the car mechanic, the house painter, the cook, and the sanitarian—to name but a few vocations that keep us functioning daily. If the decision is that the physically handicapped youngster can best be directed toward one of these vocations, he or she must be impressed by the importance—the dignity—of that work.

Does your community have the schools that will prepare a physically disabled child to learn a vocation? Is there a special high school that teaches typing skills, plumbing and carpentry, graphic arts, etc., to the young person who has physical disabilities? Can the regular vocational high school adapt and accept the physically handicapped child? Somewhere within the immediate community in which you live there must be such a place where your handicapped child—or your neighbor's child—can receive this training and become a fulfilled, contributing member of community and society.

Further, if the physically handicapped young person is in a special school or school program designed for the severely disabled, the parents must make certain that the school also schedules special extracurricular activities that go beyond the daily teaching hours. The sense of group participation and the satisfaction of competing and performing in debating, newspaper work, art exhibits, and so on, are essential to the overall education of the severely handicapped youngster in his or her drive to become a social individual. If necessary, the parents themselves may have to gain permission to organize these activities so that these isolated youngsters have the opportunity to expand their horizons.

The last question that must be answered is by far the most important: How can I give my physically handicapped child a true sense of self-worth? Without this, he will have to constantly fight his way upstream, then gradually give up, sinking to the quiet bottom of the mainstream of life immured by an implacable self-pity and self-hate. Parent and teacher must work together with insight and constant awareness to reinforce this youngster positively so that he feels a sense of accomplishment and the realization of moving forward. But to do this, both parent and teacher *must* believe that the child has worth, potential, and the makings of an important, contributing member of society. They must see the glowing possibilities beneath the twisted exterior. They must work to unbend the mind and the skills even though the body may be reluctant to straighten completely. There must be a joint dedication by parent and teacher to the future of this child. The child will feel it, know it, and will accept and integrate this trust and faith into his own self-esteem. This will act as the initial life force that will get him over the first hurdle of accepting *himself.* If parent and teacher challenge the handicapped youngster with tasks that can be accomplished considering the disability, tasks at which he can succeed, then the subsequent success can be constantly used as a positive reinforcement which encourages the disabled youngster to push just a little bit harder to reach the possible.

One of our professional friends has a severely handicapped son who was unusually bright and alert. Both parents worked very hard to give him the impression that he could attain what he wanted if he worked at it. He needed wheelchairs for mobility; he could not get to the bathroom with ease. His parents sent him to a special school for the physically handicapped where he graduated from high school with honors. But where was he to go for college? He learned that there was a college that would take him on one of two conditions: either he must have a companion who would wheel him from class to class and assist him in his toileting, or he must be mobile, walk with braces to his classes, and manage to care for his own personal hygiene. This boy had never walked alone. He faced a difficult decision. His parents offered to hire the companion, but he knew that the expense was far beyond what they could afford.

Finally one day, he turned to his mother and father and asked directly, without emotion, "Do you think I could learn to walk?" There was an immediate negative inner reaction which both parents managed to stifle. After a long silence his mother, herself a physician, responded: "Anything is possible. But it may not happen. And it will be very, very hard." He nodded. Then he said, "You must promise to let me try this my way . . . by myself. Do not interfere." His parents stared at each other for a difficult moment, then quietly agreed.

The young man closeted himself in his bedroom upstairs, asking that his meals be brought up to him. Day after day, his mother heard him lift himself out of the wheelchair and fall with a deafening, horrible thump upon the floor the sounds echoing through the small house. The parents tightened their grip on their chairs, bit their lips, cried silently, but did not move to climb the stairs and help him. Weeks passed, and the falling continued. When she brought his meals to him every day, his mother noticed fresh bruises. All she said was, "How is it going?" He would smile and comment, "Better. I'm going to make it." She would nod and say simply, "We will help if you need us," and leave his room. The parents felt the need to escape from the house more often than usual to run away from the deafening sound of their son falling on the floor above their heads.

About two months later, when she brought his breakfast upstairs, he looked at her and smiled. "Ask Daddy to come in, please." She quickly called her husband. When he arrived, the boy slowly and carefully pulled himself up out of the wheelchair, and, using two heavy canes as support, walked laboriously and awkwardly across the length of the room by himself. "By next week, I'll make it to the bathroom," was his only remark. This young man was admitted to the college and is now a successful junior. The last time one of us saw him was at the Kennedy Center in Washington, D.C., where after leaving his wheelchair at the head of the aisle and taking up his heavy canes, he walked slowly and calmly to his seat in the theater in front of his proud parents.

There are heights to which the physically handicapped can rise that far exceed the parent's, the teacher's, even the doctor's expectations. But behind these magnificent achievements lies a wealth of positive thinking, positive education, and positive parenting. Each of these people has given the physically handicapped child the will and the drive and the knowledge to try for the highest possible level.

18 The Mentally Retarded Child

Do you remember the first time you learned that your child was mentally retarded? You probably have a difficult time forgetting it.

The first "official" notification likely came through a doctor. It is possible that you were lying in your hospital bed, thanking God for the new baby, when your doctor walked through the door with his eyes downcast and his jaw tightly set. You did not want to say anything, you didn't even want to think it, but suddenly you found yourself asking, almost screaming, "There's something wrong with my baby, isn't there?" And he silently nods, and tells you about Down's Syndrome or Mongolism. You want to cry. "My baby is a Mongolian idiot!" you think. "I'm cursed, not blessed. Dear God, what have I done to deserve this?"

Or maybe the diagnosis came after an endless nightmare series of tests. You were sitting in his inner office. You intuitively knew by the way the nurse told you to make yourself comfortable that she expected you to be with the doctor for a long time. Something deep within you even knew what the doctor was going to say. But you hoped desperately that it would not be said. You have been trying to get ready for it but there does not seem to be any way to prepare for words like these. Your son is not doing the things which all the other children in the neighborhood are doing at his age. You know, also, that the child is physically immature. Your mind races and thinks: he may be just a little bit slow, but I honestly think he is retarded. The word cuts through your mind like a knife's edge. *"Retarded,* my God. I've said it, after all this time."

And finally your doctor spoke the words that told you for certain that your child was retarded. "Please, doctor, forgive my crying. I tend to get emotional when I hear bad things about my children. I'll be all right, I think."

190

The Mentally Retarded Child

But then, what were you actually told? As painful as it might be to relive this, try to remember what you were told after that first moment. And by whom? Did he give you words to memorize: like *Educable Mentally Retarded,* which means a child with an IQ of between 60 and 80 and generally capable of public school special education; or *Trainable Mentally Retarded,* a child with an IQ of less than 60, usually requiring a special placement in an institution or in a class of his intellectual equals; or *Profoundly Retarded,* that crippling phrase that suggests an almost irremediable level of mental potential; or *Adaptive Behavior,* a scale of measuring how well the child can function in learning living skills; or *Sheltered Workshop,* a special job situation created for training mentally retarded adults; or . . . the words are many and familiar to you now, but they were foreign and terrifying then.

After you were first told that your child was retarded, what happened to shape your thinking and your plans about that special child? Did your doctor advise you to send the child to an institution and "forget" about him? Less than a few decades ago, this was standard advice; and many parents did institutionalize these special children, trying afterwards to fight the guilt that enveloped this separation. Most parents bore the external stigma of "abandoning" their child. Most of today's doctors do not give this painful advice because society, child care, education, and training for the mentally retarded child have all improved so much that keeping the child in your home is not only rewarding to you but beneficial to the child as well. In the past, your doctor might have given the best advice if he suggested that you institutionalize your retarded child. Now such an action is usually the parents' last resort.

Possibly after the initial diagnosis of retardation, you were told to try to enroll your child in a day class or a class at a special residential school. All decisions were hard. Your head was full of questions: What could you do? Did you envisage your child or want to envisage him as a child who might someday "catch up" with the rest of his age group? Did you think of giving him a "head start" by enrolling him in a special nursery school? Did you consider having tutors come to your home? Did you try teaching your child yourself to see if the doctors and the psychologists were wrong? In the past, you would have been thwarted and blocked for the lack of resources and knowledge to do one of these things. Today, the educational system is growing up into the proper resources which allow the teaching of the retarded with skill and dignity.

Did anyone advise you to read the biographies of retarded children and their families? Did you hear any of the politicians tell their campaign audiences about how *special* retarded children were? ("Retarded children are love," is their message.) You find yourself looking at your child, your own "Angel Unawares" as a special trial—your passport into martyrdom. Your child has become your atonement. Did you feel this guilt? This anxiety? Did you love him freely? Did you have trouble disciplining him? Did you expect that special child ultimately to hurt you?

Part of today's educational process for the retarded must include the counsel and education of the family of the retarded child. Perhaps you met other parents of retarded children through the Association for Retarded Citizens' groups. These parents very likely shared with you the similar special problems that they were having with their retarded children. During these sessions, you might have met one of those unique parents who talked about *all* of his children; and during his conversation, you had trouble distinguishing which one of his children was retarded. "Yes, Jane is retarded," this father would finally tell you, "but Tom is terribly rebellious, and Carolyn's weight problem never stops." And as he talked about his family, you heard the story of understanding, acceptance, and equality for which you had been searching for years. Here was a parent who had realized that his retarded child was a child first and foremost; a retarded child after that. But didn't you wonder when that parent would wake up and become disappointed and disillusioned? Wasn't he, after all, just deluding himself? The child is, was, and always would be retarded. Others would know it for all of the child's life. Why shouldn't the parents? The answers to these profound and probing questions all fall within the scope of the educational process for your retarded child.

If your child was born within the last ten years, there has been a little of each of these experiences in your life; you have sampled all these feelings and expectations. Why are we asking you to remember and reassess these expectations and feelings for your retarded child? Because this book is about your "slow" child in the educational system, *and your control of that system* to get your child to the highest point of his or her intellectual mountain. Above all, it is about your battle with negative expectations about your retarded child.

Education has long been criticized as a haven for mediocrity. Ask any parent of a gifted or talented child what their biggest problem is with the school system. Often they will tell you that their problems center on trying to get specialized educational opportunities and experiences for their children that transcend those offered for the "average" student. You can figure that if one teacher has to deal with thirty students all day every day, that teacher will employ the best methods for reaching the largest number possible in that crowded situation. She will sight her targets, therefore, at the average level. When this occurs, those children who have more talents or intelligence than the average may not know that they have that larger capacity. They may even feel that it is wrong to use their intelligence. They finish faster and simply become bored. If they demand special attention, they are accused by jealous classmates of being "teacher's pet." And so such students achieve the "averageness" of their peers. The teacher is prevented from having to face her failure in reaching and teaching all children by the standard, acceptable performance of these talented youngsters in the analysis of the class as a whole.

But if the parents of that gifted or talented child, who are aware of their child's unique talents, persevere and insist on special programming, then the teacher will have to try to teach to that child's special capabilities. Thus, the parent becomes the watchdog over his child's education and the chief advocate of that pupil's special capabilities.

Can you see the parallel situation which exists in the case of the mentally retarded child?

Let us explain a little further. Being retarded does *not* mean that all the functions of a child are depressed. A child with great difficulties in abstract reasoning can still have above average social skills. Some of our best athletes came from classes for the retarded, meaning that physical abilities are not necessarily "retarded" when that all-inclusive label is applied to a whole child. A child who cannot write creatively may still function superbly in the house. A child does not have to know algebra to make change in a grocery store.

You must remember this: your retarded child is a complex human being, made up of many possible and different abilities and skills, who has a measured deficiency in most of the academic skills.

The competent special education teacher in the public school will attempt to teach your retarded child to master many of the skills that he or she will need to adjust properly to life after school. In doing so, your child's teacher should indicate that she recognizes and accepts your child as a *child* and not as a "retardate." The special education teacher also has a large number of children in her class. She has to face the task of trying to teach this many children the maximum amount they can assimilate in a single day. She, too, will tend to teach to the "average" level of that special class. This is natural—but dangerous.

In the case of teaching a mentally retarded child, it is downright criminal. And that is where you must help. You must enable the teacher to perceive your child as a child—with strengths despite his retardation. You will have to help her (or him) to see your child as Jane Clark, not as a 76 IQ. You will have to help her see your child as a future wage earner, not just a kid with a very limited vocabulary. They will need to see your child as a potential companion or a husband, not as an eternal child with freckles and blue eyes and an inability to read.

True, it is stressed constantly to these teachers that the children under their care are very different from each other—but so it is to the teachers of non-handicapped children. It is just that human nature—plus a frequent lack of time and resources—prohibits your child's special education teacher from completely "individualizing" the instruction or remembering that your child exists as an individual both inside and outside the classroom.

So, in order to serve the proper preschool, elementary, secondary, and post-secondary education for your child with retardation, it is going to be necessary for you to do some extensive homework—and then some schoolwork. Essentially, your home assignment is the honest assessment of your child's strengths and weaknesses as a total human being, and specifically as a learning person. Your school assignment is to plan your child's educational future with the special education personnel in your school by creating a continuing dialogue about your child.

A good way to start the homework is to take a paper with a line drawn down the middle, labeling the left-hand column "Strengths" and the right-hand column "Weaknesses." Start by asking yourself probing questions about your child. Try to open doors that have been mercifully closed in the past, but do not neglect the positive qualities either. Compare him or her to all of the other children you have known. Ask the essential questions: Is he capable of showing love? Is he appealing and pleasant? Does he play with others? Can he express simple ideas? sequential ideas? complex thoughts? Can he follow instructions of either a simple or a complex nature? What are his good and bad physical habits? Is he motivated toward working? toward learning? What kinds of work does he like? Can he influence other adults or children to do what he wants them to do? Under what circumstances? Does he have special interests? Are there activities that "turn him on"?

What is his attitude toward school? What does he say about the teachers and other adults at school? and his classmates? What vocational and educational games does he like to play? What sports does he like and which is he skilled at? What radio or television programs does he enjoy? What does he usually do in his leisure time? Does he have serious or continuing health problems? Who are his special friends? Are there any significant adults in his life other than parents? Do you have any discipline problems with him? How does he handle authority? What motivates him? And, finally, from what kind of a family does he come? Essentially, have you been supportive, tolerant, submissive, frightened, denying, smothering, or challenging to your child?

Take each question and decide if your answer is a strength or a weakness in relation to the total child and his or her educational prospects. Make your list and analyze each column carefully. Think of those things on the list that you particularly value and that you think you can help cultivate. Check off those traits which you think are especially reinforceable in school. Think of those characteristics which you have listed that require or will require more discipline. And decide which attitudes or desires will help him explore vocational areas or may prove particularly useful in the future.

Next, circle the traits which you feel are best handled in school by the special educators. You are now ready to negotiate with the school system about your child's future.

Armed with this homework and a desire to establish a good relationship with the special education personnel at your child's school, set up an appointment with the appropriate person—probably the child's special teacher. Keep the conversation continually focused on your child and, particularly, on his or her future.

You must now share your child's strengths and weaknesses with the special educator. After you have gone over your list, it would be wise to ask whether your observations match her opinion of your child. Probe for any further elaboration of both strengths and weaknesses which you may have omitted or not known about. Speak clinically if possible—remove yourself from the parent role and try to view your child from a distant perspective so that you can be as objective as possible, though this is extremely difficult for a parent to do.

With the help of the school personnel, you must attempt to evolve an educational plan for your child. Many of the other valuable professional personnel—school psychologist, school physician, school nurse, and social worker—may have important contributions to make to this long-range plan for the child. You must make certain that you have received the help of these expanded professional resources; your child will need all the expert advice he and you can bring together in order to structure his future. But by this we do not mean a technical plan, which predicts that "by 1988 your child will be expected to know how to hold down a job, to count change, to read newspapers, and to go unaccompanied to the movies." Rather, the plan we are proposing will inform you how the teachers will be educating your child, what the child should be learning, and *for what purpose.* Together, you and the school have to define what are the long-range objectives of your child's education; essential to this are the methods and strategies the teachers are going to use in attempting to reach those objectives.

There are four essential questions to be dealt with here:

1. What specific skills and information is the child going to be taught which, unlike the traditional school material, will be directly applicable to his or her life after school? You must not accept answers like, "He will read at a fourth grade level," or, "He will be able to do simple math." Ask specifically, what newspapers, books, and signs will he be able to read when he has finished the school program? What everyday math situations will he be able to handle with his arithmetic background? What aspects of dating or companionable behavior will he learn in school? What will he be taught in school that will help him live independently? Will he learn about sex and birth control? Where will he find the necessary information and help to obtain and hold an appropriate job? In other words, what practical skills will your child be taught?

2. What will the educational system be doing to help your child explore different interests and aptitudes with a view to his or her life after school? Will he be able to take part in vocational learning experiences? Is the school system going to offer him many possible experiences in different kinds of work in order to determine his motivations and interests? Will the school introduce him to successful retarded adults who are engaged currently in work which might prove applicable for him? Will the skills he is learning in the educational setting be useful and applicable in the work he is considering as a future job? How early will work-related words like "salary," "time clock," "vacation schedule," "employment," "job rating," and "routine" be introduced into the experience of the retarded

child? And what is being done to help the child visualize himself as a potentially successful worker?

3. What are the school's expectations for your retarded child? This is the question that really challenges the special educator to declare whether your child is seen as a person with positive and negative qualities or merely as a stereotyped "retardate." And generally, this is the question which receives the most realistic response, if it is phrased in a non-threatening way, such as: "If you were to predict where my child would be in ten years, what would you say?" The teacher's answer is vital to you and your child; you should not rest until you get it. You must realize that research has shown that if the teacher has low expectations for *any* child, the child will meet only those diminished expectations, no matter how high his innate interest or abilities. Thus it is important that both you and all the teachers involved hold the highest rational expectations possible— expectations that have resulted from close, objective observation of your child, and that have taken into account all the child's strengths as well as his weaknesses. If you are sure that you have arrived at this mutual understanding with the school personnel, then you will be more certain that your child will be encouraged to reach his or her maximum capacity. If the expectations are based on a stereotyped model and do not take the uniqueness of every human being into account, your retarded child will be only partially challenged. You will never know his full potential and he will remain on the bottom rung of the ladder.

4. Finally, where do you, the parent, fit into the educational plan? Are you an outside observer, required to report regularly to the educator on the child's noted progress? Or are you assuming an active part in the child's education? Can you receive assignments from the special educator? Are you able to take guidance from all the school personnel for the home-based problems? What can you learn from the school staff about the methods needed to teach household jobs, vocational preparation, functional skills from first-hand knowledge and involvement? Can you know, in effect, how the child's educational plan is progressing? Is there a formal or informal way to become a colleague to the special educator? Is there a good way to explain your child's education to his or her non-retarded siblings and relatives? How can you render your child's life outside school a positive reinforcement of his experience at school?

When you know the answers to these four major questions, you will have your child's educational plan. You will also be aware of his role and yours, and the objectives will be mutually agreed upon.

There is only one major problem with this plan. It must be reviewed often—probably at a minimum once per year—because children grow, change, evolve, and mature. Jobs change, expand, become obsolete, assume new requirements, change status. Teachers learn new methods, receive new books, obtain fresh personal insights, and may learn to care more deeply. And you yourself will change, progress, expand, learn to pause and contemplate your retarded child as a whole. If you can create an educational plan early enough in the child's life, you will have a blueprint to guide you. The final product will be strongly influenced by the sensitive, flexible, loving changes you make from the overall master plan. But that blueprint for action must always be in place.

It needs to be very carefully drawn up: it is the profile of the present and the future of your retarded child.

19 The Child with Chronic Physical Illness

You are walking out of the local hospital, stunned and afraid. The pediatrician has just told you that your seven-year-old son has diabetes mellitus. He had seemed so well over the summer. But soon after starting school, you noticed that he began losing weight and sleeping more than usual in the evenings. He became intermittently difficult to arouse in the mornings. Your husband noted that Richard was drinking a great deal of liquid and going to the bathroom a lot. A recent call from Richard's teacher, expressing her concern over Richard's fatigue, pallor, complaints of "stomach aches," and progressively poorer school-work, prompted you to take your son to his pediatrician. He listened to the history, performed a thorough physical, examined a blood and urine specimen, and immediately suggested that Richard go into the hospital for more extensive tests. The testing was now over and you were told the facts. Richard has diabetes—"sugar in the blood." He needs daily injections of insulin. He must be watched very closely. Suddenly you have been pushed into the unprepared position of nurse to your chronically ill child.

Standing on the sidewalk in front of the hospital, it occurs to you that you forgot to ask the hospital doctor about Richard's schooling. He had intimated that Richard could return to school as soon as possible. But what was he to do in school once he got there? What should you tell the teacher, the principal, the school nurse? How could the school help you and Richard with his diabetes? It dawns on you that for five days a week your son will be in school almost seven hours. These are crucial hours for your child: learning hours, hours of social growth, and also, now, important hours relative to the control and management of his chronic illness. Yet you forgot to ask about the role of the school in your son's illness. The doctor had carefully covered all the aspects of Richard's physical problems, meticulously outlining your role and Richard's responsibilities; but he had completely disregarded the fact that Richard would be spending so many significant waking hours in school.

It is not unusual for parents and physicians to fail to remember the very important part of the chronically ill child's life that school occupies —both in terms of actual time and emotional and intellectual significance. Usually the management of the physical and chemical aspects of the disease takes complete precedence in the parent's and physician's thinking. However, unless consideration is given to the child's return to school, the chronically ill child will find himself (or herself) without the necessary support and understanding in a neutral, under-informed environment. The school can only be expected to accomplish the necessary functions if the people within the system are fully informed and then mobilized around your child and his illness.

Let us take Richard's case to help illustrate what can and should be expected of the school system and its personnel when confronted with a pupil who is suffering from a chronic physical complaint. What should Richard's mother ask of the school in the way of assistance and necessary support for her son? What must she do to guarantee this mutual management of her son's illness while he is at school?

First, the teacher must play an extremely important role. In Richard's case, observation of his levels of awareness and alertness are essential to the management of his insulin. Daily records by the teacher of changes or variations in Richard's behavior throughout the day, continued week by week, will be of immeasurable assistance to his doctor in adjusting the dosages of insulin injected daily. Richard's mother must also inform the teacher about the symptoms of too heavy a dose and the opposite, too little insulin. Each problem will have its own specific set of symptoms. The teacher must be sensitive to these signs so that she can spot a medical emergency and alert the principal, the school nurse, or the parent—whoever the system has designated as next in line to manage the daily medical crises which might arise during Richard's school day. To substitute for the parent in monitoring Richard's chronic health problems during the hours he is under her direct surveillance, the teacher must become as informed about Richard's illness as his parents. However, the parents have to bear in mind that the teacher must teach *all* the children within her class, including Richard. Therefore if Richard's illness becomes a recurrent and persistent problem, the teacher may request that the boy's health be set on a stable basis before returning to class or that the school nurse or principal assume hourly monitoring so that she can be freed for teaching. Occasionally, the school will make the justifiable request that the child go back to the doctor for more controlled medical management before returning to the classroom because his medical problem is causing sufficient disturbance to interfere with the daily education of the other children in the classroom. Children with diabetes, seizures, chronic asthma, or low blood sugar episodes are examples of those who may need better outside medical control before the teacher can assume an appropriate level of classroom supervision over the illness.

The other person who should be fully informed about Richard's diabetes is the school nurse. The more often she is available, the more valuable a medical ally she will be to Richard and his parents. If she is frequently in school, she should become fully conversant with Richard's disease through his physician. Her ability to maintain a continuous open communication line with the boy's medical team will provide the school with the insight into changes in Richard's medications and medical status. This will permit the school to make the proper adjustments of curriculum and activities for Richard as his health changes. The school nurse can also act as liaison between teacher, principal, and the boy's medical advisers. Her ability to interpret Richard's school behavior and performance and to relate these to his current medication will provide the vitally important background for the necessary shifts in medical management. If the nurse is available either at the school or by car, she would be the logical person to deal with the immediate medical emergency that might unexpectedly happen on any one of Richard's school days. For example, knowing the signs of too much insulin and low blood sugar, the school nurse can give the boy sugar orally while waiting for the parent to assume control after the proper phone call. This relieves the teacher of the responsibility and frees the principal from the need to substitute for the busy teacher during the emergency. Both can return to their tasks knowing that Richard is in capable professional hands.

One of the very significant considerations in choosing an appropriate school for Richard after the diagnosis of his diabetes would be the availability and training of the school nurse. Several factors make a competent school nurse essential when a child has been diagnosed as having a changeable chronic physical illness. The professional nurse has the medical training and background to comprehend the disease state and its complications properly. She will be aware of the importance of

201

medication and the possible untoward reactions to prescribed medication. She will be better able to recognize the onset of crises than the teacher or principal. Communication between nurse and physician as professionals is easier. Last but far from least, the continuous availability of school nursing for the chronically ill child removes much of the anxiety of both the parents and the teacher. This allows the parents to send Richard off to school without fear—a feeling which is transmitted to the already frightened child all too often. The teacher can deal with the boy without the constant dread that she will be asked to face a medical emergency for which she has not been properly trained. Her attitude toward Richard may have been clouded by the pressures imposed upon her by his illness. She is a human being; despite her best intentions, she may become short-tempered and hostile to a boy with a potentially threatening chronic illness. You must consider the possibility of *demanding* school placement for your chronically ill child in a school that has the most efficient and available medical help—a school nurse and a school doctor. Not only will your child benefit educationally and physically but the school will be less disrupted; and you, as his parents, will be able to continue the rhythm of your own lives without the concern of frequent, unnecessary interruptions.

Richard has diabetes. But each illness has special characteristics that demand flexibility from the school. In Richard's case, he must have freedom to adjust his diet whenever he or his school observers feel that he needs more calories to prevent his blood sugar from falling too low. He must be permitted to carry a candy bar or a thermos of sweetened orange juice with him so that he may leave class and take the necessary calories to prevent a low blood sugar attack. The school nurse, principal, or teacher may be his ally in this case, storing the juice or candy bar, allowing the sudden movement from the classroom, checking frequently to see if the food prevented any serious problems. Richard may also have problems of frequency of urination when his blood sugar is higher than usual. He must be given the permission to excuse himself without embarrassment and go to the bathroom. The physical discomfort if he is refused and the emotional pain if he must frequently request bathroom privileges are examples of rigid school rules which must be discarded in the case of this particular boy. Other children with other chronic diseases require different privileges but similar flexibility. It would be extremely helpful if the physician, school nurse, or you as parents, were to inform the school officials of the special needs and considerations your child requires during the normal school day.

The Child with Chronic Physical Illness

Once informed, the system must be prepared to adjust to your child's needs as long as they are rational and not extremely disruptive to the normal school program. If you have difficulty in establishing these necessary privileges, you must stir up the system from school nurse through school physician through city health department until your child receives the proper consideration due his chronic illness and his need to attend school on a regular basis.

Richard is only seven years old. Every morning he must be injected with insulin from a needle and syringe. His diet is carefully watched by his parents. He has been told over and over again that he must not eat cookies or candy or potato chips unless his parents hand these choice items directly to him. He carries special foods to eat if he feels faint or dizzy. Does Richard feel different from the other children in his class? Of course he does—it is inconceivable that he would not.

The physician who discharged Richard from the hospital stressed to his parents that they must consider Richard's emotional well-being as well as his physical health. The pediatrician wisely suggested that Richard's parents go out of their way in an attempt to help the boy have a positive concept of himself. He should not feel strange, different, or inferior to the other children. Richard's parents have been stressing this fact to him on repeated occasions. They have pointed out the famous people who had the same chronic illness he has. They adjust his diet so that he can attend a birthday party and eat a small piece of cake without drawing the other children's attention to his empty plate. His mother and father have worked assiduously *not* to change their attitudes toward their son. His discipline remains the same; the rules and regulations around the house are unchanged from his pre-illness days. All in all, Richard's parents have done a remarkable job in helping their son not to feel set apart from the other children just because he has a chronic illness.

But they forgot one thing. How important can it be in the face of such careful home planning? The omission is of such monumental proportions that it may destroy their carefully constructed house of normalcy for their son. What Richard's parents forgot to do was enlist the help of the school in preventing the sense of separateness in their son. The personnel within the school had never dealt with a child with his illness before. They were on edge; their emotional antennae quivering in anticipation. These teachers, principal, and counsellors all act from a vantage point of compassion and caring. But they are in danger of focusing the spotlight on Richard with such intensity that he could start to retreat farther and farther into the shadows of the classroom. He may wish to become invisible, his difference having been made all too obvious and painful.

What are the school personnel doing? The teacher has moved Richard's chair to the very front of the room so that she can watch him more closely. About once an hour, she will interrupt her lesson and inquire if he is feeling well. The principal stops in every morning to ask if Richard remembered to take his insulin at home? The playground monitor only allows Richard to play for fifteen minutes at a time, forcing him to take a ten-minute rest while the other children go on playing. Richard is never kept after school even if the entire class is being disciplined; he is allowed and encouraged to leave. When he plaintively pleaded to serve his fifteen-minute punishment time, the teacher patted his head, complimented him on his bravery, and made him go home. This took place in front of the entire class. Are these isolated instances enough to make this seven-year-old boy feel odd, different, inferior to his classmates? Yes! Just one or two of them might be enough to start the chain reaction of self-pity and a poor view of himself.

The parents must help the school personnel play their proper role in allowing this boy—and all other chronically ill pupils—to feel that he is a natural, integral part of the school. Attention must not be paid openly to the child's illness. The teacher must become aware of the need to help the child be accepted by his classmates as a "normal" classmate. She or he must know only those limitations which are absolutely essential in the child's daily school existence. If physical play must be restricted, the teacher should be encouraged to plan significant alternative tasks for the child during that period—tasks that are directed toward class integration and class participation. Making signs for the class play, or setting up the display for a science class, or working with several other children on a class newspaper, are all positive activities that can be substituted for physical activity without necessarily causing the child to feel useless. Despite chronic illness, the same rules, regulations, and punishments must apply to this child. If not, he will be viewed as "special," very much the teacher's pet. The only way out of this dilemma would be openly to admit the physical illness, which most children are reluctant to do for good reasons.

Inquiries into the child's health should only be made when there is a serious question, when he actually looks ill. Then the child should be called aside or sent to the health office with as little fanfare as possible.

The Child with Chronic Physical Illness

You are Richard's parents. You assume that the school personnel will have the sensitivity to recognize the need for all of these maneuvers without you having to tell them. But ask yourselves this question. Before your son was diagnosed as having this particular chronic illness, were you as sensitive and perceptive about the feelings of chronically ill children as you are at this moment? The answer is most probably No. Just as the physician cautioned you about the need to focus on the child's self-esteem, so you must repeat the same lesson to the school staff. When they become aware of the dangers of oversolicitousness and overt concern, they will perceive (as you have) the crucial need to allow the chronically ill child to blend comfortably with his peers as much as possible.

Let us pose a problem for you to solve. You are about to enter your ten-year-old girl in a new school. You have just moved into the area, and she will be in fourth grade in the neighborhood elementary school. She is a freckled, happy, active youngster—but she has one problem. She has had moderately severe asthma since she was four years old. There is a strong tendency toward allergies and asthma in your family. She is accompanying you to school several days before the semester starts so that she can get to know the new school and you can have the opportunity to talk with the principal and the teacher. Your daughter leaves you willingly as she is introduced to a neighborhood child who volunteers to show her around. You are led into the teacher's room and sit down at a table facing a young, attractive, relatively new teacher who will be responsible for your daughter for the coming year.

First question: What information about your daughter's asthma do you want to discuss with the teacher?

(a) the strong family history of allergies?
(b) the things that appear to precipitate the attacks?
(c) the frequency of school absences during previous years?
(d) the role that emotional factors appear to play in her asthma attacks?
(e) the medications that she usually takes during the asthma season?

Consider each of the possible answers carefully, then try to think through the value of sharing each item with your daughter's new teacher.

It is highly unlikely that *(a)* is necessary for the teacher to know. The family history of allergies is important medical and historical information for the pediatrician or school nurse; the teacher will have very little use for this data in dealing with your child on a daily basis. Too often parents overload teachers with superfluous information about their child's illness. This lessens the impact of the genuinely important points that must be transmitted to the teacher so that the child will be dealt with appropriately.

But *(b)*, the factors that seem to precipitate the asthma attacks, may prove of inestimable value to the teacher and to your child. For example, if your child is highly sensitive to animal hair and dander, the teacher must be careful not to bring animals into the classroom without first excusing your child or placing her some distance away. This can prevent a sudden, embarrassing asthma attack during school. Respiratory infections frequently trigger asthma attacks in childhood. The knowing teacher can separate your child from the neighboring child who has arrived at school with an obvious cold accompanied by runny nose and loose cough. For the other child, the cold is self-limited; for your child, that same cold could be the forerunner of a serious and prolonged asthma attack. Thus *(b)* is very valuable information for your child's teacher.

As for *(c)*, children who miss school regularly because of physical illness run a very real risk of falling far behind their group and possibly failing to pass into the next grade. Special mechanisms to provide the chronically ill child with work to do at home can be planned at the beginning of the school year if the parent has had sufficient experience to estimate that a significant number of school days might be missed. If the child has already spent a school year with frequent absences, the parent may be able to advise the new teacher about which methods proved most effective in maintaining continuous learning. Talking about this ahead of time may be the key to successful functioning when such illness does occur. So *(c)* is indeed useful information.

As implied in *(d)*, emotional factors often do play a role in chronic disease. These factors may precipitate attacks of such illnesses as asthma and diabetes or play important parallel roles in such chronic childhood diseases as rheumatoid arthritis and sickle cell disease (among others). Each child has his or her own specific trigger emotional factors, which precipitate the explosion of disease or adverse reaction to a chronic disease. Many of these emotional traumas may be directly connected to the child's performance or relationship to the other children in the schoolroom. If the parent is aware of the factors within the school environment which could conceivably initiate an acute attack of a chronic disease or increase the emotional load of the child bearing the brunt of the prolonged illness, the teacher should have access to this vital information. Then preventive therapy can be attempted within the classroom to ward off any emotional triggering of the illness or reactions to it. Again, the information contained in *(d)* will prove of significant worth during the school year.

Why would it be important for the teacher to be concerned with the medications your daughter took during the last school year when she was bothered by her asthma *(e)*? The significance rests primarily in the side effects this medication may create. If the prescribed drugs appear to have no noticeable effect on your daughter's behavior or learning in the classroom, then the teacher will probably not need the full details of her medication. However, any side effects that might affect a child's school performance or adjustment in any way should be brought to the teacher's attention, with the promise that the teacher will be informed when the particular medication is begun and discontinued. Therefore, the answer to *(e)* must be a qualified Yes, if the medications create any unusual changes in your daughter's pattern of learning or behavior.

Second question: What should you expect from the school in the way of assistance to your daughter during the coming year?

(a) adjustment of her physical education program on short notice?
(b) exclusion of your daughter from outdoor sports?
(c) acceptance of her need to take medication on school premises?
(d) medical handling of the sudden, acute asthma attack?
(e) information sent home about her exposure to contagious illnesses?

The answers to this question have broad application to almost all children who have chronic physical illnesses and are enrolled in school. Parents must be realistic about what they can expect from the school for their child. If the school falls short of the ideal in the case of the chronically ill child, the parents must assume the responsibility of attempting to change the set-up so that their child (and all other chronically ill children) does not find herself shunted off into the corner of the schoolroom to experience the sense of failure in her education along with her health.

Every parent should expect the school to be sufficiently flexible to adjust the physical activity schedule of their particular child whenever health problems demand this move. Requiring the chronically ill child to participate when ill is educational malpractice. But refusing to allow the child the opportunity to participate in physical games and physical education because her attendance is known to be erratic is a thoroughly negative approach and should be fought by the parents until solved. Expect your school to be flexible in this issue—accept nothing less than this flexibility. The answer to *(a)* is a very definite Yes.

Do not expect the school to do *(b)*, however. This may be a totally inappropriate way of overprotecting a child with a chronic disease. Only when the physician who has been caring for your child over a prolonged period and thoroughly understands her illness makes the decision that all sports are forbidden should you permit your child to be totally excluded from outdoor sports. Erratic attendance at practice is not a valid excuse for excluding the chronically ill child. In some schools, this feeble excuse will be attempted as a means of keeping the less agile, less strong child off the team. Do not accept this reasoning if you are the parent. School sports are not primarily for winning; the sport is designed for the playing, social growth, and the sheer joy of physical exercise. This should not be denied the child with a physical illness unless medically prohibited. The school may be acting this way because they think they are "looking out for your child." Indicate that you can do that equally well and bring a physician's permission slip to prove it. No is the answer to *(b)* unless there is valid reason.

Many youngsters with chronic disease are quite self-sufficient and are responsible for giving themselves their necessary medication during school hours. Some take these medicines regularly; others use drugs only when they perceive the physical need for specific medications. Often arrangements can be made with the school nurse or the principal to keep such medications in the health office or the principal's office. The child can then stop by the office, ask for the medication, take the drug under supervision, and continue without hassle or constant observation by his or her peers. Parents should not have to come to school in the middle of the day to give their children necessary medications. Arrangements should be made so that the appropriate person in the school will supervise or permit the taking of the medication, depending upon the child's age and acquired level of responsibility. This is not yet a universal policy in our schools; but with the increasing number of chronically ill children being made ambulatory and capable of attending regular school, it must become so. If you have a chronically ill child needing medication, start the ball rolling by demanding this service from your school. You should expect a Yes to *(c)*.

On the other hand, no parent should expect the school to be a hospital emergency room or primary care clinic. Cuts, bruises, scrapes, and other very minor injuries may be taken care of within the school. Occasionally the school physician may be in attendance when a minor physical illness presents itself in the child, and he or she can offer immediate primary care. In some schools (as we have said), the school nurse has had the proper training and is capable of diagnosing and managing the minor physical illnesses and complaints of childhood. Beyond these minor interventions, the parents should not anticipate that the acute physical attack of any illness can be dealt with within the school. The child will have to be taken to the nearest hospital clinic or private physician's office, preferably by the parent. However, if the parent is not immediately accessible, permission for the school nurse, guidance counsellor, or school principal to transport the child to the hospital should be arranged *ahead of time* in the case of the child with a known chronic illness which has the potential of acute attacks. The response to *(d)* by the parent must realistically be in the negative.

When infections play a significant part in worsening your child's chronic illness, you must inform the teacher of this potential danger. If you have done so, you have every right to expect the school to notify you if your child has been exposed to a contagious disease. At times it is very helpful to ask your child's physician to outline the significant illnesses that should be reported to you as soon as exposure is known. This will serve as a meaningful guide to both teacher and school nurse, so that they will know exactly when to inform you of such exposure. Without a clear-cut definition of those illnesses that are potentially dangerous to your particular child, the teacher or school nurse may feel the need to call you every time the slightest sickness flares up in the classroom. With elementary school age children, this could mean daily unnecessary phone calls! This is where a line between the child's doctor and the school nurse can be of great value. The answer to *(e)* is a qualified Yes, provided that the school is given the proper list of communicable diseases to watch for.

We have used two striking examples of children with chronic illness to illustrate what parents can expect from the schools if such a child is entering the regular school system. This support of the physically ill child requires mutual cooperation between parent and school. The parent must provide the school with the proper information and the appropriate medical back-up; the school must then fulfill the educational, emotional, and physical needs of this very special child.

20 The Gifted Child

What do you do if your child is unusually bright or unusually talented and the entire school system is geared toward the education of the average child? Can you help establish a special pathway for your exceptional child? What is the correct approach for discovering the stimulation and special education your child so badly needs?

The first step is to make sure that your diagnosis is correct. Often we view our children through the rose-tinted glasses of hope and wish-fulfillment. The above average child suddenly takes on the mantle of the gifted, when in reality he or she is capable of excelling in the average study plan but unlikely to benefit from the more advanced studies available for the genuinely gifted child. Each small child moves at his own pace so that one may leap forward in the very early years while his friend of equal age may be dragging his intellectual heels. These two children may be the same in potential, but the different pacing of their intellectual maturity makes the early bloomer seem exceptionally bright and falsely gifted in comparison. It is far wiser to defer the initial judgment that you have a gifted child until at least the fourth or fifth year of the child's life—the immediate preschool period. Not only will many so-called gifted children begin to resemble their peer group more and more but the testing devices used to measure intellectual potential will be far more accurate in making a definitive assessment as to whether the child is really gifted or not.

So the first step is to be content with patient observation and assessment. Wait. Watch. If your original sense that your child has unusual intellectual or artistic skills appears to be consistently reinforced by the child's behavior and performance during the fourth and fifth years, then further investigation may be indicated.

The next step is psychological testing by competent professionals, who will assess the child honestly and tell you the truth about the level of his or her ability. This professional may be a psychologist who tests your child in a private office, or the school psychologist responding to

211

a request for assessment put forward either by you as the parent or by your child's teacher, or both. The teacher becomes an increasingly important objective observer in evaluating the level of your child's intelligence and his estimated potential in learning and artistic areas. Remember that the teacher has a classroom full of children who are probably the same age and have the same general background as your child. She is thus capable of making a broader and potentially more accurate assessment of the degree of your child's intellectual potential. The more experienced the teacher, the more children she has taught, and this ever-increasing population of children offers a more accurate retrospective comparison of your child to his peer group. It is essential that parents listen carefully to a teacher's analysis of their child. The objectivity, the experience, and the training, plus the constant first-hand observation of the child's reaction to classroom stimuli, make the teacher an invaluable observer when trying to separate the gifted from the non-gifted child.

So the second step in helping the gifted child centers on external observation of your child's potential by objective people. Whether the child is in nursery school, public or private elementary grade, or a play group, the opinion of his or her trained teacher is extremely important. Finding out that your child is above average but not gifted may save you time, effort, and energy; it may also save the child the pain of trying for rungs of the learning ladder deliberately constructed for a child of greater capacity.

If the educational professionals agree that you do have an exception-ally bright or talented child, then it is wise to seek the psychological advice and measurements that indicate exactly how gifted the child is and in which areas these exceptional skills are focused. Many times a child may be enormously talented in number concepts, excelling con-stantly in math subjects, but of only average skills in the reading and language areas. (The reverse may also be the case.) Knowing this can avert the tragedy of unrealistic expectations "across the board" in a child with exceptional skills in only one or two particular fields. Occa-sionally, the tests will demonstrate superior skills and talents in most areas. However, the child's interest levels may swing erratically so that his drive and motivation are only evident in a much narrower field. Talent and intelligence alone are not enough if the child's ambitions and interest are not of the same magnitude in a specific area. These are extremely valuable pieces of information about the gifted child. Parents must remember that, although possessed of extremely high knowledge and learning potential, the gifted child is still a child who can refuse to open this wonderful treasure chest of intellectual gifts. You cannot force a gifted child to perform as a gifted child if ambition and interest are missing. Therefore, the psychological testing should not only demonstrate intellectual potential but also attempt to chart the areas of interest and motivation, so that greater focus and attention may be paid to these current areas of highest potential.

Sometimes the school will call to inform you that group tests and classroom performance have suggested strongly that your child has the potential for exceptional intellectual or artistic achievement. Do not disregard this message. The school is asking for your cooperation in moving forward with further testing and evaluation so that the proper educational program can be designed for your gifted child.

We often automatically assume that the word "gifted" refers to a child genius with extraordinary intellectual abilities. In truth, these children are gifted. But the term also applies to children who may not fall in the top 2 percent of the child population but still possess impressive intellectual potential, far beyond that of their peers, so that teaching them the same material and by the same methods as their peers may prove frustrating to teacher and student alike. In addition, the word "gifted" must be expanded to include the child with unusually well-developed artistic talents. What a bleak and barren world we would create for ourselves if we focused only on the extremely academic and ignored the exceptionally talented! We must encourage and plan equally for each exceptional aspect in our society.

The child with artistic talents usually will not surface from among the crowd until the third or fourth grades in elementary school. Musical talents and dramatic skills may even emerge much later. The parent and the school must be prepared to seek expert opinion on the child believed to have extraordinary artistic qualities; psychological tests cannot delineate these talents. In fact, some of the youngsters may test only at an average or slightly above average level. However, when evaluated by someone proficient in the field (music, drama, art, etc.), the child could demonstrate an unusual level of artistic potential.

Let us assume that your child has been screened; you have talked with the teacher and you both agree that this child has "something special"; and the private or school psychologist has tested your child and found exceptional intellectual abilities, or the special artistic talents have been confirmed by the outside consultant. Where do you go from here? You are faced with a child whose intellectual or artistic potential may very well exceed your own. This unusual child is your own child. What do you do? What can the school do?

First and foremost, both parent and school must realize that they are dealing with a child! This exceptionally gifted individual is no older in years or social maturity than any of the other members of the class. If the talents have been overstressed up to this point, the child may even be somewhat more immature and less socially adjusted. You must realize that within this gifted child lives another child who has to learn to mature at a perfectly normal rate; who must adjust to the other young people who may not be quite as gifted or talented; and who must acknowledge that you cannot barter your giftedness for favors whether at home or in school. The home and the school must work together to design a special program in certain areas for this child; but they must labor equally hard at preventing the gifted child from feeling or acting "special."

School does not merely teach the information contained within lectures and books; it also teaches the child the important and necessary aspects of living and working with others. The gifted child must learn to let other children speak in the classroom; he or she must learn to control spontaneous criticism of incorrect or inappropriate answers from the other children. The school must help the gifted child contribute to the class discussion as a member of the group, not from a higher plane. Though uniquely different from his classmates in intelligence or talent (or both), nonetheless, the gifted child is still a member of this group, who must learn how to assimilate his special skills into the group activities. Then he will cease to be a threat and will continue as a respected but accepted member. The teacher, the guidance counsellor, and the parent must work assiduously as a team to help the gifted child learn how to accomplish these necessary adjustments.

The teacher and parent have to teach the gifted child to listen to others. Ambition must not become equated with competition—this must be averted at all costs. If the gifted child begins to try to compete with the other members of his or her peer group in the regular classroom, he will outdistance them so rapidly that he will be running in a silent, lonely desert without friends or the sounds of other children's voices. All too often the talented, gifted child is so consumed by his involvement in artistic endeavor that he shuns the common, everyday activities of his friends. The boy will avoid the ballgame; the girl will avoid the clubs and athletic events which the other girls cherish. Gradually, the gifted child becomes a loner. He begins to view himself as a singular traveler along the long road to maturity. He tacitly accepts his "difference," and it becomes part of him and his lifestyle. School and home must work together to avoid the ultimate loneliness so often suffered by the gifted child. This bright, talented child has been allowed to drift away from his peer group because of the frustrations of "losing" in the competition of commonplace, everyday games which do not test his special talents or skills. But the gifted child must be taught how to lose. He must learn that victory is exciting only if you have occasionally experienced the bittersweet aftertaste of failure.

Parents of a gifted child are often awed by their child, overwhelmed by the unexpected qualities. Therefore they find it difficult to deny the child anything he or she requests. In addition, these parents have great difficulty in placing restrictions on their child. The school may have an equally difficult time convincing the parents that they must view their talented child as a normal, growing youngster with a special gift which can become a detriment rather than an asset if it is not worked into the other important aspects of the child's life. Sometimes the school must take a firm stand when it is becoming increasingly clear that the gifted child is being "spoiled." If it is happening to a great degree, the young person may suffer permanent social and/or emotional disability. So, if you have a gifted child, don't become angry or alarmed if the school approaches you and requests that you insist on your child's participation in an extramural activity or points out improper classroom behavior. You must remember that you may be be creating a "hothouse" environment for this child within your home. The teacher has little possibility of creating such a unique environment for your child throughout the entire school day, nor should she have to. The gifted child must learn to cope with the non-gifted world in which he lives. This is an adjustment, not conformity.

This child has to mature and grow emotionally at the same rate as his or her peers. The parents also must be fully aware of the risks that these unique children run in adjusting to a non-gifted world of adults. In addition, they must work closely with the school administration and teachers to create an environment for the specially talented child that as closely as possible resembles the normal world around him without in any way sacrificing the expansion of his abilities. There are far too many talented, bright, gifted misfits who, lonely and afraid, edge around the corners of our society because this very essential step was overlooked in the excitement and glow of rearing a gifted child.

What can you expect of the school system if you are rearing an unusually able or talented youngster? The proper selection of an appropriate educational approach for the child is the obvious next step. Let us list the possible types of programs you can hope your school system will make available:

1. Mainstreaming with enrichment
2. Acceleration
3. Telescoping
4. Advanced placement
5. Special courses
6. Special schools

It is important to examine each of these approaches to the gifted child so that, as parents, you can request the one which appears to be best for your particular child.

MAINSTREAMING WITH ENRICHMENT

The philosophy behind placing the gifted child in the regular school environment with special "enrichment" programs is that the gifted child should remain among his/her peer group as much as possible. This allows the child to develop the necessary social skills within the normal age group while attending some of the "regular" classes. The extent of the so-called enrichment program may vary from school to school and be quite different from one school district to another. In some areas, the gifted child is carefully tested to delineate the particular intellectual strengths and then placed in specific advanced classes which will take advantage of these accelerated skills. Therefore some bright children may be in special math classes, while others may be in fast-paced courses of science or reading. Many children qualify in a large number of areas and the school must then decide, with the parents' assistance, which areas should be "enriched" and how many "special" classes would be appropriate for the individual child. The selection of almost all fast-paced, accelerated classes, which would remove the child from the regular classroom for most of the day, would obviously defeat the basic concept of keeping the youngster with his peers as much as possible for social growth.

In small school districts, there are usually not enough children whose skills and talents are exceptional to justify having special classes for the gifted child. Other considerations which would prevent the local school administration from offering specifically designed classes for gifted children would be insufficient funds for the necessary faculty to teach these advanced classes. The parent must bear in mind that the gifted child is a significant challenge to the average school teacher, often probing, prodding, questioning. This special child requires a special teacher. A teacher who could not cope with the extraordinary challenges and demands of the exceptionally bright child would be frustrating and counterproductive to both the gifted child and the unprepared teacher. This teacher may do very well with the average or even above average mainstreamed child; that is part of her training. But dealing with the gifted child requires special talents and skills. Therefore many school systems must search thoroughly and carefully before they can locate the appropriate people to lead these special classes for the gifted. If the faculty is restricted, then the system may be forced to attempt what might be called "enrichment."

"Enrichment" means broadening the curriculum of the gifted child to offer him or her more depth in a subject and to allow freedom of intellectual and scientific curiosity. Thus the fourth grader who has mastered long division may move rapidly into complex problems with fractions and "bases"; the eighth grader may be assigned special projects in literature or politics.

As important as what enrichment means is what it does *not* mean. All too often, "enrichment" is interpreted by an uninformed teacher as "more of the same," so she gives twenty problems on page 39 rather than the fifteen assigned to the class. That is *not* enrichment and should not be accepted by parents under that name. It is an assured way of boring a gifted child—perhaps turning him off for a long time.

Often these children use assigned special home readings or projects. Because of their advanced intellectual capacities, such special projects should not keep the gifted child from going out to play with his or her peer group during the afternoons. These extra assignments should fill up the unused evening hours left over when the highly skilled child has sped through the daily homework assignment, with a long, unfilled evening lying ahead. It is essential that the gifted child be encouraged to spend his afternoons playing with the neighborhood children or school friends rather than using this playtime for special homework or reading. Help him develop hobbies, engage in learning with adults, or broaden his knowledge with discerning television.

Most school systems are trying to deliver something special to their gifted population by utilizing this method of "enrichment." For many special bright and talented youngsters, this system will be sufficient to keep their interest and motivation in school at a satisfactory level without boring them or leaving wasted time on their hands. In addition, the system has the great advantage of isolating the gifted child as little as possible from the other children his own age. His emotional growth is being enriched at an equal pace with his intellectual growth.

ACCELERATION

Some school systems offer special accelerated curricula for their gifted children. The timing of this acceleration may differ from place to place; in some cities, the gifted child may move more quickly through the elementary courses; in other areas, the special child may pick up school speed in the junior high or senior high years. Various combinations are available in selected areas.

What does acceleration mean? It allows the child to move through subjects quickly, covering the same material in a shorter span of time than the other children. So the child "skips" a year or more but, in reality, the child has satisfactorily completed what the average student takes in the prescribed time. For example, in the Baltimore school system, for many years, there were special junior high schools and programs within the regular junior high schools which permitted the gifted child to complete the seventh through the ninth grade in two regular school years. These compressed courses taught the regular curriculum (and often went into greater depth and required return knowledge from the more advanced students), but moved the gifted child through the scheduled curriculum at a speed fast enough to permit three years to be accomplished in two.

When this occurred within a special school situation, the advantages were that the entire school body was geared toward acceleration. Assemblies and schoolwide group discussions, projects, and special events could be focused upon the superior abilities of all the students in the school. The greatest disadvantage was the "élitist" feeling that these children developed about their own capabilities. This was totally understandable; it was the simple process of human response to an unnatural selective situation. These children were separated from the rest of their peer group. They were placed in a special school. They associated on a daily basis with children of equally high intellect. To them the rest of their peers were "different." The gifted children were viewed as "special" and not always in the most favorable light.

Schools with such special programs often did not focus upon the athletic but concentrated on the artistic and the intellectual extracurricular activities, and thereby deprived the pupils of yet another possible social skill—participation in group sports. Here these youngsters would have experienced competition of a very realistic nature and perhaps learned a very important lesson suppressed until that moment: they were not always going to be the best. They were not always going to win. How to lose and how to accommodate are lessons desperately needed by many gifted children. The school which houses only the gifted may not permit this experience to be acquired as easily as the integrated school environment.

The accelerated program which is run concurrently within the regular school must overcome this isolated, élitist feeling within the gifted child. Parents should understand that it is much harder to run several different types of school programs concurrently within the same school—the cost is higher, both in terms of materials and personnel. And the effort is greater—not only must the children be taught to integrate in non-intellectual pursuits such as clubs and sports and all extracurricular activities; but the counselling, the group assemblies, the future career planning all differ dramatically for the gifted, the average, and the slow child. Thus programs which run side by side in the same school require expert administration and a very cooperative teacher/parent approach.

The parents of a gifted child must be careful not to allow their child to be too "accelerated" within the school system. In certain systems, this can happen. If the very bright child is accelerated in elementary school and "skips" a year, speeds through junior high school saving another year, and moves more quickly through high school, compressing yet another year, he or she will be three years ahead of himself at the time of graduation from high school. The main question for parents then remains: Is he only three years ahead of himself intellectually? Is he ready socially—or emotionally—for college? The answer, more often than not, is No. The repeated use of acceleration should therefore be viewed with caution by the parents of specially talented children.

Between Parent and School

TELESCOPING

This is a fascinating concept of programming for the gifted child which has been springing up within the education community. One of our children currently is experiencing "telescoping" in the gifted program in Fairfax County, Virginia. Telescoping is the intentional compression of the core material within a curriculum into a very shortened period of time, in the belief that the very bright child will be able to handle this material very fast. Once this basic material has been completed, the remainder of the school year is dedicated to a deeper handling of the subjects being "telescoped." As an example: in the regular English course, a certain level of grammar, vocabulary, and readings is expected of all children at that grade. These assignments are completed in one-half to one-third the time that might be assigned to the regular peer class within the same school. The gifted class then moves on to read special books and undertake specific individual literary projects which will benefit the individual child and the class as a whole.

Each year the basic course is telescoped, and each year the gifted child is given much more information in depth about the particular subject under study. This works exceedingly well in such subjects as English, Social Studies, Science, and Languages. The course is a strenuous challenge to the teacher, since she must not only prepare the entire basic curriculum but also be thoroughly ready to present an intensive multifaceted course over and above the regularly taught material. In essence, this teacher is being asked to teach two to three times as much as the teacher with the regular class. Is it any wonder that, although stimulating, the telescoped class for gifted children requires a teacher or a team of teachers of undeniable dedication and skill? As in all professions, these teachers are coveted and often rise above the teaching level into the administrative echelon where salary increases are possible. To keep these talented teachers at the child's level so that all special programs—whether for the gifted, the slow learner, or the handicapped child—can be continued, parents must make certain that there are significant rewards aside from salary. The only people whose voices will be heard in this crucial issue are the parents'; children do not lobby for themselves, but their parents can and must. If you have a gifted child, make certain that the special teacher remains with the children from year to year. Insist that the school system make the appropriate offer to keep her (or him) with the special children rather than moving her to a desk where her ability to help your child becomes minimal.

Telescoping has the decided advantage of keeping the gifted child within the regular school environment with the bulk of his or her peer group. At the same time, this child will move ahead during the year into subjects and books of greater complexity, which will stimulate and challenge his advanced intellect. He will not skip any years but will remain in step with his peer group in the same school, starting each year with the same subject matter, only moving faster and deeper into the area as his talents and skills permit.

Telescoping has many advantages. It does bring special children into one "special subject" class, and they may as a result develop a sense of uniqueness which must be played down by parent and teacher. But these children remain on the same time track and within the same school as their classmates, so that they can participate fully in the social and emotional peer scene which is happening around them. Does your school system recognize the concept of "telescoping"? If you have a gifted child and the idea of this special program appeals to you, it becomes your task to find out whether it exists and, if not, why not? Remember your voice. It must be raised for your child. Don't be timid if he or she has special talents or is gifted. You have as much right for your child to receive an education geared to his abilities as any other parent whose child has other educational problems or potentials.

ADVANCED PLACEMENT

Some school systems will move particular children ahead into situations more in line with their learning capacity. These children have often been extensively tested ahead of time and found to possess most of the information that will be taught in the year being skipped. The school will call the parent and ask permission to move their child a grade ahead because the administration fears a bored, disinterested child during the forthcoming year. Often this will occur in schools that permit the children to pace themselves—so-called open schools. In this self-pacing environment, the gifted child may frequently move so quickly ahead of the others that the teacher suddenly finds herself without a lesson plan to satisfy the educational curiosity of the child. It is at this point, if other types of gifted program do not exist, that the teacher and principal may suggest moving a child ahead with an advanced placement. Advanced placement most often occurs in high school, where a student may be moved into college-level courses for which he or she will receive advance college credits.

There are several questions that you, as the parent of the gifted child, must ask the school before you allow your child to be skipped into a higher level. First, will the teaching program in this upper grade be calibrated and in tune with the previous education of your child? Or will the placement leave significant "gaps" in his or her information base? Secondly, is your child being moved ahead within the same school, so that he will feel "funny" about the impact his skipping will have on his friends and the others in the old class as well as the new? Is he sufficiently emotionally mature to handle being in a classroom with children potentially a year to a year and a half older than himself? Thirdly, what stage of physical maturation has your child reached? If she is a girl who will be significantly behind her classmates in pubertal development, she could suffer from the very real pre-adolescent pangs of being "different" for a long time. If a boy, will he be dwarfed by the rapidly growing taller boys in the class and excluded from group play and group bonding? Will the language and the social scene be at an advanced stage where your somewhat naïve, quiet youngster will feel excluded and "behind" socially? If the answer to any of these questions comes back with a resounding Yes, then many of the advantages of advanced placement may be completely lost because the bright child may be so socially miserable that learning is pushed into the corner and the discomfort, frustrations, and anxieties are what occupy his/her bright but troubled mind.

If you feel that your child's physical and emotional make-up allow for a positive advanced placement, when is the best time? There are two distinct answers. First, when the current placement has literally used up all the material available to teach your child and he is left alone on an island surrounded by his own sea of knowledge. Secondly, the most appropriate time would be when the child can change schools to accomplish that placement. This minimizes the internal social conflicts which create childhood jealousies and confrontations. For example, if in your area junior high school begins at grade seven, then the fifth-grade child can be advanced directly into the new school in the seventh grade; or the sixth grader may move into the eighth grade upon entry into the new school. Because going to a new school always requires a degree of adjustment on any child's part, adding the advanced jump may not prove as difficult since it will be part of the general internal adjustment through which the child is maneuvering.

Advanced placement is not ideal. Sometimes it is necessary because it is all that your school system can offer your child; sometimes it is done because there is no other way to cope with the advanced standing of your child. However, resist the move if in your judgment as a parent you can foresee social or emotional trouble on your child's part because of an unanticipated move into an advanced peer group.

SPECIAL COURSES

To deal with the very talented youngster, some school systems create special course material within the regular curriculum to add an extra layer of challenge and stimulation while still integrating the gifted child in the regular setting. Early introduction of foreign languages is a frequent mechanism used to electrify the bright mind and keep the child on his or her educational toes. Many schools offer these language courses in the very early grades, having already identified a number of bright potential students. These youngsters are often excused from course work they have already mastered or which is given as a homework assignment so that they can attend the special course. Occasionally, the special course is given after regular school hours so that they can assimilate totally into their class activities but remain later to receive extra information and enrichment. In the Baltimore school system, the Johns Hopkins University offers an algebra course for junior high students of exceptional math talents who score quite high on the special screening tests given to all the children for the purpose of identifying the gifted. In essence, this is a college algebra course for junior high school students. Most of the children find the course the right blend of challenge and extra hard work they need to keep their minds on school—and the television screen and comic book. In contrast to advanced placement, these college courses are usually not given college credit.

There are distinct advantages to this form of giving an "extra added attraction" to the gifted child. First, the cost is less in terms of personnel, time, and money. Often only one teacher is needed for a class of fifteen or slightly more. Secondly, this course need not interrupt the normal flow of the child's school day nor specifically characterize him or her to the peer group as a "brain"—which often has more negative than positive meaning at this age. In addition, this special course permits the child to develop exceptional skills in a specific area so that he can feel an inner pride of accomplishment, whether the course is in a foreign language he learns to speak with ease or special mathematics which he proceeds to master.

For the child with talents that are artistic rather than intellectual, this is a common method of providing additional stimulation and release. Special courses in art, music, drama, carpentry, and so on, are frequently made available either during or after school for the child with demonstrated ability and interest. Occasionally, a school system will overlook this aspect of the gifted program, focusing primarily on the intellectually exceptional children and forgetting the artistically talented youngsters. Again, if you are the parent of a talented child, there is no reason why you cannot request and even demand some form of artistic stimulation for the gifted children within the school. Many parents do not have the funds to experiment with the possible talents of their obviously artistically versatile child. However, once the school program has uncovered genuine artistic talent, the family should find the resources to implement the school's findings so that their special child receives full exposure and training for such talent.

For many intellectually gifted children, one or two "special courses" may not be enough. The regular curriculum is not sufficiently stimulating to hold their interest throughout an entire school day. If your child fits this category, then search through the preceding programs for a better one and try to have it implemented within your child's school system. However, the "special courses" system will suffice for many youngsters as just enough outside stimulation to keep them learning at peer level without feeling frustrated or bored.

SPECIAL SCHOOLS

Occasionally, school systems provide special schools where the gifted or talented may go for a thoroughly enriched environment. Many times these schools offer accelerated programs for the intellectually bright, with opportunities to excel in specific areas of skill and mental agility. These schools are quite expensive to run and maintain. They are considered an educational "luxury" in many school systems rather than an educational necessity. Today, with school financing being so tight, special schools are closing rather than new schools for the gifted being planned. Is this totally wrong? Probably not. If the first four methods of handling the intellectually gifted children prove effective, why should they be isolated within a special school for the gifted, labeled as "different" and feeling élite, isolated from their peer group, and unprepared for the sudden immersion into general society that entrance into college so clearly signifies? These young people often find themselves withdrawing from general peer relationships and limiting their friendships only to those special children who attend their special school. This isolating, restrictive behavior may persist throughout their adult life and deprive them of the great wealth of meeting and knowing the heterogeneity of the world around them.

The best excuse for a special school for the intellectually gifted is when the system has such a limited number of special youngsters so widely spaced geographically that attempting separate programs at different schools is both economically and administratively inappropriate. Bringing all these mentally superior students together under one roof permits the development of faculty, of special curriculum, and the use of resources at a level of control that is not possible when you have children scattered all over the place. If your area falls into this category and you have a gifted child, accept the special school. It may be all that your school system can afford; all that is practical or feasible in the special educational handling of your child. It may be a case of the special school or nothing. But accept this only if inadequate or poor-quality programs for the talented exist in the regular school. Efforts at school improvement should focus first on upgrading the regular school; only when this is impractical should the special school be advocated.

A fine example of the special public school for the gifted child with artistic talents is the New York City High School of Performing Arts. Here under one roof are gathered children from all walks of life with one common virtue—a very real artistic talent in one of the vital cultural areas. These youngsters may be budding musicians, embryo actors, potential artists. Each has been screened, auditioned, and selected. Each has entered a school where there is a strict core curriculum that demands a very basic and satisfactory intellectual education but also requires full participation in the artistic education that runs concurrently with the basic curriculum. This is not a "play" school. These young people have two curricula to satisfy: the regular and the artistic. They must be dedicated and disciplined very early to be able to accomplish this double burden; but that is essentially what this school is attempting to teach by isolating and concentrating on these young people. To be an artist is not the romantic technicolor dream that so many young people imagine. It is a life of constant, continual practice and self-improvement within one's sphere of talent. This is the invaluable aspect of having a special school for young people of artistic brilliance: it teaches them the structure and essence of their artistic field; but it also inculcates the hard work and constant commitment that this field demands. Many drop out—and so they should. They return to the regular public high school having received an important lesson. Although they had the talent, they did not have the necessary interest, the dedication, or the drive. Without these qualities, education for this student in the special school would be a waste of the youngster's time, the parent's hopes, and the taxpayer's money. The search for "sudden stardom" in any of the artistic fields is doomed to ignoble and frustrating failure. The special school for the artistic screens these youngsters out at an early age and prevents many painful adult losses. In addition, this special school provides the foundation for many fruitful and creative careers in the arts, which not only enrich the lives of the students but also the quality of the community and often the nation.

It is extremely difficult for the average integrated junior and senior high school, which is attempting to deal with many types of students, to dedicate time and energy to a full program for the artistically talented young person. Despite our concern about the isolation and lack of heterogenity, we feel that such a school has sufficient merits to warrant that each school system give serious consideration to implementing such an institution at the high school level. It need not be a large special school: the teachers are available; the students exist undiscovered within the community. All that is needed is the place to bring out the talents of teachers and pupils alike, fused in a new and exciting adventure in education for the talented. If such a school does not exist in your community, fight to see that it becomes a reality. Even if your child is not eligible, such a school has the long-range potential of enriching the life of your community and ultimately the life of your child.

We have outlined six possibilities that exist within various school systems to handle the very special needs of the gifted child. If you have a child with exceptional intellectual or artistic talents that would classify him or her as gifted, consider the options for education available within your community for your child. Ask your school administration what can be done for him. Then consider the six alternatives listed here and question your school system about the method you feel would be best for your child. There may be a very good fiscal or administrative reason why it cannot be implemented. On the other hand, these reasons may be a smokescreen. If what you want for your gifted child is or could be accessible, and all that is needed is the first voice to start the chorus that could result in the implementation of such a program, then let your voice be the first. Begin the tactful and thoughtful discussions with your school system that will bring about sufficient options for the gifted children in your community. Do not let us have discrimination in reverse. For years, the slow child has had to have advocates to assure him a proper education; now we are turning the corner for programs for the educationally handicapped child. In moving around that very important corner, let us not lose sight of the other educationally exceptional child—the gifted child. Be sure there is an educational system that is conscious of the full potential of this exceptional child, and makes the most—not the least—out of his education and his future.

21 The Child with an Acute Illness

What can you do for your child's education when he or she is suddenly struck down by an acute, long-lasting physical illness or disability that will remove him from school for a long period of time? This problem faces many parents during the course of their children's school careers. Even for the very young child in the elementary grades, the lost time could throw him significantly far behind his peer group and prey on his mind during the physical mending process. The older the child, the more serious is the loss of long periods of school time. Not infrequently, these children will find themselves unable to catch up on the voluminous amount of work missed during their illness. Many are faced with the prospect of going to school during the summer, while others must live with the expectation of repeating a grade and falling behind their peer group.

The emotional impact of the lag in education during acute illness can occasionally become a significant factor in the state of mind and overall state of health of the acutely ill child. Children who have been in the hospital for prolonged periods sometimes develop a deep and extended depression, which leads in turn to poor eating, refusal to take medications or accept medical advice, and antisocial reactions to the nursing and medical personnel. The root of this behavior lies in the anxiety over the loss of school days and the fearsome prospect of failing or being asked to repeat a grade. Such anger at the worrisome illness and the ominous people associated with it is a natural human response —especially in a child.

Many types of illnesses can precipitate the extended absences from school that bring about this transient but very real problem of too many lost school days. Fractures of certain bones require prolonged bed rest, occasionally in traction or special positioning, special beds, and so on.

The Child with an Acute Illness

Rheumatic fever, kidney disease, repair of congenital defects of the heart, bowel, kidney, or lung—all will cause the child to be temporarily out of the school setting for a long enough period of time to cause significant delays in learning. These are only some of the possible types of physical problems that create a situation parents must learn to solve.

Basically the parent has four viable options in approaching the school about how to bring education to the sick and *temporarily* incapacitated child. These are:

1. Parent functioning as teacher
2. Hospital school
3. Hospital or home itinerant teacher
4. Special tutor

For the parent to be an effective teacher, he or she must understand that the relationship between parent and child must differ to a major degree during teaching sessions. In times of illness, children tend to regress and become much more dependent upon their parents than is appropriate for their age, and far more than they were before the illness. If the parent is to be a successful teacher, this regressive behavior cannot be permitted during the teaching periods of the day. No unnecessary "giving in" is permissible if the child is going to attempt to use his or her available intellectual resources and learn at the same pace as his classmates. The ability to assume a firm though understanding demeanor becomes an absolute necessity for an effective parent-teacher.

In addition, the parent must establish a working relationship with the child's teacher. The teacher must have faith and confidence in the parent's ability to teach this absent member of the class so that when the child returns, he or she will be allowed to remain in step with his classmates unless his performance indicates otherwise. This requires that the teacher knows well how the parent intends to function as the teacher of his/her own child. It is also vital that the weekly materials being used at school by the classmates are available to the child. The teacher must meet with the parent on a weekly basis and go through the lesson plans for the coming week. She must provide the parent-teacher with whatever materials and text references are necessary for the child (hemmed in as he is) to grasp the total concept of what is being taught by the parent.

The parent-teacher must assess the overall progress of the child on a regular basis, and, using this as a barometer, measure the effectiveness of the teaching. If it becomes apparent that things aren't working out, then another means of education must be sought. This regular assessment by the parent can be supplemented by the teacher supplying regular tests for the child. If the teacher grades the papers and evaluates the success of the parent-teacher, she can also assess the child's progress objectively. In this way the teacher remains the primary evaluator of the child's education; and she receives regular information as to the pace of the absent child's learning. Then the child can return to the classroom at a proper level, having been monitored throughout the home educational process.

Often the parent-teacher relationship functions very successfully, particularly in areas where other options may not be available to the convalescent child. But frequently too the process is a doomed and unsatisfactory one; parent and child are equally unable to shed their preconceived attitudes and therefore cannot enter into a parent-as-teacher relationship. In these cases, the process should be discontinued at the earliest moment failure becomes evident. To continue might not only damage the educational growth of the child but seriously harm the parent-child relationship as well.

Many children must spend an extended amount of time when they are ill inside a hospital. Often children with fractures, burns, or postoperative convalescence are required to be quiet and immobile for long periods of time. In this case, the school has to come directly to the child. For this reason, some of the major children's hospitals have been able to make arrangements with the local school systems to incorporate a regular schoolteacher as a member of the hospital staff. The teacher functions as instructor for all of the children who are hospitalized over extended periods of time. Usually, the hospital school is actually designated as one of the recognized schools within the educational district. Thus the temporary education that the child receives in this hospital school setting is officially recognized as acceptable and appropriate upon his or her return to the regular classroom. The hospital schoolteacher is a trained, specially qualified teacher, who usually possesses the extra human qualities so necessary for teaching and understanding individual hospitalized children. The hospital teacher should keep in constant communication with the child's regular teacher so that the lessons in the hospital parallel the regular school material as closely as possible. She must take her cues not only from the regular classroom teacher but from the child's medical and nursing attendants as well.

She must schedule only the number of hours of formal teaching that the doctors and nurses feel the sick child can manage and which will not interfere with the therapy scheduled for the child's recovery. Often this type of hospital instruction increases in time and intensity as the child's convalescence shows signs of steady improvement.

The hospital school is a superb concept—one that brings a proper understanding of the child's educational and emotional needs into the sterile hospital setting. A child derives many benefits; particularly emotional ones, from working with a recognized teacher, and this often has a very positive healing effect. Just like adults, children need a great deal of reassurance during hospitalization that they will get well, that the illness is limited, and that optimism is the prevailing medical opinion about it. The realization that a concerted effort is being made to continue his or her education gives the individual child the real sense that those around him are being truthful when they tell him that he will get better and be back with his friends and classmates very soon. This has a subtle but definite impact upon the confused and often discouraged psyche of the hospitalized child.

Parents should find out whether the hospital in their neighborhood which primarily cares for sick children has attempted to implement the concept of the hospital school. A special school requires the sanction and administrative support of both the educational system and the hospital authorities. If nothing has been done, then the parents of all children, healthy and ill, should band together and begin pressuring for action to make the hospital school a reality. Don't be put off by the argument of cost. There is no human measure of "cost effectiveness" when one is dealing with the education of a sick child and the psyche of a hospitalized child. In addition, if these children can be kept at the same level as their classmates, the time dedicated to assisting them in catching up versus the additional school time needed if they must be held back favors hospital teaching on a cost basis.

Many children have extended illnesses which need not be monitored for prolonged times within a hospital. These youngsters are sent rapidly out of hospital to convalesce at home. Thus the children whose absences from school are spread out over weeks and months may not all be contained within a hospital setting but are often dispersed over distant neighborhoods in their homes. Many educational systems have attempted to deal with this problem by instituting the itinerant teacher in a "homebound teacher" program. In this special program, teachers are sent out to the hospitals and homes of children whose illnesses last over a specified number of days. These teachers will consult with the child's teacher beforehand to make certain they arrive at the child's room or home armed with the proper learning materials. They will spend one or two hours teaching the child; often they leave the children with detailed instructions for additional study until the next visit. Occasionally the home teacher will ask the parent to assist in reinforcing the work, or, actually to participate as a co-worker in instructing the child. Each school area designates the number of days that a child must be away from the classroom due to illness to qualify for the services of an itinerant home teacher. Most states specify that the child who has missed two weeks of school because of an acute illness or physical disability is eligible for home or hospital instruction by the itinerant teaching staff.

It must be stressed that the concept of the itinerant home and hospital teacher *is* a sound and necessary one within the school system if the child with prolonged illness is to be protected against educational failure and subsequent emotional frustration and anger as one of the complications of his or her illness. If this sytem is not currently part of your local school system, you must ask why such valuable educational assistance to the sick child has been overlooked. Parents should not wait until they are personally affected to take up the crusade. The parents of well children must join forces with the parents of sick children to create a voice powerful enough to be heard by both the educators and the legislators.

What about those parents faced with the problem that their child is ill and will be in the hospital or at home for weeks but who find that the local school system is not geared to teach their child? To crusade is extremely important. However, equally urgent is the immediate need of the youngster to receive and assimilate lost information. Not infrequently the parent does not feel qualified to do the teaching, or is extremely busy with other children, or is working while the child is being cared for by a third party . . . in these rather common situations, what is the parent to do?

Here is where the tutor may be extremely useful. Ask the school to help you pay for a special tutor, since this may be the most appropriate way of solving the problem. In most communities, there are married women who have given up teaching but who would be willing to give the sick child individual tutoring for one or two hours per day for pay. The school occasionally keeps a file of such individuals for parents who need tutoring services for a sick child or the child with special learning problems. If this list is not available through the school, the parent should check with the central school administration. This is where the hiring of teachers occurs, and these people may know of others who have applied requesting part-time teaching or substitute work. Finally, advertisements in the local newspaper may result in locating a tutor for the convalescing child. Again, these teachers must keep in constant communication with the child's regular classroom teacher(s) so that the pacing and content of the material is consistently on target.

If the family's and/or school's financial means do not permit hiring special tutoring help when the educational programming for these children is deficient, then the parent must improvise by seeking out the person most readily available to teach his sick child. Relatives often can assist here. However, the parent should be as critical of the qualifications of the volunteering relative as he has been of his own capabilities and commitments. A very good source of help for the shut-in school-child is the friend or classmate. The youngster who is bright enough and mature enough to keep his classmate abreast of the material may prove an ideal tutor if the family's funds are limited. The child's parents must help the classmate tutor by checking with the teacher, who will assess whether he or she can handle the work. In addition, the teacher can participate in the daily tutoring by passing along tips and handouts as part of the day's lesson. Homework assignments which are graded, as well as intermittent testing devices, also graded, will give the convalescent child the sense of constant contact with his classroom, as well as informing both the friend and the sick child about the effectiveness of the teaching. As with the parent-teacher experiment, if the peer-tutor relationship is apparently not an effective or workable technique for the sick child, then it should be swiftly discarded. However, if it works, it has several side benefits besides the positive learning experience. The convalescent child maintains a social relationship with one of his peers during his illness. In addition, the other important daily social and athletic happenings within the school can be shared so that the youngster does not sense such a gap on his return to the classroom setting.

Many states and school districts now function under laws which require that they provide educational services to all children. (This will be reiterated in Chapter 25 on Parent's Rights.) Therefore, your school district might be obligated to pay for tutors or offer reimbursement.

Check this not only with your local school administrators but also with your state Director of Special Education. When you have ascertained your child's rights, you can act accordingly.

It is obviously possible to combine several of these methods of instruction for a child with an acute illness, while being very careful not to overtax his or her energies. One should also watch for redundancy between various teachers and the content of their lessons. Let the child help in deciding which of the learning appears to be most profitable for him. Combine this with the classroom teacher's appraisal of his work with each of the methods being tried. With this information, the parent can then concentrate on whatever special instruction seems to best fit the child while ill.

No child should be condemned to the constant worry about falling behind in school as he lies in bed trying to get well. The parents, the teacher, and the school system must work together to provide him with the special support that will help him return to his classroom prepared to keep pace with his classmates.

PARENT POWER

22 Parent Power– Becoming a Child Advocate

You are facing the school principal in a dimly lit office at the end of a long corridor in an old building. Only anger is lighting up your mind at this moment.

"Then I guess we're at an impasse, Mr. Allen. But let me recap our conversation just to make sure I have understood you correctly. I've come to tell you that my son, who has a learning disability, has been diagnosed by three professionals, all of whom stated that what would be best for him is continued integration in his regular class, with help from a resource teacher. I'm asking that you provide that resource teacher for him, knowing that you have two such teachers employed here at the present time.

"You're telling me, in return, that you cannot offer my son such a resource, because (a) your resource teachers are working at the maximum caseload allowed by the state department of education, and (b) you don't have enough money to hire another resource teacher. Therefore, you're saying that I can't get the school help for my son which he needs because of your manpower problems. You're also saying that the problem can't be solved this year because there are eight children on the waiting list for resource teachers who will receive help before my son.

"You offered to place my son in what you call a 'self-contained learning disabilities class' where, you admit, he would receive the right kind of academic work but be isolated from all the classmates he started school with. You offered this as an answer to three professionals who stated very clearly that my son needed the social setting of the children in his regular class more than he needed a segregated special class.

"And you're asking me to accept your decision on this compromise —me, his parent!

"Mr. Allen, I find the decision impossible to accept, and I refuse to do so. I have made my own decision—that my son should have a resource room teacher and that no compromise should be made. I insist that you find a way to do this.

"Goodbye."

Hurried steps. The door closed with a sharp, firm sound. Deliberate, angry motions at putting on an overcoat, darting a look at the school secretary who could overhear the heated confrontation. The heavy strides down the long hallway. Then, midway down the hall, you stop. You are suddenly assailed by a painful vision of a beautiful red-haired boy fearfully entering a strange class filled with children in various stages of frustration, and sitting next to the window to stare sadly outside at his third grade classmates as they play during recess a half hour ahead of his new schedule.

Remember the first chapter of this book? Here is an example of how a school sometimes acts when it become immovable, conservative, traditional. And often parents let the matter drop here because of their own fearful experiences with school principals as authoritarian figures. Many parents at this stage may even rationalize the school's position, saying things like, "Surely, the special class can't hurt my child too much if that experienced principal recommended it. After all, he's much older and more experienced, etc., etc." This is a true cop-out, dear friends. Parent advocacy starts right here. If that child needs a resource teacher, he—and all the other children who need that resource teacher—should have one.

And you must see that he gets one. You must become a "child advocate."

A child advocate usually faces two kinds of tasks. The first is known as case advocacy. Here he or she recognizes a child who needs something more out of the school system than he is getting, and sets out to find it—or its equivalent. The case advocate acts *on behalf of* the child because the child cannot speak for himself among the adults from whom he must get this special something. The advocate, then, is a person who has grasped the needs of the child, the available resources of the school system, and the alternative resources outside that system, and who sets about to create a workable match between the child's need and the resources available.

The second type of child advocate works for class advocacy. This advocate realizes that a whole group of special children—such as all mentally retarded children or all learning-disabled children—need special provisions from a school system; understands the resources that do and should exist within that system; and again, seeks to make a match of children's needs to available resources.

Does this sound easy? It isn't. It is very hard work. An effective child advocate is not a person who rushes about "doing good" for his or anyone else's child. An effective child advocate is a person who works very hard at discovering the full story behind children's needs, the total picture of the available resources, and the most appropriate method of blending the two. If a child advocate works well, he changes the system —for the better. If he works poorly, he may obtain short-term results at long-term expense (like getting Mr. Allen to move that child to a resource room and teacher at the expense of another equally needy child whose parents were just not as vocal).

What qualifies a person as a good child advocate? Essentially, the intrinsic quality of being truly motivated to help children—*but in a systematic way.* He is committed to finding out all the needs of the child or children he is helping. He probably lists them on a sheet of paper; and he justifies these needs by making quite certain that they have been professionally determined (an example is the case at the beginning of the chapter—three professionals who recommended a specific action). He also reads the literature and speaks to the experts in the field so that in the case of class advocacy or group decision making, he is backed by reputable surveys or observations. A good advocate makes sure that what he is about to advocate is *not* just his own need, but the actual need of the child, of the group of children, of the society at large. He must also be certain that his recommended action is the choice recommended by leaders in the field of child education.

Then a good child advocate (whether case or class advocate) sets out systematically to pursue the resources available. Perhaps he or she finds that other children who need resource teachers are obtaining them from private schools. Or he finds that some parents are paying qualified special tutors for their children—tutors who make frequent contact with the teachers in the public school system to maintain a continuing dialogue about the child. Or perhaps he finds that the resource people already employed are underqualified and should be replaced before any other children are referred. The picture of the process is becoming clear: the child advocate starts with a problem and lists *all* the possible solutions, knowing that eventually he will have to select the best.

Finally, having selected the best of his or her alternatives, the child advocate carefully thinks through the actions needed to guarantee those resources for that special child or special children. The choice of a strategy is bound to be a difficult one, which must be made with the help of objective parties. Will he use a direct confrontation? Will he organize a parent protest to embarrass the special personnel? Will he tap the militancy of labor unions? Will he turn to a court action or a lawsuit? Will he employ the pressure of powerful political figures? The decision ultimately must be based on two factors: Whether the strategy will accomplish its objective; and whether it will pave the way for a long-range continuation of the practice of supplying the resources needed.

A child advocate is rarely employed or selected to play his or her role. He generally appoints himself, because he loves children and wants to help them. Thus, as parents, you qualify as child advocates. When your child needs an advocate, you will appoint yourself. And you must learn to become a good one.

The child advocate has a parallel in the field of intelligence and detective work. You must systematically gather all the information you can, using whatever leads you uncover, and then, wherever possible, verify all the facts with more than one opinion. After you have processed this information, you must phrase your findings in the vocabulary and language of the persons or agency for whom you are gathering the facts (in this case, the school). Unless the school understands exactly what a child advocate is saying and requesting, the break in communication can defeat the fulfillment of the child's needs.

There are some tools to help you in this fact-finding operation that detectives and agents do not have. One of these is the Freedom of Information Act, a federal law which states that parents can request and must be given all documents pertaining to their child that are on file in any public agency. You don't have to guess what your child's current teacher said about him—you can look it up in his file. Ask the school·secretary to hand over your child's file. You may state that you are requesting it under the provisions of the Freedom of Information Act. Generally you will have his file before you can turn around twice.

If not, report it to the school board—they do not want to lose the federal money coming into their district—and they will see that you get it. (There will be more about this in Chapter 25.) Similarly, this action will be successful with the school psychologist, or even with the pediatrician who submitted a report about your child to the school. You will be able to inspect all the reports; if any of these professionals have stated in writing that your son needs a resource teacher, you have evidence which can be used in any court-directed legal action to gain the child his rights.

Another tool you have as a child advocate is something called an Equal Educational Opportunity philosophy in the schools. This states that all children, regardless of potential or limitations, have a right to as much education as each can handle successfully. Furthermore, this philosophy states that education ought to be modified to meet the special needs of handicapped or disabled children so that they, too, may have an equal educational opportunity. Much of the current federal money going into schools is based on this philosophy, and schools in every state have said that they are committed to comply with this ruling. Court suits on behalf of children not receiving equal educational opportunities have been won by the plaintiffs (parents) as courts interpret the law to mean that state constitutions are subject to this philosophy. As a child advocate, if you are pointing out to a school system that they are not providing equal educational opportunity, they may be both professionally and fiscally embarrassed—especially if you are armed with facts, figures, and illustrations. Your school system may be able quite suddenly to provide those services a great deal faster than they originally thought was possible in order to avoid that charge.

A third tool at your disposal is the fact that another stated aim of the public schools (also accompanied by much federal money) is for "career education." This philosophy as worked out through various demonstration programs states that all children, and particularly special children, should be exposed to the world of work at the earliest possible moment. If indicated, the child must be prepared to choose a vocational future by the time he or she finishes secondary school.

The school administrator can be reminded of his or her delayed plans to assure that career education is practiced in that school. The ruling even suggests such programming at the preschool level. An administrator would "lose points" if the absence of provisions for career education in your child's school was made known to the general public and the educational community, local and national. He should, therefore, be helpful in implementing career education goals for special children or special cases.

Finally, each state constitution establishes a school system within its state and mandates that children be given a "free" education; that is why public schools cannot charge tuition for residents in their states or districts. Furthermore, the courts are interpreting these constitutions as having the intent of insuring that the school district is responsible for the cost of educating children with special needs in private schools or in other districts when there is a reasonable explanation why the local school district cannot provide the service within its own boundaries. Thus, parents often can send their children to other nearby public school districts, or to full-time special private schools, to obtain needed services; and they will not be charged additional educational costs for their child. How many parents know this? Now you do! And that knowledge can be a powerful persuader for improving services for your child.

Given these tools, you, as a "certified" parent and child advocate, can now pursue the solution of the case of the special child within the public school without a resource room teacher.

First of all, you can probably obtain the written verification of your child's immediate need for the resource room teacher. Check your child's files; ask for the verification documents from the diagnostic professionals; and, if necessary, copy the documents. Then by asking other parents or P.T.A. groups, you should attempt to find out how many other children need the same type of resource room help but are not receiving it. You may discover that you have more allies than you ever realized. Find out exactly what the professionals mean when they speak of a "resource room teacher." Does this match what the school is now offering through its "resource room teachers," or does it actually mean something else? If you ask them to clarify the diagnosis further, it might emerge that they mean simply a minor modification of the curriculum, with a brief intensive teaching period once a day by a teacher skilled in perceptual remediation. If this is indeed the case, you could accomplish it without having to find a trained learning disabilities resource teacher (who has received a master's degree in special education).

Check out all the possible resources. If there are not enough resource room teachers in the Elmwood District, are they available in the Oakhurst District, which is separated from your school by only three blocks? Or do the two private schools in the district have the necessary teachers? Or are there teachers who have the credentials for being good resource room teachers but who have been improperly assigned to do regular duties? Can the school provide alternate opportunities to help your child? Does the school need further clarification of the diagnosis and educational plan by the professionals who made them? Check the educational rules and regulations pertaining to the provision of resource room teachers which have been handed down (by the state department of education) to the local districts. Do they mandate a resource room teacher for each child who has been determined to need it? Such mandates do exist. Investigate the local and state funding of resource room teachers. Does your state reimburse them, as many states do, from state funds? If so, an economic argument by the local district against hiring more resource room teachers because of "low funds" is both inaccurate and dishonest. Check whether trained personnel in this field are available in the nearby universities. Are teachers being graduated from these institutions who cannot find jobs? Probably so, in this day and age. If there is a lack of proper teaching personnel for your child and there are unemployed, well-trained teachers searching unsuccessfully for jobs, demand an explanation of this discrepancy from your local school board, your state educational agency, your mayor, your governor, and your federal representatives. You will need this evidence for your next step as an advocate.

Once you have gathered all the information, you are ready to plan your future strategy. If one of your findings is that the school administration has consistently dragged its feet on hiring appropriate resource room teachers, then you might want to make a public issue of your fight for your child's education, so that the foot-dragging will be highlighted and stopped. If on the other hand the school is really tight for money but has made every effort to find the proper financial resources without success, your next move might be to concentrate on the state and federal financing agencies who have the funds to alleviate your child's and school's needs. It is usually more effective for a group to lobby for this. If the state regulations do not support the need for resource room teachers, then you may have to try court suits or decisions handed down by the state Attorney General. In cases where the state laws are vague, you may have to try to stimulate the introduction of legislation. And if the proper personnel are not available for hiring even though there may be money available for their salaries, then you may have to help your local school agency hire the talent from the faculties or personnel of adjoining universities, or discover ways of supplying training to the already intact school faculty, or use personnel who are currently working in adjoining districts or private schools on a cooperative basis. Whatever moves you outline in your advocacy, you must select a strategy, pick your allies, set a time schedule and delineate roles—then lights, camera, ACTION!

By now you've gathered that being a child advocate is no easy task. It is a particularly difficult job if you attempt to do it on your own. Most people do not work best alone; they function most effectively with the thoughts and support of others who are intensely concerned about the same issues. The greatest educational change and progress comes from advocacy groups rather than the dedicated but isolated parent. The history of change in education is replete with ancedotes about "parent power" as the major force in moving schools off dead center.

If you are the parent of a handicapped child, for instance, it is highly possible that a nearby group of parents is already advocating for the needs and problems related to your child. Examples of such organized advocacy groups include the National Association for Retarded Citizens; the United Cerebral Palsy, Inc.; the Easter Seal Foundation; the Association for Children with Learning Disabilities; the National Association for the Deaf; the National Foundation for the Blind; the American Foundation for the Blind; and the National Association for Mental Health.

It is usually much harder to locate the exact group you need if you are advocating a new or innovative idea or a previously unpublicized area of child concern. However, there is good news in this area now. A federally sponsored group has surfaced in Washington, D.C., called Closer Look, which is dedicated to helping parents combine to exert parent power. This group, funded by the Bureau of Education for the Handicapped of the U.S. Office of Education, was initially created to assist parents of children with handicaps locate a proper school placement for their child. Parents were alerted to the agency's existence by television spots produced for Closer Look and played on television stations throughout the country. They were encouraged to write to Closer Look in Washington, and were told that they would be sent a computerized list of possible school contacts in their particular geographical area. However, it became quickly apparent to the staff at Closer Look that they were getting a great deal of mail inquiring about parent groups. As a result, Closer Look began to process and distribute information on advocacy groups of parents with special child interests; in addition to the school contacts. This means that if you write to

Closer Look, you can get their accumulated material about parent groups, which has been written for, by, and about you—a parent in need of a group! (See the Appendix for details of this and other addresses.)

As you delve into advocacy, there is one other resource with which you should become familiar. A number of experimental child advocacy programs have been established by several federal agencies to demonstrate that systematic child advocacy is possible and does work effectively. These demonstrations are just about finished and can be visited by interested parent advocates. Further, many of the programs will be publishing their findings and methods. If you are willing to make a commitment for your child, you might want to pursue this. Write to the Coordinator of Child Advocacy, Bureau of Education for the Handicapped, U.S. Office of Education, Washington, D.C. 20202.

For general information on other advocacy programs throughout the country which are not necessarily sponsored by federal funds, you should write to the Director, Office of Child Advocacy, Office of Child Development, Department of Health, Education and Welfare, Washington, D.C.

And now some words of advice as you prepare to become involved in the field of child advocacy, which can be translated into parent power:

1. Don't build monuments to yourselves. Define a child advocacy task, get it accomplished, and then move on. Successful agents for change start the job and let someone else finish it. If your child is that important to you, it makes no difference who ultimately gets the credit for his or her improved education.
2. Stay cool. Advocacy will always raise heated passions and bitter confrontations, and objectivity is all too easily lost sight of. Change always creates this atmosphere. Develop the technique of cooling down: slow, well-thought-out responses; recesses in important conferences; the use of third-party mediators; and the like. If you lose control of your emotions, whether as an individual parent or as a parent group, you will lose the advocacy fight.
3. Be far-sighted. Think of what you want for your friend's or neighbor's child who might have the same problem. Make sure that your actions prepare the way for this other child too. This will ensure that the changes achieved are permanent ones.
4. Be aware of when you are gaining ground in your struggle. Before

you start your strategy, plan periodic checks along the way which will tell you that the action is proceeding as planned. Check the minutes of school board meetings to make certain that your problem was discussed and acted upon by the committee. Set dates for the completion of actions with the school principal and monitor the progress of the school personnel at those times. Ask other parents to report to you what is happening to their children in the school system. Talk to teachers to find out what faculty actions are being taken to modify, change, and improve. If your action is just being given lip service, you must know this and initiate another strategy which will set the change in motion.

5. Stay with the task. Initially you will define clearly the advocacy task which you feel needs to be accomplished. Along the way, you will collide with people whom you feel should be fired, moved, or changed. Forget them and keep to the job in hand, or you may lose the battle. Distractions such as this take your eyes off the objective.

Ask an experienced, conscientious, committed educator how to create change in education. He or she will tell you to demonstrate the need, explore that need, write a monograph detailing the changes that must be made, set up an evaluation system, initiate the first stages—and maybe, in *fifty years,* the change will be made.

Ask an experienced parent advocate how to create change in your school, and he or she will tell you that changes in the system have been effected in *fifty days.* Do you have the courage and devotion to be this fifty-day wonder—the parent advocate? If you do, you may be making your most important contribution to your child's educational future.

25 Helping Many Children —Not Just Yours

This book—we have said many times—is an attempt to provide you, the parent, with the tools for ensuring your child the best possible education available. It treats the school systems of this country, both public and private, as institutions which, although in constant change, retain certain consistencies and values that make it possible for you to develop expectations and objectives through which you can obtain what you need for your child. If you maintain objectivity, plan alternative ways of action, and keep your child's needs in mind, you *can* procure the best available education. You can become an effective child advocate.

In this chapter we briefly want to discuss the responsibilities that you as parents have when you accept the challenge of changing or modifying the schools to meet the needs of your child. Let us call these responsibilities the four "ethics of child advocacy." You'll see the need for these ethics as they are explained.

The first ethic is this: *Make sure that the goals you set for your children are truly objective ones.* As parents, you do *not* instinctively know what is best for your children in terms of education. How could you? You probably came through school systems much poorer and less well equipped than those your children now attend. You have no models. So you must think through the aims that you have in mind for your child. Check them out with other parents and with the authors of books for parents. *Always* check them out with a qualified educator —who is not your cousin or your client or your child's teacher. Try your very best to be objective in setting these goals. But set them and then hold to them.

Secondly: *To obtain needed services for your child, don't rob another child.* If your child needs a service and there is a waiting list, don't insist that he/she be pushed up to first on that list. Some other child will suffer. Instead, consider ethic number three.

The third ethic is this: *As you advocate for your child, advocate for all children who share his or her needs.* Instead of fighting to become first on a waiting list, advocate with vigor to get sufficient personnel so that the waiting list need not exist. Think big in your advocacy. Your child will *not* be alone with his needs, but you may have to seek out the other children and parents. If your child's needs are based on a handicapping condition, then it may not be too difficult to find other parents whose children need services. It certainly should not be too difficult to enlist their aid in a campaign for increased educational opportunities for children with disabilities similar to your child's.

But, under this ethic, services should not be all that you advocate. You should explore *why* the services were not available in the first place; you should seek to change permanently the provisions of services for children like your own who will follow with similar problems in future years. To do this, you may have to consider asking the school board to increase the budget. You may have to petition services from the state department of education. Or you may even need to change your state legislation to help those future children who will resemble your child. Do it for your child—and receive the unspoken "thank you" of the vast battalion of future children with the same handicaps, the same problems, and the same needs.

The fourth ethic is this: *Let the changes you make be as gradual as possible, giving credit to the people who must institute them.* This ethic recognizes that change in any institution must always be somewhat traumatic to that institution. If the change occurs too quickly, it will be as quickly rejected. If the power behind the change is viewed as coming from an outside force, it cannot and will not be easily accepted by the persons who must live daily with the change. As a change agent, you will have to make some decisions about the changes you want to see initiated. Try to make sure they will be permanent. Allow them to emerge subtly as ideas which emanated from the school personnel. Try to enlist their support early. Let change *grow* into the system as gradually as your child can stand it. Then it will remain to help other children in the future.

Try to find someone who has acted as an effective change agent and ask him or her about these proposed ethics. He will acknowledge, as we must after many years of experience, that these have been the only ethics that could convince people of sincerity of purpose in effecting a major educational change. Also, they are the only ethics that consistently assure the most good for the most children—a principle that no educator or administrator can criticize.

Join or form organizations. Practice these ethics. But most importantly, remember that three ethics are one too few; only with all four ethics in complete operation will you help other children while you reach out to help your own.

In addition to the four vital ethics of helping your own child and the other children outlined above, there is also the extremely important aspect of using the existing organizations that can have a local or national impact on the educational and emotional problems of schoolchildren of all ages. These organizations range from the broad and expansive Parents Teachers Association to specific, well-delineated organizations for children with particular school problems, such as the Association for Children with Learning Disabilities or the National Association for Retarded Citizens. To belong to any of these organizations is to become part of the wider movement to analyze, interpret, and motivate for positive change in education. There are so many important special organizations to which parents can apply and belong as functioning, vital members that we would like to present a list of some of the more noteworthy for your consideration (it is included in the Appendix in the back of the book). This list is not all-inclusive, but it incorporates a large number of those organizations that have taken effective action in the past and promise to do so in the future. There are many worthwhile groups which have been successful in dealing with the educational system in an effort to create an enlightened atmosphere of progress for children in the school system. Working with them may be another important way you can help many children, including your own.

24. Educational Jargon and Educational Games

"Thank you for coming to see me, Mr. Haring. I've been wanting to talk to you about Betty. It appears that she's having some problems in my class. Yes, I know that you probably don't see these problems at home, but school is such a different and complex institution that it's hard to see the carryover activities in the home situation. But the problem appears to be more than an academic one. There seem to be problems of a motivational nature, particularly in the areas of artistic endeavor. There have been frequent confrontations with peers and teachers alike over the aesthetic qualities of certain songs and poetry. Many of the children are questioning the faculty's selection of instructional tasks. This has to stop, or the school will not be able to fulfill its task of educating well-rounded children for today's society. Could you have a talk with her?"

What would you say to Betty? "Betty, I want you to become more motivated in art and music and stop those confrontations with teachers and peers"? She wouldn't know what you are talking about.

Would *you* know what you were talking about?

Mr. Haring, you've just been given the "works" by a defensive teacher who is personally threatened because your daughter, Betty, knows more about art and music than most of her classmates and is bored out of her mind by the music and poetry that her teachers are selecting for her class. She is challenging their choices by requesting more relevant works which would illustrate their points. She had a similar class last year in private school and knows what she is talking about, even though she uses an eight-year-old's tactics to deliver her message.

You've just had a sample of educational jargon and educational games. A teacher wishes to communicate with a parent but uses words and attitudes that clearly indicate certain assumptions in her mind. These assumptions are:

(a) The school is always right in its overall teaching plans.
(b) Students learn best by listening without question. Learning is the accumulation of facts transmitted by teachers.

Educational Jargon and Educational Games

(c) Parents should take over the discipline of the child when the school cannot succeed in conforming the child.

(d) A full explanation of the school process need not be given to parents because they would not understand it.

(e) A teacher has to maintain her/his dignity at all times, but particularly when speaking to a parent.

And her words—her jargon—reflect these assumptions.

Let us hasten to say that this use of jargon is *not* a condemnation of schools and school people. Indeed, everyone uses some jargonese in their conversation. People use jargon to accomplish different things. How many times have you been talking to another adult about something in which both of you are interested and your child interrupts with the request that you explain what you are talking about? Haven't you been guilty of giving him or her a technical answer that is over his head so that he will leave you alone? Or haven't you occasionally extricated yourself from a long and potentially boring conversation by saying, "It's too complex a situation to get into"?

These natural and human ways of relating will also affect your conversations with school personnel. These people, like you, have needs: they need to feel professional; they feel an innate responsibility to your child, and consequent guilt if they cannot meet his or her requirements. There are times when a teacher cannot understand a child's behavior and, as a result, feels psychologically threatened by that child. There are times when a teacher feels that she must do things with your child of which you might not approve. She is threatened and concerned about telling you. She may have the natural tendency of the teacher to try to make school appear in the best possible light. Whatever the reasons, you must remember that during your communications with school personnel, while you are advocating the needs of your child, you are liable to encounter a world of educational jargon and educational game playing. You will be stopped or stymied if you do not know how to plow through this overgrowth of technical slang.

This chapter gives you some hints to help you make your way through the morass.

The best way to deal with jargon is to stop the conversation and ask the other person to explain what is meant by that foreign term. Listen carefully, and then try to repeat the definition in your own terms. Once you both understand the meaning of the special term, then it no longer becomes jargon but a workable vocabulary. If Mr. Haring had asked for a definition of "motivational problem," "confrontations," "faculty selection," and "well-rounded children," he probably could have learned almost three

251

times the amount of information. He also would have found many of the hidden *personal meanings* covered by the strange terms. The father would have learned how to deal with Betty, if, indeed, dealing with Betty would have proved necessary once he understood the language. This translating of educational jargonese can be difficult and will often be threatening to the people with whom you are speaking, because it forces them to account for and define their words. To minimize the friction, practice the gentle approach; for example, "I'm sorry but I guess I just don't understand what you mean by the term 'normalizing.' Would you explain it to me?" When explained, repeat the sentence, using the definition. That way you'll both see if it fits the child, the case, or the issue.

"You're saying that Betty doesn't want to sit still in class and patiently listen to a familiar musical number when she thinks that a piece by a 'contemporary composer' is a better piece of music and makes the same point to her class. She told this to the teacher, and the teacher refused to bring the Tchaikovsky to class. Then several of the other students also requested the contemporary composer and the teacher felt that Betty had stimulated them to do so. So are you asking me to tell Betty to remain silent in class, not comment on the musical selections, and discontinue sharing her opinions with her classmates? Since the teachers obviously feel that their approach to music teaching has been successful for them many times before, are you suggesting that the same approach is appropriate for all students?"

Stated in this way, the conversation initiated by the teacher assumes an entirely different perspective. By working through the jargonese, Mr. Haring has defined the terms of the previous monologue, made it into a dialogue, and outlined several additional options for action.

This dissection of the underlying meaning has to be undertaken whenever you are hit by jargonese in the educational system. Let us look at some common forms of jargon. Because each of the words or phrases cited can be—and has been—used differently in various contexts by educators, we will not attempt to define the terms. Actually, that is up to you when you are confronted by them. We are just giving you the "red-flag" words— words and phrases that can lead you astray if you are not absolutely sure you know what the other person means when he uses them.

Things Everyone Says

In this category are words and phrases that you will frequently hear from all sorts of educators. You may have heard them so often of late that you actually think you know what they mean. But be careful; you may not. Often they are used to try to say something but, in reality, mean nothing. Like the term "well-rounded child." Doesn't everyone want a "well-rounded child"? Or do you? In the illustration above, it is questionable whether the child is better "rounded" *by listening to one composer at the exclusion of others?* The teacher is making a value judgment which can be debated. Watch out for the following confusing clichés:

We're interested in educating the whole child. Of course they are. Have you ever tried to educate just part of a child? Ask what the teacher feels makes up the "part" child and what makes up the "whole" child.

We use a team approach to teaching children. Is it team teaching or the team approach? Who is on the team? And does the team really work together to prepare lessons, or do they do their homework and teach the children individually? What is the advantage of this so-called team approach over a good single teacher approach? And ask the most provocative and important question: "Am I, the parent, part of the team? If so, how do I work for my child?"

We use an interdisciplinary approach. For what? Which professionals are involved? What kind of situations need this approach? Are the same professional disciplines always represented or do they change? Do they come out with one plan of action for the child or a different plan for each discipline? What's the advantage of this multiple professional approach over a good school psychologist or a good school nurse or a good school social worker?

We try to individualize the instruction of each child. So does the child. So do you. So does every teacher who has been trained in the past ten years. Sometimes this means that Miss Smith may pick up an extra book for James when it strikes her fancy, or it may mean that she laboriously plans for fifteen different students each day. It is very important to define this term, since it is vital as an educational philosophy for the handicapped child. The acid test of individualized instruction is this, "May I see Johnny's individualized instructional plan?"

Our parents are our partners. This often means, "We teach them, you house them." Or, modified, it might mean, "We have parent conferences four times a year." It might even mean, "We have three room mothers who change once a month." However, in the ideal and appropriate situation, it should mean, "Our parents learn how we teach and even work in the classroom with us for a short while to learn how to teach their children at home." You should fight for this chance of "parents as partners." If your child is handicapped, you will not want to settle for less. See what the school means, if anything, by this slogan. Try to make it *mean* a partnership in the true sense.

We do educational diagnosis. In the very best sense, this means that the school personnel assign the child to a separate room where an experienced teacher evaluates him or her and sets up educational hypotheses about him. She then tries varied ways of teaching the child to find out how he is best taught. Was the phrase used in this context? More than likely, this tired sentence meant that when a teacher became frustrated in trying to teach your child, she tried other materials and games until she found something that worked. Unless the child is *systematically* diagnosed by a clinical educational diagnostician, beware of the validity of "educational diagnosis." The term is often glibly used.

Things to Put You Off

If your child is getting into serious difficulties, or if you are perceived as becoming too aggressive (a palpable danger if you are brave enough to follow the advice of this book), you are liable to be given the phrases which will tend to limit your access and communication with the personnel of the school. These are the phrases which may forecast a slowdown of responsibility by the school. They may also try to make you feel guilty for having created a problem or for having pushed the school into a corner. You must investigate the meaning behind these glib phrases rather than be put off by them—a task easier said than done. Sometimes they are valid statements; at other times, such responses are merely put-offs. We highlight them for your guidance and to offer you some of the possible questions you can ask in investigating these generalizations.

Your child is retarded, so naturally she belongs in Mrs. Axon's class. This is one of the trickiest kinds of statements you will hear, because it is so seductively simple. It implies that *a problem can be solved by a process.* If a child is retarded, he goes into a retarded class. *Wrong!* A child who is retarded, as the chapter on the retarded child states, should first be given enough of an examination to determine what his or her strengths and weaknesses are. Test profiles *never* show a child to be a "straight line" intellectually; he always has his mental peaks and valleys. After determining these, an educational prescription, complete with clear-cut objectives, should be drawn up for him. Then the child must be placed *in that environment that can appropriately meet those goals.* That may or may not be Mrs. Axon's class. It is Mrs. Axon's class only if she represents someone who can meet those goals. The placement is *not* Mrs. Axon's class if the objectives are greater than can be accomplished in her class considering its large size. Don't settle for this "process" statement. Ask *why* Mrs. Axon's class? What will she accomplish? Have your child's goals been discussed with her and has she said that she can accomplish them? Are there other ways of meeting these goals besides the placement in Mrs. Axon's class? Why is that class better than a mainstreamed one? The best defense against any "process" statement is: "O.K., what will my child be doing in that situation six months from now?" Ask that frequently. Expect an answer. And check in six months time to be sure it has come true.

Educational Jargon and Educational Games

The experts agree that we ought to try . . . This often-used introduction might signal an insecurity in the school's decision about your child, or it might represent a valid request for more help in understanding his or her situation. So you must ask: What experts? By what standards are they considered experts? And in what field? Exactly when did they say you ought to try (whatever is suggested) and why? What did they say would be the results? Were they unanimous in their opinions? When can I meet them so I can question and better understand their conclusions? Or where can I find their writings?

I'm afraid that if we can't correct the situation we may have to con-sider excluding him/her from school. Generally this is an out-and-out bluff, particularly in this enlightened day and age. Ask under exactly what authority expulsion of your child can be effected. Ask about the appeal rights of parents. Ask what the school will do about continuing the child's education after he or she has been expelled. Ask the teacher or the principal to delineate the specific conditions or circumstances that would definitely lead to your child's expulsion.

It is my (or my colleagues') judgment that the problems are serious enough to warrant your seeking help. Often this is a serious and sincere statement. At other times, it may simply mean that the staff member cannot understand your child's behavior patterns or has become personally threatened by his or her actions. Therefore, he/she is taking a preventive position by stating, "Since I don't understand what he does or agree with what he does, your child must be sick." You must ask for a clarification of this statement. Who is making that serious, branding judgment? What are the behaviors which require a professional opinion? What kind of help is being suggested—a psychologist, a psychiatrist, a marriage counsellor, an academic counsellor, a social worker? What are the outcomes that the staff member is hoping to see as a result of this external help? How would such an outside consultation increase the child's functioning in school? Before you go bounding off for expensive, time-consuming professional consultation, you must make certain that real problems do exist which require such help for their solution.

I think we're going to have to refer your child to a professional outside the school system. What are all the facts leading up to this decision? In other words, what questions could not be answered by available school personnel? How can a person outside the school system relate to my child's needs within the school system? Does this mean that the school system will be turning away from its responsibility in the case of my child? Or is it simply that the school is requesting another confirmation from an outside consultant about a particularly difficult and complex case—my child? Be sure that the basic issue of responsibility of the school in this matter is faced—and solved.

Between Parent and School

Things to Protect the School

Statements in this category are generally used to keep parents at arms length from the inner workings of the school. Every parent must recognize that this isolation is occasionally necessary. Parents, using the human response of concern, can become over-involved with their child in school and may begin advocating for him or her too vigorously for the child's own good. They may also be advocating the wrong solution. So if you hear any of these distancing statements from the school personnel, you should investigate them, and think about the motivation behind the remarks. Are you becoming too aggressive and actually undermining your child's education? Might you be wrong? If you pursue this route in the school situation, are you going to alienate the school system completely to your point of view? Stop. Investigate. Think. Only when you have corroborated the correctness of your actions should you move through the protective games of the school.

The system you're asking about is too complicated to explain right now. The first question which should immediately come into your mind must be asked silently: Too complicated for whom? It is a bit insulting to have this statement flung at you, even though the remark may be made in good faith. Perhaps the person who uttered this statement realizes the full complexity of the background details of your child's school problems and thinks that it really will take too long to explain "the ramifications." But when you hear this statement coming at you, it is best to smile knowingly and murmur in return, "Try me." You'll soon know how complicated your child's story is, and you will be able to judge the need for extensive explanation. A good method of simplifying any complicated explanation about a child's problem is to ask for it on a piece of paper. This often forces the complex into a simple, concise mold. When you are confronted with long-winded solutions, simply inquire what that solution will accomplish for your child in six weeks. Both of these methods will get to the heart of the matter and prevent you from getting an overly "professional" explanation.

I think it would be wise if we delineated some roles here, particularly the roles of the parents and the teacher. Any time you get into role definitions, you are usually entering an exercise that limits the participation of certain of the members. These restricted "members" are usually the parents. In addition, by setting specific roles, you run the risk of establishing standards of behavior that become unchanged even when the underlying situation changes and evolves. When this occurs, it is best to ascertain the reasons behind the need for "role delineation" if they are not clear to you. Attempt to get to the feelings of the school personnel that prompted this delineation. Avoid allowing these roles of parent and teacher to be-

256

come formalized. If you are advocating for your child, you may need the ability to be totally flexible in the role you assume for the problem of the moment.

Let me interpret his/her test scores for you. This is acceptable, because you will need some help in understanding these important test scores, particularly if they are presented in quartiles, stanine, standard deviations, and the like. It will even be helpful to know the general impressions of the psychologist or teacher who administered the tests. But always ask for the "raw scores" too. The raw scores are the results before the impression of the examiner influences the final interpretation. By noting the raw score vs. the interpretation you have a balance and check on the subjective impressions which the examiner who is interpreting the scores to you applied to the test. You may need all of these scores at some later time to give to another examiner. You can have them; they belong to your child. Insist on them, but don't use them or be influenced by them unless they have been carefully interpreted for you in terms which you know and understand.

We're going to discuss Susan on Thursday and I'll contact you afterwards to set up a conference date. Not on your life! You need an invitation to that conference. It is your child they are discussing. They should have your responses—and you theirs. Now very likely this demand will go against the grain of many administrators and special educators. Parent involvement in child conferences has not been attempted very often in the past. Those conferences were held with only school personnel present, and the conclusions were carefully worded in jargonese that allowed the school to act as the helping professional and place the parent in the role of the compliant client. Now you are asking to become an active part of the treatment team—a professional parent. The school people may not know quite how to handle this request. But they will learn; you will teach them. Make certain you are at that conference about your child.

I think it's best that we try Efram on this schedule for a probationary period. Probationary? He has to prove something? An "experimental" or "pilot" trial may be acceptable in progressive education, but what is "probationary"? Does that mean he has a certain number of days to accomplish something? Who will set the specific number of days? And what is that "something" to be accomplished? Isn't that probationary action shifting the responsibility onto the child rather than appropriately being assumed by the school? The term "probation" usually creates a sword of Damocles hanging over the head of the student. Is that what the school wants? This might be the desirable option in a severe disciplinary case, but generally it is an inappropriate method. Check the philosophy behind the probationary period. And if your child must enter such a tentative phase in his or her education, you should be aware of the exact

257

conditions which have to be met by the end of this "waiting" period. It would be best to have these conditions in writing.

Important Words to Know

For children who have special needs, whether long-term or short-term, there are new educational words which schools are using in an attempt to describe the improved services being offered. You won't be able to talk to many educators for very long before you start hearing a few of these words. Generally, they are not defensive; in fact, many are words of hope, verbal ways of considering educational services helpful to children. We list these words to alert you to their popularity. When you hear them, ask what they mean. Their definition could be very important to you, your child, and the school.

Federal Alphabet Soup. If you have a handicapped child, the numbers and letters which are influencing his or her education often get very mixed up in school language these days. Many millions of dollars are flowing into the local schools to help handicapped children. Many other federal dollars are helping poor children, bilingual children, college students, and all types of students with special needs. You probably already know HEW (Health, Education, and Welfare), and possibly USOE (United States Office of Education). If you are advocating the handicapped child, you may recognize BEH (Bureau of Education for the Handicapped). But watch out for SRS, NIMH, OCD, Titles III, VI, and I, OCD, P.L. 94–142 which amends P.L. 93–380, and national organizations like CEC, NARC, NASDSE, WICHE, and so on. The point is, whenever you hear the alphabet, or legal numbers *as a noun,* ask for a definition. You will probably learn about more resources than you ever dreamed possible.

Shorthand Initials. Besides the federal acronyms, educators lately have been abbreviating everything from P.E. (Physical Education) to S.E. (Sex Education). When letters are used *as an adjective,* it is also wise to ask their definition, particularly if you are talking about handicapping conditions. L.D. means Learning Disability and, as we stated in Chapter 12, this definition varies from state to state. E.D. means Emotionally Disturbed, and the definition of this term can influence your child's future educational life, as described in Chapter 15. Then there's M.R. (Mental Retardation), OHI, D and H of H, B and VI (Other Health Impaired, Deaf and Hard of Hearing, Blind and Visually Impaired). Again, we will not list all the possible initials because they only become important when they are applied as descriptions of your child.

Behavioral Objectives. These are stated goals such as: "John will be able to multiply single numbers by the end of the month." This is an important concept in determining what progress any child should make. It is a valid way of stressing individual educational planning. Is your school using the behavioral objective approach?

Functional Curriculum. This term supposes that the materials which a child learns in school should have direct applicability to his/her post-school life. If the term is used, become familiar with the extent to which it is important. If it is an effective program, it should help you feel better about your school's offerings.

Normalization. This is an important, but often badly used term. It is sometimes used as an educational philosophy. Generally, it refers to the training of a special child which attempts to create the most normal schooling situation possible and has, as its ultimate goal, the preparation of this child for a normal post-school life. Let's hope it is being used and not abused in your child's special education program.

Mainstreaming. This is a term used to describe the integration of children with special needs and problems, particularly handicapped children, into regular classes of non-handicapped children. It is not yet known whether this new approach is going to prove effective. Perhaps the lack of research is responsible for the many varied interpretations and definitions of mainstreaming. If your school uses this term, check into the meaning of your local definition. Will it be helpful for your child? Or will it be harmful? You can only decide if you know what the term signifies in your school.

Resource Room. Generally, this is a room which a child with a special problem, such as blindness or deafness, can visit for part of a day in order to receive the specialized training he or she needs to help him cope with his handicaps during instruction in mainstreamed classes. But in some schools resource rooms are quite different. What does the term mean in your school?

Words are funny. They can explain, attack, defend, denigrate, praise, love, comfort, insult, destroy, commit. They are your primary tools for your child's best education. Treat them seriously—use them well.

25 The Rights of Parents and Children

The image of the school as an authority figure in our lives is an easy one to evoke. All of us have been through the process of having our lives disrupted by the compulsory attendance laws which said that we *had* to march off to the neighborhood school when we were only six years old and which seemed years before our mothers thought we were ready. We remember that our weekly allowance, the promised presents from grandmother, and the delighted bear hug or the remorseful parent talks hinged upon what the teacher of the moment wrote upon that report card. If we continued on to college, our whole careers literally hung on the nods and whims and the "(e) all of the above's" of the professor.

Small wonder that none of us dared to challenge the authority of the school. This powerful control is something we have always taken for granted; it remains solid, unchanging, immutable. That is, it has been untarnished until recently. Within the last few years, our country has gone through the intense pain of questioning its figures of authority. As disillusioned believers, we have found many of the major figures to be weak and dishonest. Our leaders, too, often have been self-serving people who developed myths to surround them and rituals to protect them and their hidden pleasures from our eyes. In this newly developed awareness, the universities have also been questioned by their angry students, who have discovered that a college education is almost worthless in the future world of competitive employment.

These discoveries of irregularities in previously revered institutions have prompted us to take a good hard look at our elementary and secondary schools for the first time. And without shock or surprise, we have discovered problems there as well. We have found that the textbooks used in these schools for years are full of biased material, required reading which fosters sex discrimination, non-traditional ideals, and distorted history. Corruption in the use of federal and state monies has been uncovered. There is a great waste of money, supplies, time, and talent in administration and poor teaching in the schools of our country. The searchlight of truth has thrown its beam across the defects and deficiencies of our nation's educational system.

And so the schools of this nation are facing their first serious test of authority. Each year they are riddled with hundreds of lawsuits, investigations, audits, and allegations. And each year spawns many new books by prominent and sensitive authors suggesting reforms, changes, even the elimination of the traditional school.

Both parents and children have felt themselves victimized by the schools when they learn of the scandals. Many parents, like you, want more out of education for their children and have taken steps to ensure parent and child rights in the future. Recent laws have guaranteed these rights, and new books and papers have spelled them out in clear terms. You should know about these rights. They are your—and your child's—legacy for the future.

The recent clarification of the rights of parents and children in education primarily came about because the parents of handicapped children felt that they were being "ripped off" by the school system. They found themselves desperately fighting for even the smallest concession for their child's education from school systems that were characterized by apathy, resistance, indifference, and incompetence in dealing with special problems. Parents were being forced to tolerate the burden of a handicapped child as an "act of God," forced to suffer in silence, and wonder when and where their child would receive a fair deal in this world. Each morning, watching children leave for school, they realized that their neighbors with non-handicapped children were sending their children to a school which was paid for out of the same taxes that the parents of handicapped children had to pay. Yet these "normal" neighborhood children were getting a better, happier, and more suitable education than were the handicapped children, some of whom received no education at all.

Some parents of retarded children in Pennsylvania decided that the whole educational system, which seemed to be patently discriminatory against handicapped children, should have that power checked. These parents sued their state school system for unfair practices. They claimed that Pennsylvania had a state constitution (as do all states) which guaranteed each child of that state an education. They further claimed that the 14th Amendment of the U.S. Constitution guaranteed "equal protection of the law." Therefore, if the handicapped children of that state were getting less educational benefits than were the non-handicapped children, the school system was acting illegally to deny those handicapped children that "equal protection."

These determined, advocate parents brought suit in federal court— and won! The statements of the rights of children and parents which resulted from the subsequent actions of this court case and other similar court actions, as well as subsequent federal law (known as Public Law 94–142), provide the basis for the rights statements in this chapter. Naturally these statements apply to the rights of non-handicapped children and their parents as well. They apply to *all* children.

A fundamental right of your child is a *right to education*. Perhaps this sounds too simplistic or too obvious. If you take that right for granted, probably you have not yet had to face a school system which wants to exclude your child because it does not have the appropriate teacher or class for him. You have not faced the administrator who proposes to expel your child because the school cannot cope with his troublesome behavior. You have never had to face the prospect that your child might have to grow to maturity without an education. If you have never faced this, then very likely you can be expected smugly to take the right to education for granted. But to a large number of school misplacements, "pushouts," expelled, or excluded children, they cope with a violated right—the school's failure to fulfill the right to a proper education.

From the moment your child becomes of "school age" to the moment he or she exceeds the upper limit of school age as designated by your state, he is entitled to the most appropriate educational opportunities available in your school system. He must have teachers, classes, curriculum, and counsellors as appropriate in meeting his individual needs as are those which are provided for the star football player, the student body president, or the mayor's daughter. And if he has not been offered these educational provisions, then you may appeal to the school administrators and, failing this appeal, you may sue for "equal protection." This appeal process will be called the "due process" right and will be explained further in this chapter. In this age, the need to resort to the latter action, a legal suit, will be rare.

The second right your child has is to *all of education*. Perhaps his or her school automatically places him in a vocational track when you want him in a pre-college track. It is possible that the school does not provide him with a modified physical education program, even when you have informed them that he has a "rheumatic heart." Or your son is prevented from taking the home economics course because he is a boy. These could be violations of that "equal protection under the law" clause of the 14th Amendment. Translated into simpler terms, this means that everything which the school offers has to be available within reason to all students who may appropriately want to participate. The school can counsel your child not to take part in a specific course or try to steer him into an alternative course which they feel fits him better. However, if you really want one of the courses available in the school for your child, you should be able to have him enroll in this subject. The school must prove that the course is inappropriate in order to deny it to your child.

The court battles that are fought to obtain these rights are generally fought on behalf of handicapped children. Many are specific cases of handicapped children who are being excluded from various available school programs merely because they are handicapped. A simple adaptation of that particular educational program could have made this course accessible for the handicapped child.

And then the raised consciousness of women discovered that many of the favored activities of the school also were closed to girls. The reason for this exclusion was simply traditional—they were girls taking boys' courses—and not because of any physical differences. The reverse of these discriminatory actions—boys not taking girls' classes—was also practiced. Like the parents of handicapped children, concerned parents took their case to the legislature. They received legislation from Congress which guaranteed equal educational provisions for girls and boys.

In effect, these provisions stand for the principle that all that is within the school has to be available for *all* the students. However, that principle does not guarantee that just because you want little Henry to have Mrs. Stephens for American History rather than Miss Merkle, you will get the teacher of your choice. These rights mean that if you want Henry to have American History and he could not previously take the course because he could not get his wheelchair all the way up to the second floor where it was to be taught, now Henry will be offered American History. The course will either be taught on the first floor, or an elevator will be installed to take him to the second floor, or Henry will be carried by an attendant to the second floor. That fulfills his guarantee of receiving the full spectrum of that school's educational offerings.

An important third right, possessed by every child, is that of *an appropriate education.* If your child is not an average child, then this provision becomes the foundation of your fight for his or her proper education. Indeed, this right of every child to receive appropriate education was the cornerstone of the landmark Pennsylvania court case that clarified the rights of handicapped children. When the courts acted on behalf of the retarded children of Pennsylvania, the judgment stated that each handicapped child had to be placed in a class or educational activity that would meet as many of his broad educational goals (academic, social, physical) as possible.

But how do schools know enough about a child to make accurate placements? The guarantee of the rights of children for an appropriate education might be interpreted as meaning that any child who cannot be expected to profit from a regular classroom setting in a regular school should be *identified* by the school, evaluated by the proper professionals such as the school physician, the school psychologist, or the special education teacher, and *placed* in an educational setting that should do him the most good *as determined by the professionals and their evaluations.*

What does this mean to you, the parent? It means that if your child is recommended for a special placement, the school has the obligation to justify that placement to you—and should be able to back up this decision by factual test scores, professional data, and the like *before* the child is moved. This provision also means that if the school has *not* placed your child in the educational setting deemed appropriate by you and you question this situation, the school administrators must be able to justify your child's current placement with the same professionally determined facts and figures.

Furthermore, the school is charged with the responsibility of *finding* children who need special help. The school should not wait until a child falls off the wagon of school success before beginning an evaluation. This specifies that if a child's parent reports that his child has a problem which might be handled better by a specialized educational program, then the school has to investigate and allay or remedy this fear. In simple terms, the school is mandated to evaluate every suspect child and, if needed, place him or her in the proper special school setting. The school must assure your child of an appropriate education—one which fits your individual child's needs.

Of course you may not always agree with the school, even when they have "fully" evaluated your child before his or her placement. Know that you have a right to appeal both his evaluation by professionals inside the school and his placement. In the next section on "due process," you will learn how to go about an appeal and how to find its various levels and procedures; but it is sufficient to state here that you, as a parent, have a right to have your child evaluated by professionals outside the school system. If their opinion differs from that of the school personnel, you have a right to appeal the school's decision. A situation occasionally arises where such an appeal is necessary.

You should never accept an evaluation or placement during the initial explanation. Think it through. See if the material you were told about your child fits with the bits and pieces of information and observations you can assemble from your past personal experiences with the child. Discuss the school's decisions with the members of the close family unit and with friends. What are their thoughts and observations? You must then decide whether to support the school's decisions or demand that they investigate further. The right of an appropriate education for your child is one right you cannot afford to neglect.

The wording of the 14th Amendment to the Constitution also gives us the title of the fourth right of a child and his parents, the right of *"due process* of law." This means, in basic terms, that a school cannot arbitrarily or capriciously assign a child to only part of an educational program, exclude him from any part of a school program that he needs, or keep him in specialized educational classes without the parents' prior knowledge. "Due process" is the guarantee that parents will be consulted in all administrative procedures regarding their child within the school. Included in the "due process" right is an appeals process which assures a parent some leverage in all the important school decisions affecting his child. Each school system in the country that receives any sort of federal money (which covers most school systems) is required to have a written document of the procedures of "due process" available to the parents of that school system. Write to your school superintendent for a copy of this document, asking him for his manual of procedures to implement due process requirements. If he does not have such a document to give to you, or appears reluctant to share this information with you, then you must write to your state's Director of Special Education in your State Department of Education, c/o the State Capitol. Explain your frustration with your local superintendent and ask for a copy of that valuable manual. You can be reasonably sure you will get the document if you must resort to this approach. When you do, you will find that the following are your rights under "due process."

A. You have a right to receive a written notice before your child is evaluated. Naturally, if you receive such a notice and do not wish the child tested, you may object. And if the school wishes to test him or her anyway, you can appeal that action. There are certain circumstances where the school has a right to test a child without your permission; but, in most cases, you could successfully prevent a testing or evaluation session which you perceived as being potentially unfair to your child. However, we must put forward a general word of advice: Do *not* stop the evaluation session if it appears well intentioned. It is a general truism that the more you know about your child, the better decisions you will be able to make about him. The same holds for his school and the people working in it.

B. You have a right to written notification before your child is removed from his current classroom and placed in a different educational setting (special class, etc.). Again, as before, you have a right to appeal any placement. It is in this particular area that many appeals are currently being fought. As a rule of thumb, it is best to exercise this right only when you have the data and information provided by outside professionals who will objectively and factually uphold your placement decisions. In any case, you should never agree to a change in your child's school placement unless you fully understand (1) what actions and/or scores indicate that he needs such a change in placement; (2) what new or different educational goals can be realized best in the new setting; and (3) how long your child will need this placement and what will be the expected next step after the change. Guard granting your permission for an educational change as your most important tool in learning the whole truth about your child, his schooling, and what is truly appropriate for him.

C. Your child has a right to a periodic review of any non-ordinary educational placement. This means that the school should retest or otherwise systematically reevaluate your child's school assignments at regular intervals, preferably each year, to see if the child is receiving maximum benefit from that class setting or if the current school placement should be changed or terminated. This right speaks to the fact that in the past, children who were occasionally misdiagnosed during the initial evaluation by the school psychologist or special education teacher remained in special classes for the rest of their school life. Consequently they often faced minimal expectations and reduced challenge in classes inappropriate to their capabilities. With periodic evaluation, these children will be found and removed from the inappropriate programs, then returned to more realistic educational settings.

This right should have a very significant meaning for you as a parent. Not only does it offer you the chance of repeated assessments to determine whether your child really needs that specialized education; it also allows you the unique opportunity to get a proper look at his school progress through the years. Insist on a schedule of periodic evaluations when you have that first conversation with the school administrator about agreeing to enter your child in a specialized school program. This is your child's right, which you as his parent must protect, demand, and monitor.

And then exercise that right to know the information gained in the reevaluation. Request the scores of all tests and ask for the interpretation and significance of the results. Make every effort to have your child's classroom progress explained in terms of these test results. This information will allow you to compare your child's maturity and adjustment in class to his potential. Such insight into your child is what all parents should have the opportunity to discover.

D. If you are dissatisfied about any aspect of your child's schooling, and particularly if your child is a handicapped child, the school system will have to recognize your right to a fair and impartial hearing. The school system has to adjust its practices to accommodate the findings of such hearings. All hearing practices and procedures (as stated before) are clearly outlined and categorized in a manual, and any citizen may obtain copies of these manuals either from the local school administrators or from the state department of education. You should read these standard practices and procedures over carefully before starting an appeals process which will ultimately result in a hearing.

Why is it important to know what is in this manual? Because the practices and procedures manual will show how you can:

*receive timely (enough time to be thorough, but not so much time that your child is harmed) and specific written notice of such a hearing. You'll find that the school can start a hearing as well as you can, so this right of a prior notice becomes important to you not only as the originator but also as the recipient of the appeal process.

*review all records. At a hearing about your child, nothing should be used to support a school's position of which you are not aware. With few exceptions, you should have access to *all* school records pertaining to your child. Read every page of that record thoroughly and have Xeroxed copies of each page whenever possible.

*obtain an independent evaluation. "Independent" means an expert opinion from some professional outside the school system. This will become particularly important when you begin to build a factual but "child-based" case.

*be represented by counsel. Because the hearing process is quite a new procedure in many school systems, few local attorneys are familiar with the intricacies of the "hearing" process in schools. Go to parent organizations and ask for their references for legal aid or for a professional advocate. There are many people who have recently become interested and informed about hearings related to the type of special child in their own homes.

*cross-examine. This procedure is, of course, an unfamiliar procedure to most lay persons. But it may be necessary when a hearing is based upon your personal concern that uninformed attitudes are being used to make decisions detrimental to your child. This cross-examination is best done by your experienced counsel or advocate.

*bring witnesses. Select these people very carefully, for each represents another important source of data and helpful information.

*present evidence. It may be necessary to "build a case." This may involve the use of witnesses, evidence, outside professionals' opinions, and cross-examination procedures. Here the parent is again advised to have the advice of an outside agent in the presentation of such evidence.

*receive a complete and accurate record of the entire proceedings. Read the manual of procedures to learn what kinds of notes will be taken at the hearing and who will be responsible for getting these transcripts or minutes to you. When you think that a reasonable time has elapsed after the hearing, phone to request your copy. Often there are untimely delays in getting these notes processed. You—actually your child—cannot afford this delay.

A right you probably have never heard of is the right of the child for the *least restrictive educational environment*. This is terminology that resulted from significant court cases and is now being used as the philosophical basis for much of the "mainstreaming" activity that is taking place in American schools. "Least restrictive environment" means that when a child is being considered for placement in a specialized educational setting, he or she must be placed in the setting where he can function as comfortably as possible within as non-handicapped a group of children as he can accommodate.

In the educational perspective, a special class of 100 percent handicapped children in a residential school where there is little if any contact with non-handicapped children is the *most* restrictive environment possible for a child. At the other end of the spectrum, the class with twenty-eight non-handicapped children and two handicapped children, all learning to their maximum capacity through the skills of a superior involved teacher, who offers each child adequate help and supervision, is the optimal *least* restrictive environment. Each child is different. The classroom needs of children include both extremes—and middle-ground classrooms as well. Many children will have to progress from one type of class to another during their educational journey.

Thus the right of the "least restrictive environment" is a relative right. It is relative to the child's problem, his growth, his potential, and his needs. But that right gives you, his parent, access to the privilege of questioning his educational setting. For instance, has your child been transferred to a special education classroom because the school is convenienced by this change or because this move represents the best placement for your child? Could the same child be placed in a normal classroom if the teacher were given special help? If this is the case, then his school should provide that help. You may be able to force this specific action by the use of due process and possibly a hearing. But first you must be fully aware of your facts and figures. You'll be fighting a vague and ambiguous concept or policy; and you'll need data—lots of data—from outside the school. If your child ends up in an environment that appears much more restrictive than you believe appropriate for him, you should ask for a calendar of progress which clearly delineates under what conditions and when he might be able to move to an enviroriment of lesser restriction. Then you have the periodic reevaluation for use as a decision-making process for a more positive future placement.

Often parents of handicapped children are intimidated by the public schools, who force the parents to send their children to other schools because "we just cannot handle him here and will not be able to do so for some time." Thousands of parents have paid millions of dollars in tuition to other public and private schools for education of their children which should have been available in the local schools.

This inequity should not occur any longer. The clarification of rights has indicated that parents of handicapped children who must turn to private education by necessity have as a matter of law (P.L. 94–142) a right to a *reimbursement* of all costs. *Handicapped children should not be a financial drain on the family,* particularly in education, just because they are handicapped.

Because many school boards are finding themselves paying expensive tuition rates for private schools on behalf of children in their districts, they are attempting to add more sophisticated and comprehensive educational services for those special children in their local schools. This development should always be encouraged. It will help your child stay with his friends and grow with his family.

But if your school district is still one of the thousands that do not have the proper provisions for your child, and probably will not have these provisions in the foreseeable future, investigate the private schools and the payment of tuition from public school funds. Ask the school principal and then the school board if necessary to pay the costs of this special program for your child. Do not be put off by the statement, "I'm sorry, but that's just not our policy." Insist on reading that policy. Appeal such a restrictive local policy to the school board. Question the legality of these financial restrictions directly with your state department of education. You probably can win the reimbursement of costs for the outside education of a handicapped child. But you may have to fight.

A final right that you should know in detail is the right that gives you *access to your child's records.* This right is assured by federal legislation called the Family Education Right and Privacy Act. This legislation grew out of the concerns of the authors of the law that much material could be put into a child's record that was negatively biased against him or her unless some way was legalized of having that record checked against the truth. The legislation allows you, the parent, to check that information—and then insist upon changes in the record if that folder appears to contain biased or blatantly incorrect statements.

Whereas most of the rights discussed in this chapter arose from the extremely unfavorable conditions of education for the handicapped child, this right, the right of access to records, resulted from a feeling of concern for all people. Whether your child is handicapped or non-handicapped, bright or slow, social or antisocial, you are urged to check his/her records. You need to look at these school folders to be sure that they are correct, helpful, unbiased, and objective.

Try some advocacy. Sit down and write a letter to your local school principal saying:

Dear Mr. Robinson:

It is my understanding that the federal law now allows me full access to my child's school records. Therefore, I would like to request permission to examine all of the files of my child, John Jenkins, on Friday, March 23, in your office. I will call you on March 20 to confirm this appointment and to receive directions to the room where these records are kept. I will then request copies of relevant documents.

Thank you.

James Jenkins

This letter should bring a response within the week, and a positive one. If it is not, then you have two sources of appeal: (1) the state department of education, and (2) the federal government. You will get a response. And you will have a chance to view your child's records.

If, in perusing the records, you come across some information or opinion that could be damaging to your child and his/her education if the file is read by others, then you should seek to have the material removed. Again, if the school lags over this, there are sources of appeal.

But rather than progress into the adversary process of appeals in upholding your fight for access to your child's records, we refer you to an excellent booklet available from the Children's Defense Fund (1520 New Hampshire Avenue, N.W., Washington, D.C. 20036) entitled *Your School Records*. This booklet tells you exactly what are your rights to information, how to get them, how to effect needed changes, and what other agencies are available to help you make these changes. This noncopyrighted booklet is a must for any parents concerned with their child's school image as it may be adversely reflected in the school records.

The Appendix of this book contains lists of agencies and organizations in this country which are dedicated to helping children obtain and keep their rights to full, appropriate, free education. They exist to serve you and will entertain any question about which you may care to write or call them.

But most of these agencies only exist to consult with you about your child's rights; very few of them will fight the individual battles your child may need. You must do the tough work of ensuring your child's rights. You must gather all of the facts, make the decisions along with the school administrators, aggressively unearth all available information, and collect school and outside data. You should trust your intuition; but, at the same time, attempt a high level of objectivity. You should try to coordinate long-term and short-term goals for your child. Finally, you should be placed in the position of assisting in the decisions about the best method of educating your child.

Being a parent in this society is not an easy task; in fact, sometimes the job seems impossible. It can be done. Very likely, your parents tried to work at their roles as parents with common sense and determination. You must credit them with their successes. You have even more tools as a parent than they had: you have stated rights for your children. You also face a future of creativity and flexibility in education which was never dreamed possible.

Consider his education as the greatest opportunity your child will ever have. It is his right. Make sure you know *your* rights to see that he gets the most out of this experience.

26 The Parent-Child-School Team— The Parent's Role

Your child's education is the canvas upon which he will imprint his life. On this background, he will etch and draw his own individual patterns, which will ultimately represent his identity and his contribution to himself, his immediate world, and society in general. A meager, constricted educational canvas limits the amount that one can paint upon the surface. The patterns will be elementary; the outlines not original; the final picture of a lifetime emerging too small and too simple for the size of the potential person depicted. As the child's parents, you are instrumental in making certain that the educational foundation which your child receives is broad enough to shoulder any dream, any ambition, any talent. You bear a large percentage of the responsibility in molding the future life of your child. A good deal of this responsibility occurs in the form and content of his education.

But as we have demonstrated in this book, you are not alone in this endeavor. There is a vital and important institution that stands imposingly in the middle of your child's pathway. He cannot go around this edifice. He must walk through it for the many years that he will be receiving his education. Within this building which we call "school" are the learning waystations that will offer your child the information he often cannot receive at home. Also within this building (and others like it), your child will be assessed, evaluated, disciplined, rewarded, molded into a social or antisocial being, and directed toward a future career. The people who work and interact with your child in this school setting assume extremely important and meaningful roles in your child's life. These people may have more influence on your child's future than even you are willing to admit. No matter how strong and tightly knit the nuclear family may be, the impact of the school experience on the child is powerful and often irreversible.

It is little wonder that many parents dread the day when their five- or six-year-old leaves the predictable interior of their home and takes the first steps toward a strange, unknown, but extraordinarily influential school experience. A certain degree of control is lost. New thoughts are being transferred to your child from foreign sources, ideas are being implanted over which you have little censorship. The school has assumed the co-leadership role in your child's education, whether you wish to relinquish total control or not. How can parents deal with this powerful force in their child's life? There are several steps we have outlined which yield the necessary information parents will need if their communication and interaction with their child's school is to result in an effective "team":

1. The parent should understand the roles of the school personnel—what is the responsibility and capability of each and how each should affect the child.
2. The parent should be aware if he/she has a "special" child. If so, the parent must become familiar with the educational needs of that special child. In addition, he must be knowledgeable about the school resources he can expect for that child.
3. The parent must learn how to approach the school with calm intelligence and the right attitude to help the child receive the very best from the school environment.
4. The parent should have some familiarity with current educational policies and educational terminology so that conversations with the educators do not perplex and confuse the parent, and thereby harm the child.
5. The parent must know the rights of the child and the rights of the parent in the current school environment, so that if these rights have been abused and remediation is not being attempted, the parent may fight the system appropriately to ensure the most appropriate education for the child.

Parents should view their role in the child's school experience as a helping one. As we have tried to show, there is so much more to be gained if the parent, the child, the teacher, and the other school personnel can work together to provide the best possible educational experience. Parents should not automatically assume the role of adversary in dealing with their child's school. This antagonistic attitude usually creates an immediate defensive response on the part of the school officials and prevents a rational, thoughtful approach to the child's problems by the important people in his educational life—the school and the parents. The wise parent approaches the school with a sense of cooperation, of working together to ensure the child's adaptation to school and to facilitate his/her education. In other words, unless there are specific irremedial differences which the school refuses to correct and resolve, "Don't fight them, join them."

As a member of this team, what can the parent do to make the most out of the school experience for his child? What positive contributions can the parent make?

Children approach school on the first day with preconceived ideas about the total school experience and its importance. Much of this attitude emanates directly from the home. Often the parents instill these feelings into their child unknowingly; older siblings also play a very important role in preparing the younger members of the family for school. One of the most important tasks that the parent has as a member of this team is to instill a positive feeling about education in their young child prior to that first day of school. School must not be viewed as a mandatory evil. Education should be a very high priority in the home. Rewards for positive school participation must be part of the family pattern of living; the more positive the child feels about the school experience, the better will be his performance. There are very subtle ways that a parent can undermine the child's concepts of the educational process and the activities at school. Keeping a child home from school for flimsy reasons is a common parent misdemeanor. Dismissing a "good" report card or a "bad" report card without the appropriate response is a negligent action by the parent and has a definite underlying message which the child cannot overlook. Forgetting to ask the child to discuss "what he is learning" demonstrates a profound disinterest in his educational efforts and suggests to the child that the parent puts little value on the school experience. So will the child. These are but a few examples of how a parent can unwittingly create a negative feeling about education within the home and within the child.

Parents must also prepare their children for the authority which they will be facing in school. From the beginning of kindergarten or first grade, the child will enter a somewhat regimented, controlled environment, where the teacher is the "boss." How well the child accepts the concept of that authority figure will impact dramatically upon whether he or she does poorly or well in school during those crucial early adjustment days when so many long-range school attitudes are being formed. The wise parent begins the use of authority within the home, no later than the year before the child goes to school, so that the child is accustomed to it and knows and accepts the required responses.

It is important that the parent takes an active part in the activities and governance of the child's school. This is how the parent can gain the respect and appreciation of the school administration and then be able to suggest and initiate any necessary changes. There are many jobs within the school which will assist the busy teachers and also enrich the education of the children. Parents can act as "class parents," who accompany the teacher when the children go on educational or recreational outings. Or they can act as "class aides," actually assisting the teacher in her or his daily class management. In many schools, the parents function as school librarian. This saves the school system money and enables the parents to stimulate their own children to recognize the value and importance of books. Most schools have P.T.A.s where interaction between faculty and parents can take place, with the school the primary focus. P.T.A.s usually deal with the material as well as the socio-cultural aspects of school. These organizations can help the principal in his/her efforts to improve or upgrade the school or its programs. A raised chorus of parents can have an awesome impact upon the sluggish school administration. Action may be forthcoming at a more expedient rate when parents are behind the issue than if the principal is attempting to fight the crucial problem alone.

One of our children's teachers initiated an interesting experiment within her elementary school classroom that proved delightfully successful. She invited the parent(s) of each child to visit the school on specific mornings and discuss their profession or vocation. All types of jobs and professions were represented by the parents. In this way, the children were exposed to various new concepts about the world around them. Each child could take pride in the contribution his or her specific parent was making to society. The parents became integral to the social studies lesson plan designed by this clever and resourceful teacher. Here the parent was an active member of the teaching team. The positive parent-child-teacher rapport during this experience reached an all-time high and stayed at that level. This is the type of process that can originate from one parent and grow as success becomes the obvious result. You can be that parent—you can suggest this experiment to your child's teacher.

In the society of the seventies, the schools are an ever-changing landscape. New rules and regulations from the state or federal governments are altering the districting and child composition on a somewhat chaotic, unpredictable timetable. The school administration within your child's specific school has little to say about the timing or the content of the new regulations. All that the school principal and the other administrators can do is to react and implement these proposals with as little turmoil as possible. Parents can be of immeasurable help if they will realize that the local school principal cannot refuse to accept the new guidelines. The parents can object at the higher levels if they wish; but they should assist the local school in changing to meet the regulations with calm and dignity so that their children can be taught in an atmosphere free of tension and unrest. Learning cannot occur when children are surrounded daily by stress. A fine example of this situation is the current strife over the desegregation rulings. Little is gained by the refusal to send children to school. Little is gained but so much is being lost . . . their education. Picketing and noisy demonstrations outside school buildings distract the children who have been sent to school to concentrate and to learn. No one wants to deny the parent the right to vent his anger or displeasure at a particular ruling. However, this should be done at the appropriate location—a city council meeting, a state education meeting, or via a letter to the federal representatives (senators and members of Congress). These actions will be heard. The only individuals reacting to the local school disruption are the innocent school administrators and the children, who cannot learn because of the external stimuli and noise.

Certain schools have been restructured to experiment with new concepts in education. The regular classroom may be changed to the freer, less structured "open classroom." Combining grades may be advocated by local school authorities. Overcrowding may necessitate "shifts" during which children go to school from 8:00 A.M. to noon or from noon to 4:00 P.M. These are changes which will certainly displease many parents. Again, remember that the principal and other school personnel are not responsible for the rulings but must implement them. Help from the parents can convert a potentially disruptive situation into a workable one. Objections should be processed to the proper authorities at the same time that the parents are making certain that the school atmosphere is as conducive to learning as is possible under the current conditions. If the parent can exhibit a degree of patience, he may find that the experiment has had intrinsic value. On the other hand, he may discover that the exercise was as unsatisfactory as he had predicted and is being abandoned by the school officials. His voice should be heard—but only at the right place and at the right time. He must help his children learn while he is pushing and maneuvering for change.

Other areas of parent-school cooperation are the key subjects of sex education and drug education. Many parents resent the removal of this type of education from within the home and the shift of such material into the school. There is some error in this reasoning since the schools are not assuming *primary* responsibility for the child's education in these vital areas but are supplementing and implementing the educational process because of the extraordinary importance this information will have on the child's entire future life. The home still has the primary role in delivering information on sex and drugs to the child. If a parent questions the appropriateness or expertise of the school in imparting this information, he has every right to request that his child be excused from these specific classes. We do not recommend this action; we merely indicate that it is legitimate and should be honored. What we do not condone is the parental wish to deprive *all* children of receiving this information within the schools. Many children will never get it in their homes and without it will reach maturity with distorted street talk as their sole source of sex and drug education. To be a sincere and informed member of the parent-child-school team, the parent must weigh all actions against the school process carefully, trying to look always at the total picture rather than his particular biases and concerns about his individual child. The parent should not handcuff the entire school process unless he is convinced that the process is harmful to *all* children involved.

Parents can and should become an integral part of the teaching team on a regular basis. You ask, "Is this possible?" If you keep up with what your child is learning in school, you can reinforce such learning enthusiastically at home, and so make the whole educational process an exciting cooperative venture between parent, teacher, and child. This is particularly true when the child is exposed to social studies and history in school. Taking the child to the library to look up books about the subjects discussed, visiting the local museums to see paintings and other art pieces of the period or country under study, saving magazine articles that comment on a foreign country, a time in history, or a famous individual, past or present—all of these are ways to reinforce the learning and excite and stimulate the imagination of your child. He or she will clearly receive the positive message that what he is learning is important and meaningful. As a result, he will learn far better and with greater delight.

As your child matures, be prepared to read some of the things he will be reading in school. This will permit you to discuss the play, novel, short story, or essay with your child. You can act as a sounding board, and challenge the growing mind to stretch and expand the limits of past analysis and thought. The teacher is trying to open your child's eyes to the world around him through books, numbers, lessons, reports, and so on. When he comes to you, keep his eyes open. Don't let his lids close because the home is in intellectual darkness.

As we have attempted to show, if you have a "special" child, you must follow the five guidelines at the beginning of this chapter with continuing zeal. You must become a dedicated child advocate. Above all, you and your special child must become active participants in the team that is monitoring your special child's education. One of your prime responsibilities as the parent of a special child is the education of the teacher. How strange that sounds! But it is a vital aspect of your teaming function. You must instruct the teacher in everything you know and have been told about your special child. There are three reasons why this is a crucial aspect of your interaction with the teacher:

1. Many of the problems discussed here are familiar to the teachers, i.e., mental retardation, learning disabilities, neurological hyperactivity. However, many emotional and physical illnesses are unknown to the teacher. He/she has not learned about the cause, the signs, the consequences of these problems. To the teacher, these special areas are as foreign as they were to you the first time you were forced to cope with the reality of your child's problem. Therefore, to manage your child with the greatest expertise within the classroom, the teacher must know all about the nature and scope of his problems.

2. Each child is different. Every child is unique. Therefore, though the teacher may have a general grasp of certain special educational problems, your child most likely offers exceptions to many of the established rules. To instruct and manage your child effectively in

class, the teacher must know every unusual aspect of your special child's problem area.

3. There are other children *like* your special child. As you relate the entire story of your child's problem to the teacher, she will learn to deal more effectively with your child; and she will also add to her knowledge so that she can understand and manage the next child who presents her with a similar problem.

So, as you work on the team with your child and his or her teacher, try to keep the teacher (and the necessary school personnel—school nurse, doctor, etc.) continuously informed about external consultations, advice, medications, changes in therapy, and new diagnoses. Often the teacher or other members of the school health team can be a very valuable informant to your physician or child psychiatrist or physical therapist. This is where the teaming plays a vital role in the handling of your child. The teacher monitors the child's responses, guides the physical therapy, or applies the appropriate psychological approach during the school day while you carry on during the hours at home. Only in this way can the child receive maximum benefit from both therapy and education.

On occasion, such functioning breaks down—or has never existed from the beginning. The parent stands alone, without the necessary resources to guarantee his/her child the proper and most appropriate education. Either something is *not* being done that should be, or something *is* being done which the parent feels is wrong and detrimental to his child. When the barriers to communication and response between parent and school system are so great that the parent cannot cross them, then the parent must seek his and his child's rights and fight like hell for that educational excellence which is legally guaranteed to his child. Parent power can be effective for the single child through the strong voice of the parent who understands his rights and knows how to obtain them. Parent power can be dramatic when it comes from local parents or parents in a national organization shouting out a clarion call for action to remedy an educational process felt to be against the best interests of a specific type of child or for all children. Parents must no longer be intimidated by the austerity and bureaucracy of the educational system. They must not be fearful that it is "just too damn big to fight." If your child needs an education better suited to his needs than he is getting and no one at the local school level is listening or reacting, then arm yourself with the facts about your child and his rights and fight for every single one of those rights and promises.

As you reflect back upon the previous chapters, you will understand fully the significance of the parent working in concert with the school personnel to mold and shape the very best educational experience for every child, whether that child be average and without unique qualities or quite special in needing particular educational patterns and focus. The parent cannot be the teacher and the teacher should not attempt to become the parent. But on the effective team, the edges between teacher and parent do blur to the degree that each is capable of supplementing the role of the other when needed. This is the basis of the ideal parent-child-teacher team.

There is a power in being a parent: the power of teaming with the responsive school system to help your child . . . and the power to force a sluggish school system to educate your child in the best and most appropriate way possible. Use that power. It is your intrinsic right as a parent.

APPENDIX

RESOURCES
FOR PARENTS

Throughout this book we have referred to potential resources for parents: organizations that advocate certain types of problems common to children; agencies that provide information parents might find helpful; groups that help parents define issues, plan actions, or educate others. Those references are the substance of this appendix.

How exhaustive is this listing? It only scratches the surface. Most of the listings are of *national* organizations or agencies; they may not be as helpful to you as your *local* chapters or affiliates of these agencies. When you contact them, ask about local representatives. Also, ask anyone you contact about *other* organizations, groups, or agencies that might be interested in the same types of advocacy you are seeking. Soon you'll have your own—more valuable—reference list.

And if you do not find what you seek on this list, write to the Committee for the Handicapped, People to People Program, Suite 610, La Salle Building, Connecticut Avenue and L Street, Washington, D.C. 20036, and ask for the Directory of Organizations Interested in the Handicapped. This directory can be invaluable in finding all sorts of useful organizations for special children. In addition, it covers agencies that are interested in problems other than handicapped as well (rural service, civic services, sex education, safety, etc.).

The listings below are not in any order of priority, nor are they necessarily the most important ones. They represent those groups that have proven reliable in responding to parental concerns. The list is not exhaustive; it does not even include federal agencies (we suggest you write your congressman or congresswoman for help in sorting out such agencies). But it will at least serve to get you started.

Ask yourself, Where can I find out more about . . . parent organizations dealing with the common problems of children?

1. National Congress of Parents and Teachers
   700 Rush Street
   Chicago, Illinois

2. Try your local P.T.A. Just ask your school superintendent or principal who the president is. He'll know.

3. American Association for Health, Physical Education, and Recreation
   1201 16th Street, N.W.
   Washington, D.C. 20036

4. National Safety Council
   425 Michigan Avenue
   Chicago, Illinois 60611

5. Child Study Association of America
   50 Madison Avenue
   New York, New York 10010

. . . parent organizations dealing with special problems?

1. Association for Children with Learning Disabilities (ACLD)
   5225 Grace Street
   Pittsburgh, Pennsylvania 15236

2. National Association for Retarded Citizens
   2709 Avenue E East, Post Office Box 6109
   Arlington, Texas 76011

3. National Association for Mental Health, Inc.
   1800 North Kent Street
   Arlington, Virginia 22209

4. National Association for the Deaf
   814 Thayer Avenue
   Silver Spring, Maryland 20910

5. National Society for Autistic Children
   169 Tampa Avenue
   Albany, New York 12208

. . . organizations with useful information for both parents and professionals?

1. The Council for Exceptional Children
   1920 Association Drive
   Reston, Virginia 22091

(When writing to this organization, ask also about their specialized divisions, e.g., learning disabilities, teacher training, physically handicapped, etc., and their work in collecting and advocating state and federal laws for handicapped children. This agency also has a clearing house of research information about children with special educational problems, including the gifted.)

2. United Cerebral Palsy Associations, Inc.
   66 East 34th
   New York, New York 10016

3. National Easter Seal Society for Crippled Children and Adults
   2023 West Ogden Avenue
   Chicago, Illinois 60612

4. American Association on Mental Deficiency
   5201 Connecticut Avenue, N.W.
   Washington, D.C. 20015

5. American Foundation for the Blind, Inc.
   15 West 16th Street
   New York, New York 10011

6. American Public Health Association
   1015 18th Street, N.W.
   Washington, D.C. 20036

7. American Speech and Hearing Association
   9030 Old Georgetown Road
   Washington, D.C. 20014

8. Epilepsy Foundation of America
   1828 L Street, N.W.
   Washington, D.C. 20036

. . . how to find, or start, a special interest group in my area?

No matter what type of problem you are advocating, if you locate several other interested people willing to work to solve it, you may want to find or start a group. The best material for finding or starting groups can be obtained by writing to:

Closer Look
1201 16th Street, N.W.
Washington, D.C. 20036

. . . the legal rights of children and their parents?

1. The Governmental Relations Department of the Council for Exceptional Children
   1920 Association Drive
   Reston, Virginia 22091

2. Children's Defense Fund
   1520 New Hampshire Avenue, N.W.
   Washington, D.C. 20036

3. for your state, write, c/o The State Capitol,
   (a) your state's Attorney General
   (b) your state's Office of Child Development, or
   (c) your state's Superintendent of Schools

. . . local provisions of services for children with handicaps?

If your local school superintendent or director of special education cannot help you, try:

1. Closer Look
   1201 16th Street, N.W.
   Washington, D.C. 20036
   (computerized listings)

2. Division of Special Education
   State Department of Education
   c/o The State Capitol

3. *Porter-Sargent Handbook of Private Schools* (1975)
   (This book is often available either in local libraries or in your school's department of special education. If not, you may obtain it from Sargent Publications, 11 Beacon Street, Boston, Mass. 02108)

4. *Porter-Sargent Guide to Summer Camps and Summer Schools*
   Sargent Publications
   11 Beacon Street
   Boston, Massachusetts 02108

Index

289

Index

cal problems, 200, 201, 202, 207, 209; emotional problems, 116, 202, 203–04, 206–07; failure in school, 116; and guidance counsellor, 209; parents, 119–203 *passim,* 205–10 *passim;* and peers, 203, 204, 205, 206; physical activity, 204, 207–08; and private physician, 201, 202, 205, 206, 208, 209

chronically ill child: and school nurse, 72, 82, 84, 91, 200, 201–02, 203, 205–06, 208, 209; and school physician, 73, 75–76, 202, 203, 209; and school social worker, 98; and teacher, 200–07 *passim,* 209; teaching at home, 205, 206; *see also* health and medical problems

cleft lip/cleft palate, 56, 58

Closer Look, 244–45, 288

Committee for the Handicapped, 285

communication specialist, 46–58; hearing problems, 46, 47, 48–49, 55, 145, 173; and hyperactive child, 145; language problems, 51–52, 53, 55–56, 145, 175–76; and learning-disabled child, 51–52, 53, 56; and parents, 50, 53–58 *passim;* school social worker, referral by, 99; and special education teacher, 51–52; speech problems, 46, 53, 54, 56, 145 (abuse by peers, 48, 50; articulation, 47–48, 51–56; articulation, lisp, 51, 52, 54, 58; cleft lip or cleft palate, 56, 58; dialectical, 49, 52–53, 57–58; neurological malfunctioning, 56; physical disorders, 56; stuttering, 50, 52, 57; stuttering, "normal non-fluency," 53–54, 57); voice problems, 50, 56–57

Council for Exceptional Children, 287; Governmental Relations Department, 288

counselling, guidance, and therapy (for child): chronically ill child, 209; emotionally disturbed child, 161–66 *passim;* gifted child, 214; hyperactive child, 134, 146, 147; physically handicapped child, 180, 183, 185, 186, 280; by school social worker, 97, 98–99; *see also* psychiatrist; psychologist; vocational training

counselling, guidance, and therapy (for parents): ascertain real need for, 255; of emotionally disturbed child, 161, 163, 164–65, 166; of failing child, 121; of mentally retarded child, 192; by private psychologist, 70–71; special education programs, 42; *see also* individual school personnel

crippled child, *see* physically handicapped child

cystic fibrosis, 73, 74; *see also* chronically ill child

daydreaming: by failing child, 110, 112; by hearing-impaired child, 171; *see also* boredom

deafness, *see* hearing, problems with

death or family illness (and child's fear), 67, 98, 113, 136–37

desegregation, 277

diabetes, 73, 74, 201, 206; *see also* chronically ill child

divorce or separation, effect of, 67, 98, 136–37

doctor, *see* physician

drug abuse, 159; drug education, 278

dyslexia, 127; *see also* learning-disabled child

educational games and books, 35, 132

educational jargon, 6, 22, 30, 129, 250–59, 274

Educational Resources Information Center (ERIC), 43

emotionally disturbed child, 4, 106, 155–67; abuse by, 158, 159, 165; and administrator, 157–58, 162, 164; exclusion from school activities, 106–08; expulsion from school, 106, 163–64; hyperactivity, 137, 138, 142; National Association for Mental Health, Inc., 244, 286; parents, 106, 107, 108, 155, 158–67 *passim;* and peers, 158, 159, 162, 163, 164, 165; physical education, 107; and psychiatrist, 161, 162, 164; and psychologist, 161; and school nurse, 164; and school physician, 79–80; and school social worker, 161, 164; special education, 157–58, 161–63, 167; and teacher, 162, 163, 164; teaching at home, 106, 163–64

emotional problems, 4, 159; abuse by peers, 4, 18, 48, 50, 94, 113; chronically ill child, 116, 202, 203–04, 206–07; convalescent child, 116, 228, 231, 234; death or family illness, 67, 98, 113, 136–37; faked illness, 112; and field trips, 16, 67; gifted child, 214–15, 219, 222, 223, 225; hearing-impaired child, 174; hyperactive child, 136–37, 138, 142, 146, 147; learning-disabled child, 127–28, 131; physically handicapped child, 181, 183; "school phobia," 67, 112–14, 152; teacher-child conflict, 4, 17, 21–22, 64–65, 113, 115–16; visually handicapped child, 169–70; *see also* behavior/behavior problems; failure, factors in/failing child; peers;

Index

physical abuse; psychiatrist; psychologist

Epilepsy Foundation of America, 287

exclusion from school activities, 4, 16, 106–08, 263; *see also* legal rights; physical activity/physical education

expulsion from school, 4, 16, 103–06, 255; education, provisions for, 105–06, 262; emotionally disturbed child, 106, 163–64; learning problems as excuse, 104; parents, 22, 103, 104–05, 108; teaching and structured activity at home, 105–06; as punishment, 103, 104; and teacher, 103, 105, 106; term of, limit to, 105

extracurricular activities: chronically ill child, 204; failing child, as motivation for, 119, 122–23; gifted child, 214, 215, 217, 219; physically handicapped child, 181, 182, 187; visually handicapped child, 177; *see also* exclusion from school activities; physical activity/physical education

eyesight, problems with, *see* vision, problems with

failure, factors in/failing child, 4, 109–25; and administrator, 109, 116; "educational immaturity," 110–12; extracurricular activities as motivation, 119, 122–23; and guidance counsellor, 109, 116; hearing problems, 116; hyperactivity, 116; illness, 116, 206, 228, 232; learning disability, 116, 118, 124; motivation low, 115, 119–20, 122–23; older child, 117–24; and parents, 110–24; rebellion against authority figures, 118–19, 122; rigidity of school environment, 123–24; "school phobia," 64, 112–14, 152; sibling rivalry, 121–22; and teacher, 109, 110, 111, 113, 115, 116–17, 120, 124–25; teaching poor, 115; testing, 109, 110, 116, 117, 121, 124–25; unreal expectations by parents, 120–21; vision, problems with, 116; young child, 110–16; *see also* emotional problems; learning problems

Family Education Right and Privacy Act, 270–71

family life, *see* death or family illness; divorce or separation, effect of; parents; siblings/sibling rivalry; teaching at home

field trips, 16, 67, 276

Freedom of Information Act, 240

Genêt, Jean, 105

gifted child, 4, 192–93, 211–27; artistic potential, 211, 213, 219, 224, 225–26; boredom, 193, 217, 218, 221, 224; Council for Exceptional Children, 287, 288; emotional problems, 214–15, 219, 222, 223, 225; and guidance counsellor, 214; parents, 192–93, 211–17 *passim,* 219–27 *passim;* and peers, 214–19 *passim,* 221–25 *passim;* physical activity, 219; and school psychologist, 211–12, 213; special education, 192–93, 212–27 *passim;* and teacher, 193, 212, 213, 214, 215, 217, 220, 221–22; testing, 211–12, 213, 221

grade, failing a, *see* failure, factors in/failing child

grade, repeating a, 111–12, 228

grade, skipping a, 219, 221–23

guidance counsellor, 41; and chronically ill child, 209; and failing child, 109, 116; and gifted child, 214; and hyperactive child, 146, 147; parents, and referral of child to psychologist, 66, 70; and physically handicapped child, 185

handicapped child, 241; exclusion from school activities, 106–08; "mainstreaming," 40, 259, 269; organizations and agencies, 43, 244–45, 285–88 (Bureau of Education for the Handicapped [United States Office of Education], 245, 258; Committee for the Handicapped, 285); parents, 43–44, 45, 106, 261–62, 270; physical activity, 107, 263; vocational training, 41, 181, 185, 186, 187, 191, 195, 196; *see also* legal rights; special education; individual handicaps

health and medical problems: acute temporary illness (and convalescent child), 4, 116, 228–34; chronically ill child, *see* chronically ill child; drug abuse, 159, 278; drugs and medication, 77 (chronically ill child, 201–02, 205, 207, 208–09; hyperactive child, 128, 145–46; learning-disabled child, 127, 128, 130); emergency problems, 82, 84, 91, 201, 202, 207, 209; faked illness, 112; organizations and agencies, 286, 287, 288 (American Association for Health, Physical Education, and Recreation, 286; American Public Health Association, 287); physical examination, 73–74 (of hearing and sight, 173; yearly, of "special education" children, 74–75); serious or long-term problems, referral to outside medical services, 75, 76–77, 82, 83, 91; and speech problems, 56; teaching in hospital or at

Index

Index

outside medical services, 75, 76–77; referral of child to psychologist, 66, 69);
and school psychologist, 59, 60, 61,
63–71 *passim*, 121, 212; and school social worker, 52, 94, 96–97, 98, 99, 121,
161; sex education, issue of, 67, 77, 88,
278; special education, 40, 42, 63, 64,
259, 269; *see also* transfer of child
below; and special education teacher,
40, 42–43, 43–44, 45, 69, 195, 220–21;
and teacher, 23, 29–37 *passim*, 62, 63,
109, 110, 111, 116, 141, 142, 219, 250,
251, 279–80 (as "class aide," 276; communication, lack of, 19, 29, 32, 33, 97;
referral of child to psychologist, 61–62,
66, 69, 70); as teacher at home, 105–
06, 229–30, 232; educational games
and books, 35, 132; tests: consent to,
266; insistence on, 110, 116, 117 *(see
also* records *above);* transfer of child,
22, 63, 116, 123, 124, 262, 265–69
passim; unrealistic expectations for
child, 120–21; *see also* counselling,
guidance, and therapy (for parents)
parents organizations, 43, 80, 242, 268,
276, 280; National Congress of Parents
and Teachers, 286; *see also* Parents
Teachers Association
Parents Teachers Association (P.T.A.), 3,
20, 80, 132, 242, 249, 276, 286
peers (and problems with): abuse of, 158,
159, 165; chronically ill child, 203, 204,
205, 206; convalescent child, 228, 233;
"educational immaturity," 110; emotional abuse by, 4, 18, 48, 50, 94, 113;
emotionally disturbed child, 158, 159,
162, 163, 164, 165; gifted child,
214–19 *passim*, 221–25 *passim;* hearing-impaired or visually handicapped
child, 169–70, 171, 174–75, 177; lack
of exposure to, 114, 135; motivation
low, 115, 122–23; physical abuse by, 4,
15, 66, 113, 152–54; physically handicapped child, 182; and punishment,
18; repeating a grade, 111–12; school
psychologist, help from, 64; speech
difficulties ridiculed, 48, 50; and transfer, 18, 19; tutoring by, 233
physical abuse: by emotionally disturbed
child, 158, 159, 165; by peers, 4, 15, 66,
113, 152–54; by school authorities, 17;
by teacher, 4, 149, 150–52; *see also*
punishment
physical activity/physical education:
American Association for Health,
Physical Education, and Recreation,
286; chronically ill child, 204, 207–08;
emotionally disturbed child, 107;

gifted child, 219; handicapped child,
107, 263; physically handicapped child,
107; visually handicapped child, 170
physically handicapped child, 4, 179–89;
Council for Exceptional Children, 287,
288; emotional problems, 181, 183; exclusion from school activities, 106–08,
263; and guidance counsellor, 185; National Easter Seal Society for Crippled
Children and Adults, 244, 287; parents, 106, 107, 108, 178–89 *passim;*
and peers, 182; physical education,
107; and physical therapist, 180, 183,
185, 186, 280; and private physician,
74, 180, 183, 185; and private psychologist, 180, 185; and school nurse,
280; and school physician, 74–75, 183,
185, 280; and school psychologist, 180,
185, 186; special education, 39, 41,
180, 182–87 *passim;* and teacher, 185,
187–88; teaching at home, 106–07;
transportation for, 183–84; vocational
training, 41, 181, 185, 186, 187; *see
also* handicapped child
physical therapist, 180, 183, 185, 186,
280
physician, private: and chronically ill
child, 201, 202, 205, 206, 208, 209;
examination of child, 73, 74; expelled
child and return to school, 104; and
handicapped child, 43; and hyperactive
child, 134, 137, 142, 144, 145, 146; and
learning-disabled child, 127, 129, 132;
and physically handicapped child,
74, 180, 183, 185; and school physician: cooperation with, 280 (referral
by, 76)
physician, school, 72–80, 83, 280; and behavior problems, 79–80; and chronically ill child, 73, 75–76, 202, 203, 209;
and emotionally disturbed child, 79–
80; health education in school, 72, 77–
78; and hyperactive child, 145; learning
problems, 79–80; and mentally retarded child, 195–96; and parents,
74–78 *passim*, 80, 121 (referral of child
to outside medical services, 75, 76–77;
referral of child to psychologist, 66,
69); and physically handicapped child,
74–75, 183, 185, 280; safety in school
monitored, 78; and school nurse, 77
(referral by, 76, 82, 83, 87; yearly
check-up, 74, 75); and school psychologist, referral to, 69; and school social
worker, referral by, 99; and teacher, referral by, 76
*Porter-Sargent Guide to Summer Camps
and Summer Schools,* 288

Index

Index

57; *see also* communication specialist; language; voice problems
stuttering, 50, 52, 57; "normal nonfluency," 53–54, 57
superintendent, *see* administrator, school
suspension, *see* exclusion from school activities; expulsion from school

tardiness, 15–16
teacher, 25–37; and administrator, 20, 21, 23, 142; American Federation of Teachers, 29; and child, conflict, 4, 64–65, 113, 115–16 (transfer to another class or teacher, 17, 21–22, 116); and chronically ill child, 200–07 *passim*, 209; and convalescent child, 229, 230, 232, 233, 234; discipline and punishment, 16, 113 (physical abuse, 4, 149, 150–52); and emotionally disturbed child, 162, 163, 164; expulsion of child, 103; work at home, 105, 106; and failing child, 109, 110, 111, 113, 115, 116–17, 120, 124–25; and gifted child, 193, 212, 213, 214, 215, 217, 220, 221–22; and hearing-impaired child, 168, 171, 173, 174–75, 178; and hyperactive child, 134–35, 137, 139, 140, 141, 142, 145, 146; and hyperactive child, so-called, 135–36 and parents, 23, 29–37 *passim*, 62, 63, 109, 110, 111, 116, 141, 142, 219, 250, 251, 279–80 (as "class aide," 276; communication, lack of, 19, 29, 32, 33, 97; National Congress of Parents and Teachers, 286; referral of child to psychologist, 61–62, 66, 69, 70; *see also* Parents Teachers Association); personal life should be exemplary, 14; and physically handicapped child, 185, 187–88; and school nurse, referral to, 76, 86–87, 88; and school physician, referral to, 76; and school psychologist, referral to, 61–62, 66, 69, 70, 212; and school social worker, 97; sex education taught by, 88, 89; and visually handicapped child, 168, 169–70, 173, 178
teacher, special education, *see* special education teacher
teaching at home: chronically ill child, 205, 206; convalescent child, 229–34 *passim;* educational games and books, 35, 132; emotionally disturbed child, 106, 163–64; expelled child, 105–06; mentally retarded child, 191; physically handicapped child, 106–07

teaching in hospital, 229, 230–31, 232
tests/testing: and failure in school, 109, 110, 116, 117, 121, 124–25; gifted child, 211–12, 213, 221; hearing, 48–49, 145, 172, 173; hyperactive child, 143–44, 145; interpretation of results, 257; learning-disabled child, 128–29, 131, 172; neurological, 143–44, 179; parental access to results, 257, 267; parental consent to, 266; psychological, 5, 6, 32, 61, 62, 63, 64, 68, 69–70, 120, 144, 161, 211–12, 213; by psychometrist, 61; standardized achievement, 14, 32, 64; vision, 168–69, 173; vocational, 121; *see also* health and medical problems, physical examination
therapist, *see* communication specialist; counselling, guidance, and therapy; physical therapist; psychiatrist; psychologist
transfer (to another class or teacher), 18–19, 142; parental role (questioning, consent, appeal), 22, 63, 116, 123, 124, 262, 265–69 *passim;* and peer pressure, 18, 19; as punishment, 17, 18, 21–22; teacher-child conflict, 17, 21–22, 116; *see also* special education
tutor, special, 232–33, 239–40; peer as, 233; physically handicapped child as, 182; *see also* teaching at home

United Cerebral Palsy Associations, Inc., 244, 287
United States Office of Education (USOE), 258; Bureau of Education for the Handicapped (BEH), 245, 258; Closer Look, 244–45, 288

vision, problems with: American Foundation for the Blind, Inc., 244, 287; blindness, 4, 168, 175, 176–77; emotional problems, 169–70; failure in school, 116; National Foundation for the Blind, 244; physical activities, 170; reduced vision, 116, 168–71, 175; special education, 39, 40, 41, 169, 170, 175, 176, 259; and teacher, 168, 169–70, 173, 178; testing, 168–69, 173; *see also* handicapped child
vocational skills and training, 241; handicapped child, 41; hyperactive child, 147; mentally retarded child, 191, 195, 196; physically handicapped child, 41, 181, 185, 186, 187; testing, 121
voice problems, 50, 56–57